To rate

D1187808

Declan maguire

BSc Aviation Management

2008

FLY *BUY* DUBAI

Published by Media Prima

Europe Office:
Formations House
29 Harley Street
London W1G 9QR
Great Britain
Tel: (+ 44 207) 6124118
Fax: (+44 207) 1827078

Middle East Office:
PO Box 29997
Dubai, UAE
Tel: (+971 4) 3452020
Fax: (+971 4) 3450707

Copyright © Dubai Duty Free 2008

Editorial Support: Kate Simpson
Editing: Roger Thiedeman
Suplimentary editing: Mike Simon
Design: Willow Design

Colour reproduction and printing by
Emirates Printing Press, Dubai,
UAE

FLY *BUY* DUBAI

25 years of Dubai Duty Free

by Graeme Wilson

Media Prima

Contents

66 The path of excellence and distinction does not stop at a certain stage - on the contrary, we consider any success we achieve as an additional incentive to achieve greater success. 99

HH Sheikh Mohammed bin Rashid Al Maktoum
Vice-President and Prime Minister of the UAE
Ruler of Dubai

Introduction from
HH Sheikh Ahmed bin Saeed Al Maktoum
President of Department of Civil Aviation Authority and
Chairman of Dubai Airports

In 1985, less than 18 months after it opened, Dubai Duty Free was feted by the duty free industry as a shining example of the direction in which the industry could go. Winning a Frontier Award, and being named Airport Retailer of the Year, was a quite remarkable achievement so soon after the company was formed.

Just as it was unexpected, winning a Frontier Award was, however, quite apt. Even then Dubai Duty Free was at vanguard of the industry. We have innovated and led, pushing the envelope and building what can be argued to be the most successful duty free business the world has ever seen.

I am proud that Dubai Duty Free has been a major component in enhancing the Dubai brand. Through an *avant guard* approach to corporate communications, the company had played a role in developing the image of the emirate and, indeed, the UAE as a whole. As we have seen, especially through our renowned tennis tournaments and in supporting some of the world's finest thoroughbred races, Dubai Duty Free straddles the world stage both as a successful corporate entity and as a brand ambassador for the emirate of Dubai.

The days when international airports around the globe manage their duty free operations as an afterthought are now over. Dubai Duty Free stands as a symbol of the direction that the industry is heading in the 21st century.

Ahmed bin Saeed Al Maktoum
Dubai
October 2008

Introduction from
Colm McLoughlin
Managing Director, Dubai Duty Free

Exactly a quarter of a century ago, eight Irishmen arrived in the tiny emirate of Dubai and into the unknown. Their brief was to create a duty free operation in Dubai's fast emerging, yet small, airport. Airport retail was in its infancy in the Middle East. By the end of 2008, we expect our annual turnover to reach $1.2 billion. This will establish Dubai Duty Free as the biggest duty free in the world.

Our 25th anniversary is a time of great celebration, and a time to reflect upon a quarter century of successes. We have received many awards and accolades over the years, but my staff and I have never lost sight that the greatest achievement is the personal satisfaction of a job well done.

I am proud that, from among our 3,000 hard-working staff members, this is a celebration that I will share with 60 pioneers. Of the 100 staff who joined Dubai Duty Free in its first year, 60 remain with us today. That is a remarkable statistic and indicative of the corporate culture that we have attempted to imbibe into the fibre of this company.

None of this would have been possible without the vision of HH Sheikh Mohammed bin Rashid Al Maktoum, Vice President and Prime Minister of the UAE, Ruler of Dubai, and the leadership of HH Sheikh Ahmed bin Saeed Al Maktoum, President of Department of Civil Aviation Authority. The Dubai government and the Ruling Family have underpinned the success of Dubai Duty Free.

Our Silver Jubilee year had been a juncture on which we can reflect — yet also one that lends itself to anticipation. The opening of C2 and T3 at Dubai International Airport and the recent opening of our own new Head Office and Distribution Centre are just several developments that will drive Dubai Duty Free forward over coming years.

Colm McLoughlin
Dubai
October 2008

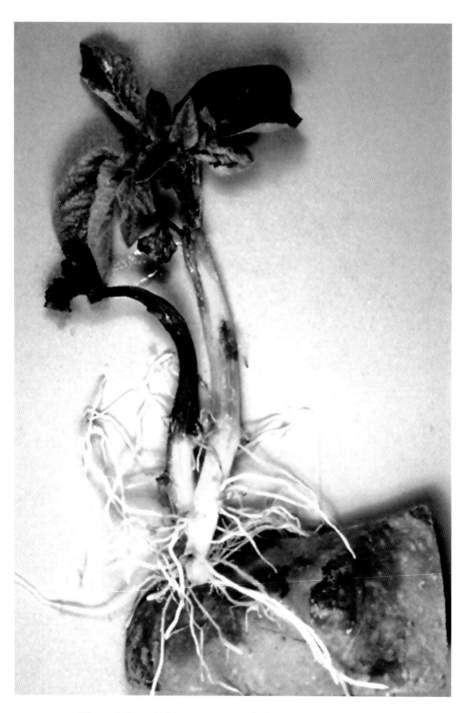

Phytophthora infestans, commonly known as potato blight,
would cause millions of Irish to starve.

Chapter One

An Gorta Mór

Just as energy is the basis of life itself, and ideas the source of innovation, so is innovation the vital spark of all human change, improvement and progress.
— Ted Levitt, American economist

During the 1930s, the town of Rineanna on Ireland's west coast enjoyed an excellent reputation as an ideal spot for shooting wild duck and geese. Enthusiasts of the sport flocked to the north side of the town's Shannon estuary to bag their game.

Hunting waterfowl was no phenomenon of the 20th century. Indeed, since prehistoric times, they have been hunted for their food, down, and feathers. Ducks, geese, and swans appear in European cave paintings from the last Ice Age. A mural in the ancient Egyptian tomb of Khum-Hotpe depicts a man in a hunting blind. Muscovy ducks - shown in the art of the Mochina culture of ancient Peru around 200 BC - were likely hunted by many peoples of the vast American continent long before then. And in Ireland, waterfowl hunting would, for a time, be as much a part of the country's culture as Guinness and the sport of hurling is today.

The rise of modern waterfowl hunting and the history of the shotgun go hand-in-hand. In the 19th century, the seemingly limitless flocks of ducks and geese crossing the Atlantic and landing on the west coast of Ireland were the basis for a thriving commercial waterfowl hunting industry. The Irish took this sport to their hearts, especially those of Rineanna, a town which lies close to the River Shannon. Most were poor peasants, drawing meagre income from the land, thus the arrival each hunting season of the rich hunters from municipal Dublin and other major cities was a boon to the local economy.

At the time, the Irish nation remained scarred by the events of An Gorta Mór - the Irish Potato Famine - which, between 1845 and 1852, had reduced the population of Ireland by nearly 25 per cent.

Pathogenic water mold - or *phytophthora infestans* - commonly known as potato blight, had ravaged potato crops throughout Europe during the 1840s. When it spread to Ireland its human cost was exacerbated by a host of political, social, economic, and climatological factors which still remain the subjects of heated historical debate.

One observer, the Quaker, William Bennett of Mayo, wrote of seeing '...three children huddled together, lying there because they were too weak

Fly *Buy* Dubai

The unpalatable image from that era shows an Irish family suffering during the worst deprivations of the Irish Potato Famine.

to rise, pale and ghastly, their little limbs perfectly emaciated, eyes sunk, voice gone, and evidently in the last stages of actual starvation...' The famine was a watershed in the history of Ireland.

Debate on the British government's response to the failure of the potato crop in Ireland and subsequent large-scale starvation - and whether or not this constituted what would now be called genocide - remains an historically and politically-charged issue. Jeremy Rifkin, in his book *Beyond Beef*, writes:

'...The Celtic grazing lands of Ireland had been used to pasture cows for centuries. The British colonised the Irish, transforming much of their countryside into an extended grazing land to raise cattle for a hungry consumer market at home...

'The British taste for beef had a devastating impact on the impoverished and disenfranchised people of Ireland. Pushed off the best pasture land and forced to farm smaller plots of marginal land, the Irish turned to the potato, a crop that could be

An Gorta Mór

Millions lost their homes during the famine — cast onto the street by monsterous absentee landlords.

grown abundantly in less favourable soil. Eventually, cows took over much of Ireland, leaving the native population virtually dependant on the potato for survival...'

With the grim famine still fresh in Ireland's memory, the town of Rineanna had attempted to rebuild itself. Its population had been decimated by the famine, through both death and emigration.

An excellent snapshot of Rineanna is provided by the Irish National Census of 1901. The district was split into two electoral divisions, but the trends were one. Of the 83 souls listed, all were Roman-Catholic, all males over 16 years of age worked in farming, and all were born in County Clare. Arguably the most diverse life was that of a Miss Jane O'Donoghue, the unmarried 27-year-old daughter of a farmer. Her father had passed away, leaving her mother Maria to manage the farm. In order to make ends meet, Jane went to work with her needles and listed her occupation for the Census as 'Dressmaker'. She was unique in Rineanna, with its strong agricultural tradition.

Fly *Buy* Dubai

By the early years of the 1930s, the pastures of Rineanna - seasonally at least - rang out with the sound of gunfire. The huge numbers of wild duck and geese brought the wealthy to the town in droves. The population was, understandably, only too keen to accommodate and profit from this.

And in time, not only the residents of Rineanna but every citizen in this economically-challenged west coast region of Ireland would come to enjoy another bounty from the air. Just as the area benefited from its position along the migration routes of wild birds, so the same region was well placed for manned flight as humankind began to take to the skies.

It was the muddy, flat land near the sea which gave the area its ideal hunting qualities and, equally, also offered the authorities a large, flat terrain - perfect for the emerging aviation industry.

Trans-Atlantic aviation in the Shannon estuary commenced with a seaplane base at nearby Foynes. The flying boats, which began service in 1937, took off from Foynes and landed in Botwood, Newfoundland some 18 hours later.

On July 5, 1937, two experimental trans-Atlantic commercial flights took off: a Pan American Airways Sikorsky S-42B flying boat, named *Pan American Clipper III*, flew from Botwood to Foynes while simultaneously, a British Imperial Airways Short S.23 C-class 'Empire' flying boat, the *Caledonia*, flew from Foynes to Botwood. The trial was a success and heralded two years of test flights. It was the start of a new era not just for the region but for the world at large.

The early North Atlantic Ocean flights, setting out from the west coast of Ireland, were indeed pioneering. Communications were in Morse code (wireless technology) and a radio officer was on board each flight, his job to keep in contact with the ground stations in Ballygirreen - a receiving station near Foynes - and Botwood in Newfoundland. In 1939, between June and October, the flying boat season, 46 of these aircraft crossed the Atlantic. It is a testimony to the skill of early airmen that none were lost.

Soon, Foynes was also connected to outposts of the British Empire when a British Overseas Airways Corporation (BOAC) Short 'Empire' flying boat service began operations. En route to Australia, the BOAC boats landed at what was then the tiny trading entrepot of Dubai, on the Trucial Coast in Arabia. Few had heard of Dubai in 1937, but the Sheikhdom, under its progressive ruling family - the economically-minded Ruler, Sheikh Saeed bin Maktoum Al Maktoum, ardently supported by his son, the Crown Prince, Sheikh Rashid bin Saeed Al Maktoum - had assented to a British request for landing rights on its sheltered Creek.

An Gorta Mór

(top) A Pan American Airways Sikorsky S-42 flying boat landed at Foynes in Ireland in July 1937, heralding the beginning of a new era for the country.

(right) The interior of the Sikorsky was all about passenger luxury.

(top) *The Empire flying-boat Canopus was the first civilian aircraft to land in Dubai.*

(left) *The interior of the Empires reflected a need to keep passengers comfortable during weeks of travel.*

An Gorta Mór

Both Foynes and Dubai now sat along an expanding Empire Route. But the similarities did not end there. Both had suffered the deprivations of economic meltdown for, like Foynes, Dubai too had ridden the storm of the demise of its mainstay industry - in its case, pearling. The two events - the crash of pearling, and An Gorta Mór - had, in a way, set each on a course that would see their interests collide. An amazing parallel though they were continents apart.

The Maktoum administration, like its counterpart in Dublin, had witnessed the very depths of despair. Both had pulled through, although not without considerable suffering for each of its peoples. Neither Dubai nor Ireland had been helped by their subservient roles to British interests. But both were to emerge with strength, thanks to their progressive, forward-looking governments who were to search for solutions to the problems afflicting their respective peoples.

And, indeed, one of the many solutions conjured up in Ireland, and based upon that nation's position as an aviation hub, was to bring the two countries together a generation later, in a manner that would have a far-reaching impact on both.

The first aerial photograph ever taken of Dubai, in 1931. (inset) The progressive Ruler of Dubai, Sheikh Saeed, with his Heir Apparent, Sheikh Rashid

Éamon de Valera, one of the greatest Irishmen on the international stage and a former President and Taoiseach.

Chapter Two

Shannon

The human bird shall take his first flight, filling the world with
amazement, all writings with his fame, and bringing eternal
glory to those whose nest whence he sprang.
— *Leonardo da Vinci, Italian polymath*

As early as October 1935, the Irish government of Éamon de Valera took the decision to initiate a survey 'to find suitable bases for the operation of seaplanes and landplanes on a transatlantic service'.

A progressive, de Valera — one of the dominant political figures in Ireland — was to serve his nation in public office from 1917 to 1973. For many years he worked as a member of the League of Nations (forerunner to the United Nations), and in 1932 was elected President of the League of Nations Council. The principal author of the Constitution of Ireland, he went on to be Taoiseach (Prime Minister) on three occasions, his last term ending in June 1959, and to serve as President. One of the first Irish political figures to recognise the relevance of aviation, de Valera took a keen interest in developments in the west of Ireland — in particular the outcome of the trans-Atlantic air service survey.

The Department of Defence, which provided technical advice to the Civil Aviation Section of the Department of Industry on the project, was tasked with carrying out the survey and, on November 21, 1935, a working party set out from Dublin for County Clare in the west of Ireland. Their brief was to survey a number of sites and, in order to complete the task quickly and efficiently, the party split into teams.

One of the groups discovered a land area to the west, at Rineanna, which, although wet, was deemed suitable for landplanes. For County Clare, and indeed the descendants of the families of O'Brien, Lalor, O'Donoghue, Henchy, and McNamara — all mentioned in the census of 1901 — everything would change. From a remote farming outpost, 135 miles from Dublin, Rineanna was to quickly become a major international destination.

Following a satisfactory report, de Valera and his government approved the choice of site and directed work to begin on preparing the country's first trans-Atlantic airport. It was to be the biggest civilian engineering project ever undertaken in this sleepy, backward area of Ireland — but it was surrounded by controversy.

Whereas the Foynes terminal was on the south bank of the Shannon

Fly *Buy* Dubai

River, the 760 acre site at Rineanna was on the north bank. Critics charged that de Valera represented Clare in the Dail (Irish Parliament) and the jobs created would benefit the Taoiseach's constituents.

But, despite the protests, work on Rineanna Airport (later to be known as Shannon International) forged ahead. A first priority was drainage, which began on October 8, 1936. Then work commenced by laying some 135 miles of pipes. Four grass runways were marked out, the longest being a mile in length and 400 yards wide, running almost southwest to northeast. The other two grass runways were 200 yards wide and laid out in such a way that there was an angle of approximately 45 degrees between each adjacent runway.

The project was far from complete when Rineanna was visited by a man who was, at the time, one of the most famous in the world.

Charles Lindbergh, 'The Lone Eagle', made the first solo, non-stop flight across the Atlantic, from Roosevelt Field, Long Island to Paris, France in 1927 piloting the Ryan NYP monoplane '*Spirit of St. Louis*'. Lindbergh became the world's best-known aviator and indeed his family predated the Kennedy clan as 'American Royalty'. The Lindberghs had become a national obsession in the United States when, on March 1, 1932, baby Charles Lindbergh II was abducted from the family home. He was just 20 months old. A nationwide, ten-week search ensued before an infant corpse was found just a few miles from the family home.

Biographers say that Lindbergh never recovered from losing his son and, indeed, the family were so devastated they were to later quit America. But before this was to happen, Lindbergh was called upon to serve his country on numerous occassions.

In the autumn of 1936 he visited Europe as an agent of Pan American Airways (Pan Am), surveying locations to establish an Atlantic gateway into Europe from America. It subsequently became known that he was also working for the American government, reporting to Washington on the state of civil and military aviation in Hitler's Nazi Germany.

The Pan Am portion of Lindbergh's trip took him to Ireland, and in December 1936 he flew over Rineanna and its environs in his Miles Mohawk. He followed this with a walk across the area with Ireland's then Minister of Defence Frank Aiken and officials from the Departments of Industry and Commerce, Defence, and Board of Works. It was reported that 'great satisfaction was expressed concerning the suitability of the site'.

Although the Second World War was to contribute much to the aviation industry, it delayed the development of the new Shannon Airport. But despite this delay, the importance of the west of Ireland as a gateway with

*Legendary aviator Charles
Lindbergh assesssed
Shannon in 1936 for
Pan American.*

Fly *Buy* Dubai

*Shannon airport received its first scheduled commercial flight
on October 24, 1946.*

the United States still grew. Flying boat services were operated by the American and British militaries during the war, and Foynes terminal played host to many leading personalities of the day. Winston Churchill and Franklin Roosevelt passed through — in secret — *en route* to strategy conferences and key meetings, while comedian and entertainer Bob Hope stopped over on his way to entertain the troops in Europe.

During the war, Imperial Airways, the forerunner to BOAC and later British Airways, operated flights into Shannon from Bristol in southwest England, to coincide with flying boat operations from Foynes. The new airport itself had been serviceable from 1942, but during the war years it had remained low-key, as civilian services were almost non-existent. But come 1945 and with Berlin in ruins, the authorities rightly predicted a revival in civil aviation. The runways at Shannon were extended to allow for an anticipated new generation of bigger trans-Atlantic aircraft and so, once the war ended, the airport was ready to be used by the many new, post-war commercial airlines of Europe and North America.

Conversely, the mid-Forties had seen the use of flying boats on commercial flights dying out and, a year after the war finished, the airboat facility at Foynes was closed. It was a similar story in Dubai, where the Sheikhdom's civil aviation era came to an end in 1947 with the end of flying boat services between Britain and Australia.

But while Dubai would be sidelined as an aviation hub for some 12 years until it created a new aerial gateway, De Valera's vision and the strategically important position of Ireland's west coast, ensured that the country would remain a key part of the growing civil aviation industry.

In 1945, Shannon had begun receiving scheduled aircraft from Trans World Airline (TWA) — a company to which Charles Lindbergh was technical advisor — and Pan American Airways. But it was on October 24 the following year that the first scheduled commercial flight landed, an American Overseas Airlines Douglas DC-4. It was a day of great celebration.

The number of international carriers using Shannon rose sharply over succeeding years for, as anticipated several years earlier, the airport had become the gateway between Europe and the USA. The limitations of the operating range of aircraft at that time — DC-4s, DC-6s, and Lockheed 749 Constellations — necessitated the interruption of journeys for refuelling. Thus, Shannon became the most convenient and obvious point before and after the flight across the Atlantic. Indeed, most of the airport's income was derived from providing fuel, food, and accommodation for these aircraft and their passengers.

The door was now open for the entrepreneurial spirit of one man to alter the course of the aviation industry just as significantly as Howard Hughes, Glenn Curtiss, William B. Stout, C. R. Smith, and other aviation pioneers had done before him.

With their distinctive tails, Lockheed Constellations, affectionately known as 'Connies', were soon a regular sight on the West Coast of Ireland.

Shannon

Irish Coffee, that symbol of Irish Hospitality,
was created at Shannon airport.

Chapter Three

Irish Coffee

If you're involved in developing an important idea, you
have to let it possess you. If you keep knocking on
the door, the door will open.
– *Dr Brendan O'Regan, Irish entrepreneur*

It was in February 1947 that the Irish Parliament passed an historical and extremely important piece of legislation that would be the first step toward the creation of a global duty free industry. Taoiseach Éamon de Valera had just one year left in office at the end of three back-to-back terms, although he would serve in the same position twice more and later as President. If Shannon was his baby, then it can be said that he is the political godfather to the duty free industry.

The Customs Free Act was a piece of legislation backed by the Taoiseach and driven through Dáil Éireann, the Irish lower House of Parliament, with the backing of the premier's Fianna Fáil party.

The Customs Free Act exempted transiting and embarking passengers, goods, and aircraft at Shannon Airport from normal customs procedures. This was a phenomenal move — not just in its foresight but in the fact that it was the very antithesis of a duty free industry which was to spread to every corner of the world. Moreover, it was to not only establish Shannon as an international centre of industrial trade and distribution, it was also to hand-rear a new bevy of professionals — men and women who have become specialists in the duty free industry. The very people who have made Dubai Duty Free, and others like it, forces to be reckoned with.

Brendan O'Regan was born in 1917 in Sixmilebridge, County Clare, not too far from Shannon city. O'Regan's father owned the long-patronised Old Ground Hotel in Ennis, County Clare, some 10 or so miles north of Shannon. O'Regan followed his father's footsteps into the hospitality industry and, by the early 1940s, was a respected and well-known figure in the business. Following studies in Germany, France, Switzerland, and Britain, he returned to his homeland in 1938 to manage another of his father's enterprises, the Falls Hotel in nearby Ennistymon. He was then appointed Manager of St Stephen's Green Club in Dublin.

In 1943, with World War Two at its height, O'Regan was appointed Catering Controller at Foynes Airport, which was an important refuelling point for flying boats travelling between the United States and Britain. Conscious that he should present an image of the Irish to visitors as they transited through Foynes, he redecorated the airport's restaurant to reflect the traditions and character of Ireland. He hand-picked his staff, choosing those who were well-educated and having the ability to convey the positive image of the Irish people.

O'Regan's restaurant was a success and word spread. Soon it was catering for politicians, military top brass, and celebrities as they passed through the tiny airport.

Two years later, with the demise of the flying boats and the arrival of trans-Atlantic commercial airliners, O'Regan was transferred to the new airport at Rineanna (which was to become Shannon) where again he set up a restaurant. O'Regan himself tells the story of the first meal served at Rineanna Airport: "... and Lord Headfort said to me: 'That's quite extraordinary, we didn't expect anything like that. Could I congratulate your chef?' I (O'Regan) said: 'But he's not on duty today.' And Lord Headfort said: 'My God, if you can do it like that when the chef is off, what will it be like afterwards?'"

There had been no chef on that opening day — the food was transported from O'Regan's family hotel, the Old Ground, in laundry baskets.

But before long, O'Regan did have a chef, who was himself to become famous for a special concoction. Joseph Sheridan invented the now-ubiquitous Irish Coffee. The beverage was conceived after a group of Americans disembarked at the airport on a miserable winter evening in the 1940s. Sheridan decided to add some whiskey to the coffee to warm the passengers. When asked if they were being served Brazilian coffee, Sheridan told the passengers that it was Irish. The name stuck — and the drink became as iconic to Ireland as Guinness... well, almost.

O'Regan's position — officially — at Shannon was that of Catering Controller. But, as during his time at Foynes, his record shows that he was not content to sit back and take a salary. He harboured a desire — to develop the entire Shannon region and bring more prosperity to this outlying region of Ireland, which had suffered so much. A century on from the Irish Potato Famine, and despite being at the heart of international civil aviation, the region was still suffering. Perhaps, he opined, there was another way?

But there was another need to make Shannon as attractive as possible. In the years following the end of the war, civil aviation was changing. Technology and techniques developed in order to gain advantage in war

Irish Coffee

were being introduced into civilian aviation. On the drawing boards were aircraft that could fly farther, longer, and offer passengers greater comfort. There was a probability that Shannon would be over-flown by trans-Atlantic traffic as the need for refuelling stops declined with aircraft becoming technically more efficient.

It was a conundrum that absorbed O'Regan. And it is one that again brings us back to Dubai.

Half a century earlier, the tiny trading village of Dubai, on the Trucial Coast, survived amid a region wracked by poverty. The then Ruler, Sheikh Hasher bin Maktoum Al Maktoum, great-grandfather of the present Ruler, oversaw a town burdened by poverty and virtual destitution. But then an opportunity presented itself.

A nationalist Persian government wrecked the wealth of its Gulf ports, leaving the region's merchants looking for a new base on the Arab side of the Gulf. There was nothing really to merit choosing Dubai over better-appointed and more-developed ports elsewhere. But they didn't reckon on Sheikh Hasher's intuitive plan to entice the merchants to his Sheikhdom. Indeed, his idea may well constitute the world's first Free Trade Zone. The Ruler slashed taxes to nil and gave land to those wishing to settle in his town.

Around the end of the 1800s the then Ruler of Dubai, Sheikh Hasher bin Maktoum Al Maktoum, created what was, perhaps, the world's first free trade zone.

(top) Pictured during his famed Presidential Debate with Richard Nixon, John F. Kennedy, the son of an Irish immigrant, highlighted the promise of the American dream. Millions of Irish crosssed the Atlantic.

(left) Seán Lemass championed the duty free concept and had a gutsy economic vision.

Irish Coffee

Thus, over the course of a generation, Sheikh Hasher transformed the fortunes of his emirate.

Halfway into the new century, the people of County Clare needed similar inspiration, although their position was hardly as precarious as what the people of Dubai had endured five decades earlier. Shannon airport was witnessing a steady increase in passenger through-flow. There was every prospect that this would continue, even in the medium term. Yet, O'Regan opined, Shannon required an angle that set itself ahead of the likes of London-Heathrow and Paris, both of which were positioning themselves as natural European hubs for US traffic. Shannon needed an innovation which would make it *de rigueur* for trans-Atlantic passengers.

O'Regan's eventual plan was to introduce goods for sale to transit passengers. In his opinion, the airport acted as an international enclave for transiting passengers and, as such, should not be liable for tax on any purchases made.

It was not an argument that would prove very popular in Dublin, with Ireland struggling economically. Ireland was growing far less rapidly than its European competitors in the post-War period. She remained very protectionist for a decade after most of Western Europe had moved towards free trade. The post-war boom saw Western Europe achieving growth rates of almost six per cent per annum while Ireland stagnated with a growth rate of less than two per cent and an employment growth rate of less than one per cent. Over the course of the 1950s, more than 400,000 Irish people, out of a total population of less than three million, emigrated.

Part of the problem was ideological; another must be ascribed to a failure of vision, which continued to see agriculture as virtually the only engine of growth. The dominant Fianna Fáil party had a negative stance toward foreign ownership.

But O'Regan had friends, and his successes had won him a voice and reputation. Within time he convinced the Irish government that the transit area at Shannon airport should not be considered part of the state.

Seán Lemass, a veteran of the 1916 Easter Rising, War of Independence, and the Civil War, served the Dublin South constituency from November 1924 until his retirement in 1969. A founder-member of Fianna Fáil, Lemass is today considered to have the economic vision that so many around him — both in his party and in the government — may have lacked.

During his years in Parliament, in a series of positions in Cabinet and later as Taoiseach, Lemass is remembered for a list of successes in developing Irish industry. Indeed, many historians contend that he remains

Of the consumer products available in the 1940s some remain familiar today, although their marketing strategies horrify.

the greatest Taoiseach ever to serve, and call him the 'the architect of modern Ireland'.

When O'Regan was extolling a dramatic and somewhat radical view for Shannon, he was lucky to be reporting to a Transport and Power Minister who was himself a progressive. Lemass took the germ of the duty free concept into the corridors of power in Dublin, and forged support for the Customs Free Act.

In May 1947 a small shop opened in the terminal building at Shannon airport, a first of its kind in the world. Offering a host of items for sale, tax free, the goods ranged from souvenirs and Irish handicrafts to local produce. Only transiting passengers were permitted to buy and the original shop was manned by one girl.

The novelty of being able to shop while waiting for their flight to take off — after enjoying a superb meal courtesy of O'Regan's highly-trained catering staff — kept transiting passengers amused. 'Shopping while you wait for the plane' fast became a winner. The concept introduced a new source of revenue for Shannon, a source that kept growing.

Lemass had gambled a great deal of political capital on the concept, against the wishes of many in his party. While Duty Free would hardly be his only legacy, this and other progressive initiatives swelled his reputation. Just a dozen years after that small shop opened at Shannon — and grew into an industry — it was he who stepped into the lofty shoes of retiring giant Éamon de Valera. Lemass would go on to serve his nation well as Taoiseach for seven years.

With a world so experienced in the buy-before-you-fly concept, has anyone ever stopped to wonder where the concept of duty free shopping actually came from? It seems incredible that it took two men with a wonderful vision, for a whole world of opportunity to open up.

And how the cash registers at Shannon airport rang. In 1951, just three years after the opening of the original store, the first Airport Duty Free Liquor Shop opened. This had started as a ship's store, where airline stewards purchased supplies for re-sale to passengers when aircraft became airborne; the same applied to cigarettes and tobacco, which began as supplies for crew only. Later, with passengers complaining that they wished to shop on the ground, the public was allowed to make direct purchases at tax free prices on a restricted basis. Quickly Shannon became famous for having the only airport liquor and cigarette duty free shop in the world.

At the time that Shannon was tasting its first success, duty free allowances in the United States were very generous, and travellers could

Irish Coffee

Brendan O'Regan's duty free concept began to take off and establish Shannon as the premium European aviation hub. (top) On a good day the shop turned over £5.

Fly *Buy* Dubai

The charismatic Coco Chanel. Her luxury perfume brand was one
of the first to find itself a top Shannon Duty Free seller.

import up to six bottles of spirits and 2,000 cigarettes each. Duty free savings often made these items cheaper than if they had been bought in the country of manufacture. The same principle applied to luxury goods — and so they became far more affordable. It was a major breakthrough and word of Shannon's duty free soon spread.

As turnover and profits grew, so did the duty free operation itself. Sensing that transiting passengers might like to buy items other than those 'Made in Ireland', Shannon's buying team began to venture further afield to source goods. As the inventory of goods on sale increased, so the team quickly realised that internationally-branded merchandise was becoming popular. Cigarettes and alcohol were mainstay items, of course, but they were soon to be joined by an ever-increasing range of luxury goods. French perfumes and cosmetics went on sale — and famous brand names such as Dior, Carven, Balmain, and Chanel were quickly joined by a range of delicate porcelain ornaments, figurines, and expensive tableware from Germany. The luxury items were fast proving a hit, and as the range available expanded even further to include top-of-the-range cameras and watches, the very blueprint for a successful duty free operation was being laid down.

As we know today, fragrances from the houses of the great perfumiers

Irish Coffee

Shannon Duty Free also aimed to boost the domestic economy.
Arran knitware was the shop floor's first big Irish success.

and designers, exquisite *objets d'art*, crystal and tableware, and photography equipment, are just some of the mainstays of any duty free offering. It wasn't long before jewellery and gold and silverware appeared on the shelves and in the display cabinets at Shannon duty free — and leather goods soon joined those. The buying team sourced the finest items and were able to buy at competitive prices to sell on to a very receptive clientele.

But while Shannon airport was bringing the cream of the world's luxury goods to Ireland, it was also bringing a renaissance to its own cottage industries. Such is the power of a successful duty free operation that it can identify and nurture a range of items which are locally produced, turning a perhaps lagging small business into a multi-million dollar operation.

And this was exactly the case in Ireland. During the early 1950s, for example, the manufacturing industry in Ireland was not the flourishing concern it was to become some years later. However, the duty free buying team saw an opportunity to promote a line of knitwear and showcase it to the world. In turn this resulted in an incredible opportunity for local artisans. The knitwear was Arran — each piece painstakingly hand-made in cottage industries. Some pieces were introduced into the duty free shop and they literally flew off the shelves.

Irish Coffee

Shannon Duty Free sparked huge industries for Waterford Crystal and (inset) Arran wool products.

Fly *Buy* Dubai

More items were ordered, and more, until a small business enterprise was turning into a thriving industry, and it seemed the transit passengers couldn't get enough of the sweaters, gloves, and scarves. Arran knitwear is now known internationally — thanks, in no small measure, to being discovered by hundreds of thousands of passengers as they passed through Shannon's duty free in those early days!

There is a similar success story with Ireland's now world-famous crystalware manufacturer, Waterford. It is recognised that by duty free incorporating a select range of this beautifully hand-blown glassware into its luxury items offerings, Waterford grew from a small family-run business into an international brand name. Its fortunes indeed turned, thanks to Shannon, and the duty free industry — and Waterford's success has never waned.

Conducting the orchestration of Shannon's success story was the indomitable O'Regan. His business acumen knew few boundaries and he has, quite rightly, in more recent times, been feted as one of Ireland's favourite sons.

By 1954 he had spotted another opportunity: mail order. Shannon began delivering goods directly to people overseas at duty free prices. In 1950, following a trip to the USA as part of a delegation under the post-war Marshall Aid Plan, his subsequent report led to a wider range of facilities for Shannon. This included the creation of an industrial free zone around the airport that would encourage overseas investors to set up their manufacturing projects. Within a decade of legislation being passed in Dublin, inward investment had become part of Shannon's make-up, the town developing to accommodate the needs of a growing population as this small enclave grew into a lively industrial hub.

Three years earlier, the Shannon School of Hotel Management had been established within the airport complex. This facility was to become world-famous and still produces highly-skilled professionals.

Continually enterprising, O'Regan, not content with the success of the establishments he had founded and mentored, saw further into the future and his focus fell on tourism which he foresaw as an additional revenue-earner for the region.

Air travel was fast increasing: both regional and international flights were quite literally taking off. The era of the holiday package was dawning and air travel, once the domain of the affluent, was embracing a wider audience. Tourism became of benefit to both Shannon's economy and Ireland's as a whole. At his prompting, a tourism infrastructure was

Irish Coffee

developed, which further catapulted Shannon Airport into a new era.

In 1957, O'Regan was appointed Chairman of Bord Failte Eireann — the Irish Tourist Board — a position he would hold until his retirement in 1973. He established and became Chairman of Shannon Development Company, a post he held until 1978. This was Ireland's only regional economic development agency. He headed Shannon Free Airport Development Company (SFADCo) from 1961, and, building on the idea that any industrial zone surrounding an international airport would need an available workforce, SFADCo purchased land for the construction of housing. This resulted in Shannon Town, the first newly-established town in the history of the Irish State.

By the late 1960s and early '70s, Shannon Town became a haven for many Roman Catholics fleeing the outbreak of sectarian, political, and religious conflict in Northern Ireland. In 1978, O'Regan founded Co-Operation North (now Co-Operation Ireland) a non-denominational and non-party organisation with the goal of overcoming violence and unemployment through widespread and ongoing economic, cultural, and social

The Irish Whisky industry also received a boost. Through Shannon Duty Free a vast new market opened.

Dr Brendan O'Regan O.B.E.
Father of the duty free industry.

co-operation between the Republic of Ireland and Northern Ireland. In 1984 he established the Irish Peace Institute at the University of Limerick.

O'Regan's work and commitment to regional development and cross-cultural exchanges have won him numerous accolades including the Commander of the British Empire (CBE) award for his contribution to peace work in Northern Ireland. In 1984 he was voted Clareman of the Year, and in 1995 was made a Freeman of the City of Limerick. Just five years later, he was awarded the Peace Dove by Co-operation Ireland. In 1999, he was awarded a Doctorate of Laws by the Queen's University of Belfast. And more recently he was honoured by the University of Limerick for his work with the Irish Peace Institute and the development of the Shannon region.

Many of these awards featured as part of an exhibition at Clare Museum celebrating the life of Dr O'Regan. The exhibition, 'Empowering the people: The Career and Achievements of Dr Brendan O'Regan', was opened by Taoiseach Bertie Ahern on February 8, 2007, then moved to the Seán Lemass Library in Shannon four months later.

At the opening, Ahern paid tribute to the founding father of duty free and commented: "I was in Dubai Airport recently where I met a proud fellow countryman, Colm McLoughlin, who is heading the world's third largest duty free business. All of that began here (in Shannon)."

Before his death, in his ninth decade, O'Regan could look back with fondness at his many achievements. When he retired in 1973, the occasion coincided with the creation of Aer Rianta, Ireland's new national airport authority. His Sales and Operations Organisation was integrated with this new entity. A decade later, and Air Rianta was to take its first tentative steps into a brave new world.

The Irish were moving outwards — and Dubai was the first in a long list of countries to benefit from their inspiration. Indeed one could question: without O'Regan's enthusiasm in the '40s, would the world's duty free industry be in such wonderful shape today? Indeed, might it even exist?

O'Regan was once quoted as saying: "We are Irish, we are different."

And indeed, as far as the duty free industry is concerned, his words hold a certain resonance which could well be the motto of all the men and women who have followed in his footsteps, while his own principal motto of 'creativity, co-operation, communication' remains the foundation on which international duty free continues to build and flourish.

*Sheikh Rashid bin Saeed Al Maktoum,
the visionary Ruler of Dubai.*

Chapter Four

The Father of Dubai

Great men are meteors that burn
so that the earth may be lighted.
— *Napoleon Bonaparte, French military and political leader*

On September 30, 1958, Sheikh Rashid bin Saeed Al Maktoum succeeded as Ruler of Dubai when his father, Sheikh Saeed, passed away. Among the largely destitute Trucial States, the new Ruler was an anomaly. He was unwilling to accept the *status quo*. The tiny Sheikhdom was comparatively well-off compared to its neighbours, as it had long nurtured a trading base and was well-established as the main commercial entrepot along the coast.

However, wealth was relative. While the people of Dubai lived in a Sheikhdom which enjoyed a certain stability compared with her neighbours, they still knew hunger. Those in the town suffered from an absence of public services, boasted perhaps two cars, had no paved roads, no electricity and no clean water. Dubai's 'prosperity' hardly ranked her above borderline poverty. Sheikh Rashid was a modernist at heart, yet oil exports were still a vague notion and the obstacles he faced — common to many leaders at that time — seemed insurmountable.

Dubai's finances were very limited. Regardless — and with a certain vision — Sheikh Rashid set about tackling the negatives to turn them into positives. He began by reforming his Customs Department and embarked upon an almost prohibitively expensive Dubai Creek Development Scheme. Within months of his accession, he launched a water company, an electricity company, began a municipality, and unveiled a platform of reforms and new initiatives. Where necessary, he borrowed money, sought grants from allies abroad, and ploughed any new revenues back into a plethora of new initiatives.

Sheikh Rashid's oft-repeated mantra from the late 1950s was: 'What is good for the merchants is good for Dubai'. Whether or not this is apocryphal, or whether the Dubai Ruler really did utter this statement, is immaterial. Through his actions, Sheikh Rashid showed a belief that only by developing his Sheikhdom, attracting more trade, and building a vibrant economy, would Dubai grow and prosper.

Each evening, Sheikh Rashid would open the doors of his *Majlis* to the people. He drew around him a cadre of the best and the brightest, nationals and expatriates, into an informal body. Businessmen, merchants, poets,

49

Fly *Buy* Dubai

landowners, *bedu*, and community leaders, all merged into a sort of 'think tank'. The vibrancy of the *Majlis*, coupled with the sense of possibility and energy that surrounded Sheikh Rashid during this period, led one British representative based in the region to dub the Sheikh 'an Arabian Camelot'. This was alluding to the Kennedy White House, which all too briefly flickered into life in the USA, until snuffed out in Dallas, Texas, on November 22, 1963.

Dubai's 'Camelot' strived to bring progress where there had been none. And where many leaders might demand sycophancy from their subjects, Sheikh Rashid asked only for free thinking from his entourage. But he was always at its centre, daring to think the unthinkable. Indeed, over subsequent decades some of the Sheikhdom's most potent symbols of progress were undertaken against a backdrop of incredulity among those who served the Ruler.

Jebel Ali Port and the Dubai World Trade Centre were two examples of Sheikh Rashid's uncanny intuition, yet both were dubbed 'white elephants' by some around him.

Conversely, on some issues there was total unity in the *Majlis*, such as the Dubai Creek Development Scheme and Port Rashid. Another of the projects championed by Sheikh Rashid which won the wholehearted backing of his people was the creation of Dubai Airport.

Although Dubai's civil aviation industry dates from 1937, when an air agreement was signed with Imperial Airways for a flying boat base on the Creek, the history of modern civil aviation in the Sheikhdom actually began in 1959. It was in this year that Sheikh Rashid — only a year into his reign and against a backdrop of British attempts to discourage aviation development in Dubai — ordered the construction of the first airfield. Located only four kilometres from the town centre on a wide, level expanse of gravel and hard sand, the site was chosen not just for its proximity to the town but with future expansion in mind.

The initial airfield consisted of a 1,800-metre compacted runway, an apron area, a small airport terminal, and a fire station. Inaugurated in September 1959, the airport was capable of handling aircraft up to the size of a Douglas DC-3 (Dakota). By 1969 some nine airlines were operating, serving around 20 destinations. The terminal, built at what was, at the time, great expense for Dubai's limited budgets and income, was very basic. Inside, arriving and departing passengers mingled, the general public milled in and out, and the few officials went about their business informally. It was, after all, an era of informality.

The Father of Dubai

Dubai's Port Rashid and Dubai World Trade Centre projects were denounced by soothsayers but quickly became the backbone of a new, modern Dubai.

Fly *Buy* Dubai

Sheikh Rashid invested everything in Dubai's progress and, slowly, the sheikhdom began to see conserted development. (inset) The Sheraton Hotel being built.

Fly *Buy* Dubai

(top) The small terminal at Dubai Airport in 1960.

(left) Inside the terminal was sparse. There was no duty free, but there was a small coffee shop.

The Father of Dubai

"There was a café in the terminal, which sold tea, coffee, and soft drinks. Perhaps some snacks," says George Chapman. "I forget who owned it, but recall that it was a concession. The café sold chocolates for a few months in the winter when it was cool enough, but not in the summer, as there was no refrigeration."

The dozen or so seats provided by the café, and its limited range of refreshments, was the only 'service' the airport could boast at the time. Certainly a duty free outlet was not considered, even by the sage Sheikh Rashid, and, after all, during the early 1960s that industry remained in its infancy.

But, on another continent at that time, Shannon, in Ireland, was building such an industry, although the rest of the world was slow to respond. Dr Brendan O'Regan may have been sculpting a major enterprise in the west of Ireland, but for well over a decade Shannon was more or less unique. Perhaps the industry can only be said to have spread to any great degree when American businessmen Chuck Feeney and Robert W. Miller formed the Duty Free Shoppers Group on November 7, 1960. The pair won a concession in Hong Kong. Over time, their enterprise spread through Europe and America, as government legislation was adopted in various countries and states which would allow duty free to flourish.

While Feeney and Miller were taking the duty free concept to the world, and O'Regan was single-mindedly concentrating on bringing the world to his home patch, in the under-developed Gulf there was a flicker of hope that it could emerge from its economic purgatory. With the advent of oil exports in the Gulf, the region was beginning to boom. The Trucial States, future components of the United Arab Emirates federation, became oil-rich in the early 1960s when the first well was spudded in Abu Dhabi. In Dubai, where oil was discovered offshore in 1966, with production commencing three years later, much of the revenue was channelled by Sheikh Rashid back into developing the city's infrastructure and developing its commercial base.

In turn, the emerging oil boom would provide a big boost to civil aviation. The oil industry itself needed support — with men and equipment flying in from all over the world, and around the region, in search of new deposits and fields. But oil was in itself only a means to an end. Some leaders, those with foresight, were not content to sit back and rely upon petrodollars. Even before the extent of Dubai's petrocarbon reserves was fully explored, the Ruler was ploughing his returns into his city-state.

Along with the workers needed for the oil business came an influx of expatriates whose skills were vital for every aspect of Dubai's growth.

Fly *Buy* Dubai

In the 1960s Dubai Airport became a small but important hub for regional aviation, showing substancial growth in traffic movements.

Fly *Buy* Dubai

Alongside lawyers, doctors, teachers, surveyors, and accountants were contractors, merchants, marketing people, bankers, and hoteliers. A diverse range of professions began to pour into Dubai — as did a great number of labourers needed for the building of the city, which was to become so significant to the region.

That first airport in 1959 kept expanding to accommodate new-generation aircraft, increasing services, and more flights. It all grew quickly due to Sheikh Rashid's far-sighted Open Skies policy. It culminated in 1971 with a new terminal building capable of handling travellers in air conditioned comfort and, externally, expansion of the runway, a new taxiway, and the installation of airport lighting throughout. This additional work enabled the airport to accept Boeing 747 and Concorde services.

In administrative terms there was also change during the early 1970s. In 1971, the Department of Civil Aviation was formed. It was responsible for granting traffic rights and operating permission for airline operators. Sheikh Rashid reiterated his wish for an Open Skies policy, which remains today.

During the 1970s, Dubai recorded a remarkable year-on-year increase in traffic movements entailing a need for further extensions to both the airport facilities and the terminal building.

It was the new airport of 1970 that saw Dubai make its first — very tentative — steps into the duty free industry.

"I think the duty free was almost an afterthought in 1970," remarks Sheikh Ahmed bin Saeed Al Maktoum, President of Dubai Airports Company. "There seems to have been no strategic planning as such, but when the new airport was being developed, the authorities accepted proposals from a number of merchants in the *souk* (market) to operate outlets. Each paid a rental, or concession fee, to Dubai Airport in return for space."

These concessionaires offered a rather haphazard approach to airport shopping. They fashioned their small stalls as replicas of their own downtown stores and thus the effect was more akin to shopping in a *souk* than in a streamlined duty free shopping concourse.

Mohi-Din Binhendi, then Director-General of Dubai Civil Aviation, inherited this situation but never found it satisfactory. Well-travelled in his own right, he passed though many of the world's biggest airports and saw for himself the spread of the duty free industry, and what its potential could be for Dubai. Even the concession system could be aesthetically pleasing if it were undertaken with some broad guidelines on presentation, he thought.

"It did not look right," says Binhendi. "At the time, Dubai had, by far, the

The Father of Dubai

The new airport was beyond anything seen in the Gulf during that era and would help cement the emirate's emerging status as the region's leading airport.

Dubai International Airport circa-1971. The emirate's Open Skies policy was seeing its aviation sector grow as new carriers arrived.

Fly *Buy* Dubai

Dubai Airport's first generation fire tenders during the early 1960s. By 1983, the airport was advertising for a third generation. The tender would lead to something new.

most beautiful airport in the Gulf. The Dubai government had invested a great deal of money and the consultants and architects had done a good job," he says. "Efficiency was a byword. From arrival at the terminal, to leaving the airport, including passing through customs and collecting baggage, we prided ourselves that passengers could often leave us in just seven minutes."

Indeed, Dubai Airport led where the others followed — much as it does today.

But times they were a-changing — although the advent of duty free shopping in Dubai was still some years away.

It is said that coincidence can sometimes make the most successful of enterprises, and it was out of a series of coincidences that Dubai Duty Free was born in 1983. In his capacity as Director-General of Dubai Civil Aviation, Mohi-Din Binhendi placed an advertisement in an international magazine for an airport fire tender — a much-needed piece of equipment to augment the airport's complement of fire safety vehicles.

And here we have the first example of coincidence. Michael Geoghagan, a manager with Irish airports operator Aer Rianta, was transiting through Dubai International on his way home from a business trip to the Far East. He picked up a copy of the magazine, saw the advertisement and, while aware that Aer Rianta couldn't provide a fire tender, it could perhaps get through

the door with the suggestion of a proper duty free facility like Shannon's.

He left a collection of Aer Rianta brochures with the airport operations manager and headed back to Ireland.

Now, it so happened that Binhendi had already been considering setting up a new retail sales area to replace the existing offerings for shoppers. Binhendi was aware that to keep pace with international shopping concepts, the airport needed to take a long and hard look at what it was currently offering. It's not that the goods on sale were not sophisticated — some of Dubai's finest merchants had concessions at the airport — but the existing retail outlets were spread over two levels and, in Binhendi's words: "Passengers wondered where to go first or where to find things cheaper and could leave without buying anything at all."

There thus needed to be a streamlining of the options — and everything operating under one cohesive umbrella.

*Shannon Estuary. By 1974 the various agencies and companies created by
Dr Brendan O'Regan were shaping the region.*

Chapter Five

A Fire Tender for Dubai

*Some people regard private enterprise as a predatory tiger to be shot.
Others look on it as a cow they can milk. Not enough people see it
as a healthy horse, pulling a sturdy wagon.*
— *Sir Winston Churchill, British statesman*

Aer Rianta International was formed as a dedicated international division of the Irish state-owned airports authority, now known as the Dublin Airport Authority. Aer Rianta International was built on over 60 years' experience of travel retailing. This experience included the establishment of the world's first airport duty free facility at Shannon and the first international duty free operation in the former Soviet Union. Either as concessionaire, manager, or operations partner, Aer Rianta International had actively promoted airport retailing in many countries.

The company is acknowledged and respected as one of the world's leading airport retailing specialists. It has earned its reputation through flexible and enterprising business culture, a world class international capability and — most importantly — an ability to consistently convert commercial opportunities into profit.

The history of Aer Rianta can be traced back to 1945, when Shannon Airport was then operating as Rineanna. From that year, until 1969, the airport was managed, in turn, by the Irish government's Department of Industry and Commerce and then the Department of Transport. In 1969, the Irish Airport Authority, Aer Rianta, assumed control of Shannon Airport as an agent of the Minister of Transport. Aer Rianta took over Shannon just as it had become obvious that a dramatic reappraisal of Shannon's terminal facilities was necessary, due to the introduction of wide-body aircraft.

Shannon was geared to handle aircraft disembarking over 100 passengers per flight, but with the new-generation airliners, it would now be required to handle over 300 per aircraft. The Department of Transport's planners had realised that a completely new terminal was required for the increased passenger loads. Government approval for a new facility was obtained in 1968 and work began within months of the first Boeing 747 arrival in 1969.

In 1974, Aer Rianta acquired the Shannon Sales and Catering Organisation which included the duty free operations, Shannon Mail Order Company, Shannon Castle Tours, and Shannon College of Hotel Management — all enterprises established by Dr Brendan O'Regan. In the

Fly *Buy* Dubai

late '70s, Aer Rianta acquired the Shannon International Hotel, now part of the Great Southern Hotels, an Aer Rianta subsidiary since 1990.

Shannon Airport did however have one enormous drawback. For all its efforts to ensure the latest technological advancements, it was technology itself which was the greatest threat to international aviation on the west coast of Ireland. Jet-powered airliners, with their capacity to reach well into Europe from the Americas, seemed to threaten obsolescence for Shannon. The question arose: what was the necessity for an airport with a very small catchment area on the northwestern end of the European seaboard, if aircraft could reach the main centre of Europe without technical stopovers? There had to be a reason to bring aircraft into the airport.

Duty free was the obvious starting point. This was followed by a campaign to draw training flights to the airport. Shannon was an airport where noise pollution would not be a major problem and where weather conditions were varied though temperate.

Terminal passenger traffic at Shannon had been adversely affected by the Northern Ireland troubles, recessions in the US, and by the world energy crisis. In 1974, Aer Rianta initiated an aggressive marketing programme to attract technical landings by US supplemental and charter airlines. This proved successful, and the airport survived a very difficult period in its history.

The search for business development led the Irish in a direction that was off-limits to many of the major Western European airports — across the Iron Curtain. In 1978, Aer Rianta executives approached Aeroflot with a proposal to store Soviet aviation fuel at Shannon for the airline to use on their trans-Atlantic services. This was the first move into a wider world for Aer Rianta, and one that would lead to greater things. In July of that year, Aer Rianta and the USSR's Ministry of Civil Aviation signed an agreement in Moscow. By June the following year, the former had built a dedicated fuel farm at Shannon.

The first Aeroflot flight to uplift fuel at Shannon landed there on July 3, 1980. In that year alone, there were a total of 240 Aeroflot landings, a figure that grew inexorably over the next decade. By 1991, Aeroflot was operating 2,000 aircraft through Shannon. The airline operated flights from Moscow, St Petersburg, Kiev, and Minsk to various cities in the United States, as well as in Central and South America. Aeroflot had traffic rights from Shannon to all of its Central and Southern American destinations, as well as Miami, Chicago, Washington DC, and Gander in Newfoundland.

The relationship between airport and airline grew, and a unique barter

A Fire Tender for Dubai

An Aeroflot Tupolev Tu-154 on the tarmac at Shannon. Under Leonid Brezhnev, Chairman of the Presidium of the Supreme Soviet of the USSR, Shannon's Aeroflot operations began.

Fly *Buy* Dubai

agreement was signed in 1983 between the two parties, whereby Aer Rianta could sell Soviet aviation fuel to other airlines, a deal which offset Aeroflot's hard currency operating costs at Shannon. The working relationship between Aer Rianta and the Soviet Ministry of Civil Aviation was further strengthened in 1987 when the former also became involved in the repainting and refurbishment of Aeroflot aircraft at Shannon. A dedicated painting hangar and refurbishing facility was constructed at the airport, which opened in August 1988.

In April 1947 American financier and Presidential advisor Bernard Baruch gave a speech in which he stated: "Let us not be deceived: we are today in the midst of a cold war..." Baruch was the first to coin the term 'Cold War' in reference to the geopolitical tensions between the Soviet Union and the United States.

But while the world suffered from the bullying of the superpowers, Shannon's successful courtship of Aeroflot did not preclude the airport from also looking West in search of competitive advantage. Aer Rianta approached the US Federal authorities to seek 'technical transit traffic' through Shannon. The concept was to establish US pre-clearance for passengers at Shannon, along the lines of similar facilities at Canadian Airports. In 1986, protracted negotiations culminated in an inter-governmental agreement between Ireland and the USA. Accordingly, a US Immigration Pre-Inspection facility was set up on a trial basis in 1986, and proved to be a great success. A permanent facility was constructed and opened in 1989. This has proved popular with both terminal and transit passengers. The first of its kind in Europe, it was yet another innovation.

Around the same time, Aer Rianta began to export its expertise, taking its highly successful duty free operations to a wider audience — initially the Middle East and the former Soviet states. Duty free shops, modelled on Shannon, would go on to be established at Sheremetyevo Airport in Moscow, Pulkovo Airport in St Petersburg (Leningrad; also Petrograd), and Kiev Airport — with further shopping facilities subsequently established in downtown locations in these cities. This was to lead to the founding of a subsidiary company, Aer Rianta International, based at Shannon Airport.

When the first duty free facility opened in Moscow, every nut and bolt had to be imported to Moscow. When the shops were ready in break-down form for transport to Moscow in the spring of 1988, they travelled in four 40-foot trucks. The shops were erected, stocked, and ready for the opening on May 1 that year, in less than a month!

Aer Rianta International, the new subsidiary, offered airport retailing and

A Fire Tender for Dubai

airport operational management consultancy expertise. Business interests would go on to include shareholdings and retail management contracts, concessions, supply contracts, and equity investments, and today it has operations in Europe (Moscow, St Petersburg, Kiev, Hamburg, Düsseldorf, and Birmingham); North America (New York, Montreal-Winnipeg, Edmonton, Ottawa, and Halifax) and the Middle East (Bahrain, Kuwait, Damascus, Beirut, Qatar, and Muscat).

Director-General of Dubai Civil Aviation, Mohi-Din Binhendi, who had advertised in an international magazine for an airport fire tender, says: "We were expanding. We were thinking big. From the beginning, Sheikh Mohammed bin Rashid Al Maktoum (then the UAE Defence Minister who also had, amongst his Dubai portfolio, responsibility for the airport) had decreed that Dubai's airport needed to be 'the best'.

"We were not measuring ourselves against the Gulf, nor the Middle East. Even in the early 1980s our yardstick was the best airports in the world. There was a long way to go, of course, but that was the intention."

Dubai's Open Skies policy was having an effect. In 1982, a total of 3,621,408 passengers had passed through the airport, a rise of 6.5 per cent over the previous year. Facilities were thus being constantly upgraded for

Beirut's Rafic Hariri International was one of the many airports worldwide whose duty free would be influenced by the Irish.

Fly *Buy* Dubai

(top) The existing duty free at Dubai Airport was decidedly low class.

(left) Mohi-Din Binhendi, Director-General of Dubai Civil Aviation, championed the concept of a fresh, new approach to duty free.

passengers and carriers, and this included emergency services. A new fire tender was required to be in place during 1983.

"I remember the advertisement, but not which publication it was in," says Binhendi. "But the outcome was unusual.

"I did not see the brochures [that Michael Geoghagan, Aer Rianta manager had left in response to the advertisement], but was briefed by the operations manager the following day," says Binhendi. "We were already considering a duty free and the options available to us. It was a coincidence, for sure, and when I looked into Aer Rianta it was clear that the Irish were industry leaders. They were natural partners, given that Sheikh Mohammed's instruction to us was that Dubai airport had to be the best."

At the time, there were six to eight duty free outlets at Dubai airport. All were individual businesses, which paid just a few thousand dirhams each year for their concession. Binhendi recalls his dissatisfaction of the status quo as it stood at the time.

"They did not fulfill our requirements, really. Although they were successful enterprises for the concerns which owned them," he says.

"They were cluttered with products, looked untidy and I remember one or two even had their staff sleeping inside when they were closed. These outlets presented little or no benefit for Dubai Airport, and while it could be said that they served the public, they were run, as one would expect, as businesses, which meant they had only the bottom line in mind."

When Aer Rianta suddenly made their presence felt, Binhendi had already been considering setting up a new retail sales area to replace the existing offerings. He was aware Dubai needed to take a long and hard look at its meagre duty free. It was not that the goods on sale were not sophisticated — some of Dubai's foremost merchants had concessions at the airport — but the existing retail outlets were spread over two levels at the airport and, in Binhendi's words: "Passengers wondered where to go first or where to find where things were cheaper and could leave without buying anything at all."

With the Irish knocking on the door, something needed to be done. Binhendi did what he did whenever a major decision was needed for the airport. Identifying a space in the airport complex, with a few rough drawings and a plan of what could be done next, he visited Sheikh Mohammed in the *Majlis*.

"Sheikh Mohammed reacted in his inimitable way. He listened to the concept I put forward, asked a few questions to satisfy himself of the details, and then said, 'Mohi, go and do it.' This is how the project was born," says

Fly *Buy* Dubai

Dubai Airport's airside shopping experience consisted of a handful of independent stores that added little to the experience of travellers.

Binhendi. "When Sheikh Mohammed makes up his mind, that's it, you have his full backing. But in order to satisfy him, it must be done well."

Sheikh Mohammed also expected his people, in all areas of government, to move speedily and without delay in order to achieve results. Within weeks, Binhendi and a small team were in Ireland on a short fact-finding mission to Shannon which was to culminate, on the last day, in a contract signing.

"Shannon was indeed very impressive. Over the course of a few days, we looked at all aspects of the business and were introduced to Aer Rianta International and what it could do for Dubai," says Binhendi. "I'm not one to get over-excited, but you could feel that this was the right organisation for us to work with, and I believed, the more I learned, that we could take Dubai's duty free from a few concession stands to a major business."

Over the course of the trip, the Dubai group was taken on an extensive tour of Shannon. It was during a visit to the actual shop floor that Binhendi encountered the man who would take the concept from an idea and make it a reality.

A Fire Tender for Dubai

"There was this fellow in the freeshop, the manager. He was so very impressive," says Binhendi. "He knew what he was talking about, he was passionate, articulate, dynamic. As we talked, I got the impression that this was the man for us. He had this outward confidence and obvious ability. That was the sort of person I wanted to work with."

One day later, Aer Rianta organised what was, in effect, a farewell dinner. The following morning the parties were to meet and sign a consultancy contract, before Binhendi was to return home. A few weeks later, representatives of Aer Rianta would arrive in the Gulf, formulate a strategy, and then, if all went to plan, bring in a team that would transform Dubai duty free.

But there were a few minor complications.

"I forget who we were dining with, but over the course of dinner I leaned over to the boss of Aer Rianta International and told him there was an addition I required to the contract — and a request I had to make," says Binhendi. "First, we wanted Dubai to have exclusivity in the Gulf for Aer Rianta's services. For ten years."

A young Colm McLoughlin was 'spotted' by his future boss when working as manager of the Freeshop at Shannon International Airport.

A Fire Tender for Dubai

Knowing full well that Dubai was considered 'cutting edge' by its regional competitors, Binhendi moved to prevent others capitalising on Irish expertise.

"And I was right," he says. "Within months of our duty free opening, three or four Gulf airports had been in touch with Shannon. At the time of the dinner, the fellow I was speaking to was shocked and very reluctant. But after a bit of haggling, something the Arabs and the Irish are both good at, we settled at seven years. We came to be very glad that this was in the contract, as it gave us an excellent head start."

The second point raised was regarding personnel.

"The Aer Rianta team for Dubai was to include a very qualified individual, who I knew would do a good job," says Binhendi. "But I had someone else in mind, the talented fellow I had met in the freeshop. I requested that he join the team."

A day later, Shannon Airports' Freeshop Manager was informed, unexpectedly, that he was to be a part of Aer Rianta's team that would shortly be heading to the Gulf.

His name was Colm McLoughlin.

Stretching eight kilometres and rising up to 214 metres, the windswept Cliffs of Moher in County Clare are believed to be the most visited tourist attraction in Ireland.

Chapter Six

Colm

It is not the critic who counts, not the man who points out how the strong man stumbled, or where the doer of deeds could have done better. The credit belongs to the man who is actually in the arena... who knows the great enthusiasms, the great devotions, and spends himself in a worthy cause.
— *Theodore Roosevelt, American statesman*

"Have you seen the entry list?" asks Colm McLoughlin. Ever-enthusiastic and, indeed, ebullient, McLoughlin brings a wide-eyed joy to his work that is somewhat inspiring when you consider that he has been employed in the same position for nearly a quarter of a century. It's now 2008. He arrived in Dubai in 1983 on a six-month secondment.

For the Managing Director of Dubai Duty Free, the source of enthusiasm on this day is the entry list for the Dubai Tennis Championships 2008. It's mid-January. The clock is ticking down towards one of Dubai's premier annual sporting attractions, a high point in a calendar packed with top class golf, motor sport, football, horse racing, and other events. Just in, the entries include nine of the top 10 women players in the world, and eight of the men's top 10. Apart from the year's four Grand Slams, such a high-profile entry is virtually unheard of.

"It's indicative of what we do. And very good for Dubai, which is, at heart, one of the most important things we do," explains McLoughlin.

This is the quintessential Colm McLoughlin, driving force behind Dubai Duty Free. The affable Irishman was called 'A Living Legend' in the book *World Rovers*, and is one of only two recipients of *Frontier* magazine's 'Lifetime Achievement Award'. Indeed, if any figure in the world's duty free industry has assumed the mantle of its mentor and leader, Dr Brendan O'Regan, it is McLoughlin.

Yet the road to captain of industry was a long and — at least in its early stages — winding and somewhat unlikely one. A County Galway man, McLoughlin was born in the small town of Ballinasloe in the west of Ireland, four years before the duty free industry began. One of five offspring, he grew up surrounded by traditional Irish influences, his father being a deeply patriotic man who even insisted that all his children, three boys and two girls, learn Irish traditional dancing.

"My father was an Irishman through and through. He spoke the Irish language whenever he could, and wore the badge in his lapel — which all

Fly *Buy* Dubai

Irish speakers wore — to indicate to other countrymen to speak the native language (instead of the regular English)," said McLoughlin. "He taught children Irish dancing until he was 91, not as a business but as a dedicated pastime.

"He was instrumental in the development of Ballinasloe and started the urban council. One of his initiatives was to put street names in Irish as well as in English. Later in his life he wrote a book about Ballinasloe. I've read it a couple of times."

McLoughlin Senior was, at one stage, invited to run for Parliament, but declined. While politics was not destined to be in the family blood, neither was retail. When McLoughlin finished high school he had his sights set on dentistry as a profession.

"That was the extent of people's ambitions at the time. You left school, you became a guard, which was the policeman, or a priest or one of the professions, such as a doctor or a dentist," he explained. "That was how things were done."

The pursuit of a profession, however, would not be seamless, and the cost of an education meant money had to be raised. In 1961, at the age of 19, he went 'overseas' to London to earn money for his university fees — but never quite made that transition from school-leaver to university undergraduate. Six years later, he had had a series of jobs which took his attention away from his chosen career, and today he says philosophically: "I never did become a dentist — I doubt, looking back, if I would have had the patience for it."

Meanwhile, among the many jobs he held while saving for the university degree that was not to be, were working on a farm in Oxfordshire, England; in a cannery; spending time in the Civil Service serving tea to visitors; and even selling encyclopaedias door-to-door.

"I was the worst door-to-door salesman. I just didn't like selling encyclopaedias on the never-never (hire purchase scheme) to people I knew would not be able to afford to keep up with the repayments. My conscience wouldn't let me!" says McLoughlin.

His encyclopaedia-selling days behind him, Colm looked for other employment. His brother joined him in London and together they painted houses for a while. Then, the young Colm worked as a bus conductor on the trolley buses which plied London and its surrounds in those days. It was a rich and varied tapestry and shows that McLoughlin was a diligent and hardworking individual who would literally put his hand and mind to anything to earn money.

It was while on the buses that his next 'career' move was to take shape.

Colm

*(top) Traditional Irish
Dancing was a feature
of the McLoughlin
family home.*

*(right) One of Colm
McLoughlin's early jobs
was on the buses.*

Fly *Buy* Dubai

Colm McLoughlin got his break into the retail industry when joining Woolworth's, the high street giant.

His route took him past a Woolworths store in Acton, West London. Woolworths was one of the original American five-and-dime stores, founded with a loan of $300 in 1878 by Frank Winfield Woolworth. The first UK store opened in 1909 and, by the 1960s, Woolworths was almost an institution in Britain.

One day McLoughlin hopped off the bus, went up to the manager of the Acton store, and asked him, "How can I get your job?"

"His name was Ginger Reed," McLoughlin recalls, adding: "He replied that you start in the stockroom and sweep the floor and you work your way up. And that's what I did…"

His approach was a bold, if not cheeky move, but was sufficient to show that the young McLoughlin had the right attitude to become a Woolworth's team member. He began his retail career as a stockroom boy in the giant Oxford Street, London branch.

"My starting salary was £9 a week — £7 and 16 shillings after tax. I had been earning £16 a week, so I had taken a steep drop to take this position,

The future Managing Director of Dubai Duty Free worked in Woolworth's flagship Oxford Street store in London.

but I was thinking about my career and with an eye on the long term," says McLoughlin.

The loss of funds required belt-tightening. In order to save on bus fares for the six-mile journey from his home in Acton to Oxford Street, he invested in a bicycle, bought from a policeman for 30 Shillings.

In Judy Garland's hit *I Can't Give You Anything But Love, Baby,* there is a line: '*...Diamond bracelets Woolworth doesn't sell, baby...*' And she was right. The company remained, at heart, a discount retailer. But there *was* a sparkling career available for anyone who understood the Woolworths' way — volume at competitive prices. Seven years on from picking up his wooden broom in the store at Oxford Street, McLoughlin was promoted to Deputy General Manager. It was no mean feat when, in those days, the average time for promotion into a managerial position was said to be 11 years.

He loved the buzz of the retail industry and enjoyed learning new things, moving from section to section, getting to know the ropes of each, and gleaning a solid overall knowledge of the business. Garland was right about the diamond bracelets, but McLoughlin found ways to shift everything else in Woothworth's.

The next step in the McLoughlin tale unfolded, again, quite by chance. During a holiday trip home to Ireland he spotted an advertisement for a merchandising manager for something called the duty free at Shannon Airport.

"I really did not understand what duty free meant," says McLoughlin. "But I went along and was interviewed by a guy called Bill Maloney — who is still a friend of mine — and his boss Tom Collins. They must have liked me a little because they took me to see Jack Ryan, Deputy Controller of what was called the Sales and Catering Unit, which operated the Duty Free. Brendan O'Regan was the Controller.

"I said: 'Mr Ryan, I want to know, if I join this organisation, how far can I go?' 'Well', he replied, 'You can always get Mr Maloney's job, and you can always get Mr Collins' job, but that's as far as you can go because I'm next.'"

Later in the interview, Ryan raised McLoughlin's relative youth as a concern. McLoughlin fired back: "Oh, that would not worry me, sir. I have loads of staff reporting to me now and they're nearly as old as you..!"

Colm McLoughlin was manager of the Freeshop at Shannon when an unexpected offer would change his life.

Colm

Despite that *faux pas*, McLoughlin got the job. Shannon and its duty free shop were to shape his life and career. He learnt from the people who had pioneered duty free. And he progressed, moving through the different departments, all the time watching, learning, listening.

"My first boss was Bill Maloney, who had arrived at Shannon in 1954 and could be regarded as the first duty free manager in the industry," says McLoughlin. "It was he who introduced branded merchandise in the industry. He was the first to introduce perfumes, design counters, staff uniforms, and write training manuals. I learnt everything he had to share."

Over the next few years, McLoughlin rose through the ranks at Shannon. He was eventually promoted to manager of Shannon's Freeshop, handling all sections except the liquor store. It was some 14 happy years later when fate stepped in again. One ordinary day, among the shelves of cigarettes and perfumes on the shop floor, McLoughlin was introduced to a delegation from Dubai. McLoughlin assumed it was a place in Saudi Arabia.

The head of the group asked a lot of questions and they got into deep conversation. McLoughlin, with his usual passion and verve, explained what he knew about duty free and how it worked. He shared some of his own ideas.

After a while the group from Dubai moved on, and McLoughlin got on with his normal daily routine. He thought nothing more about it until a couple of days later when he was offered a special assignment to Dubai.

*The Maktoum brothers were particularly successful in Ireland. Then Dubai
Crown Prince Sheikh Maktoum bin Rashid Al Maktoum won the Irish Derby in 1983.*

Chapter Seven

A duty free for Dubai

Innovation distinguishes between a leader and a follower.
— *Steve Jobs, American co-Founder of Apple*

Aer Rianta had been invited to present a proposal to set up a duty free operation at Dubai International Airport, and in June 1983 McLoughlin was co-opted into the project. The initial team was a two-man affair, and the plan was for them to fly to the United Arab Emirates to assess the operation's potential, then return to Ireland to prepare their final documents.

"I learned as much as I could about Dubai. Much to my surprise, I discovered it was not in Saudi Arabia, but was a country in its own right, part of the United Arab Emirates," says McLoughlin. "There was a notable and progressive Ruling family. What was more, as I discovered, the Al Maktoum family was well known in Ireland. Now, I was not a racing man, but if there is one thing that the Arabs and the Irish share, it is a love of thoroughbreds and 'the sport of Kings'.

"I quickly discovered how successful the Maktoums had been in racing, including such major races as the Irish Derby and the Irish Guineas."

Indeed, perhaps one of the few established contacts between Dubai and the Emerald Isle at that time was equine-orientated. As early as 1977, the emirate's ruling family had begun their extraordinary foray into the sport when Sheikh Mohammed's filly Hatta reeled off four wins on British racecourses. Hatta's 1977 campaign had been highlighted by a success in the 'black type' Molecomb Stakes at Goodwood. Top races are designated grades and are known as 'black type'.

The four brothers from Dubai were quickly bitten by a passion for the thoroughbred, and their interests broadened, both numerically and in terms of quality. In 1983, the Maktoum name first came to the attention of the Irish public when Sheikh Maktoum sent his Shareef Dancer over to the Curragh, where he triumphed in the Irish Derby, while Sheikh Ahmed's Wassl won the Irish 2000 Guineas.

Over subsequent years, the Maktoums' interests grew, and from simple ownership they became the world's foremost owner-breeders. In the process, the family invested in some of Ireland's greatest pastures, so steeped in equine lore.

So as McLoughlin learnt more about Dubai, he was to discover that the emirate was nowhere near as remote as he had first thought. The city-state

Fly *Buy* Dubai

A duty free for Dubai

The Aer Rianta team arrived in a Dubai markedly different from today. These images show Sheikh Zayed Road around 20 years apart in the early 1980s and early 2000s.

Fly *Buy* Dubai

Colm McLoughlin in the early 1980s. This is one of the last pictures taken of the then Freeshop Manager in Shannon before his move to the UAE.

was busy laying its foundations, even against the backdrop of a grim, low-level conflict between regional powers Iran and Iraq. Dubai had opened its first five-star hotels, the government had invested in heavy industries in order to diversify its oil-based economy, and several world-class ports were operating. The emirate's airport, under the leadership of Sheikh Mohammed — one of those four horse-loving brothers McLoughlin had learned about — was also growing.

It was in July 1983 when McLoughlin and Aer Rianta's finance director Michael Hanrahan flew to Dubai for exploratory talks and to get a 'feel' for Dubai and the potential its airport held. Arriving in the Gulf at the height of summer, at a time when Dubai was not as sophisticated as it is today, was a bit of a culture shock for the two Irishmen. The climate was hot, humid, and inhospitable — a far cry from a typical summer's day in County Clare with its fresh winds from the Atlantic, rolling early morning mists, and warm sunny afternoons when the barometer would just hit the 20 degree Celsius mark on a good day.

McLoughlin's immediate impression when he first set foot on Dubai's

A duty free for Dubai

soil in the summer of '83 was: "Oh, my God..."

"From the moment they arrived you could see that their ideas and concepts were just what we were looking for," recalls Mohi-Din Binhendi. "Colm was just so dynamic. He did not have an idea of what he was coming to, but quickly got a feel for it. Everyone warmed to him."

"I remember how animatedly he talked of what could be done, and how Dubai could benefit," says Mohammed Ahli, today Director Operations at Dubai Airports . "Even then, on that first visit, he essentially thought like us, which impressed everyone. People he spoke to during that initial visit came to me later to make sure he was coming back."

And McLoughlin certainly impressed the airport's Director General. On his last day in the emirate, a final meeting was held between Binhendi, McLoughlin, and Hanrahan. Hearing their proposal, drawn up in Shannon but tweaked as they came up with ideas during their visit, Binhendi grew more certain.

"I took their designs and project drawings to Sheikh Mohammed," recalls Binhendi. "As is his way, he wanted a brief, asked my opinion, and when he heard that I was keen, gave his assent — apart from one thing. Sheikh Mohammed looked at the drawings and told me to double the size of the proposed development.

"Sheikh Mohammed always thought big with regard to the airport. I don't think I, nor anyone who worked for His Highness, really knew just how great his ambitions for Dubai were at that time. But when it came to the airport and his demands for extra capacity in the new development, I think one could get an inkling as to the scope of his vision even then."

After viewing a full proposal and business plan, the two parties agreed on a six-month consultancy contract to get the project up and running.

For Aer Rianta this was great news. Yet as McLoughlin and Hanrahan got on a British Airways flight to Heathrow in good spirits, their euphoria was tempered by not-so-good news. They heard that the facility had to be open before the end of 1983 — in less than six months. Ideally, these things could take a year, or more, for everything to be put into place.

This, therefore, was not just a business development that would cheer the parent company in Shannon, it was a challenge that would push those involved to their professional limits. It meant that McLoughlin and Hanrahan had to head back to Shannon, work on an extensive plan, put a team together, and get back to Dubai — all within two months.

The project began with a concept to have a purpose-built retail area set up in a 20,000 square feet disused kitchen at the back of the departures hall. When this was operational, trading space would be leased back to the businessmen and trading companies who were already established at the airport.

It made sense commercially — based on the old way of doing things. And given the long-entrenched status of the handful of firms holding concessions at the airport there was, initially, no talk of changing the *status quo*.

But, as the airport authorities and Aer Rianta discussed the project more deeply they realised that the *status quo* wasn't going to work to the airport's benefit. The concessionaires only provided a few thousand dirhams each in fees per annum. Things had to change.

"Dubai Airport had always been an excellent proposition for us," says Gangu Batra, CEO of Jashanmal National Company, who had opened a shop at the airport in 1971. "But, given the forward motion at the airport, and a desire to see it become a world leader, I think the writing was on the wall for the concession system."

Discussions between the Department of Civil Aviation (DCA) and its guests from Aer Rianta inevitably turned to ownership. The concession system has its plus side: it brought in a very limited, though regular, income. There was no risk to DCA in terms of stock and management, no requirement to add to the bottom line with staff salaries, and certainly no hassles. But, viewed from another angle, there was no potential for the airport either.

As part of its study, Aer Rianta rolled out statistics showing the duty free revenues enjoyed in a variety of airports around the world. By the early 1980s the likes of Shannon, Heathrow, JFK, and Paris were making millions each year despite the fact that, globally, the industry was still in its embryonic stage. The Gulf, with no proper duty free history, was bursting with potential.

"Looking at Dubai airport's growth during the 1970s and '80s and the increasing number of passengers flowing through, it became obvious that we had to bring the operation in-house," says Binhendi. "There was also the issue of image. Dubai aimed to be the best in the world — even then — and, to be honest, the duty free at that time didn't look the part."

"Even based on relatively low spend per passenger, our projected figures were solid," says McLoughlin. "It really made no sense to spend so much money on a new and proper duty free facility, see turnover rise, and then allow a handful of independent businesses reap the benefit."

Aer Rianta strongly recommended an in-house approach. But reaching

A duty free for Dubai

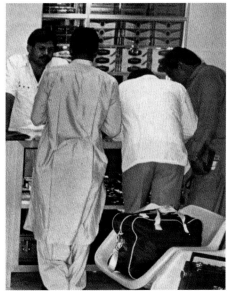

(top) Jashanmal National Company opened in Dubai in 1954 (pictured) and was one of the leading Dubai Airport sales operators before Dubai Duty Free was created.

(right) The shop floor at Dubai Airport was not what was expected when Dubai's Rulers were seeking to build a modern, world class airport.

Fly *Buy* Dubai

A viable, attractive duty free operation sat central to plans to catapult Dubai Airport from regional player into global hub.

that point was not easy. Several concessions were in the hands of trading companies such as Jashanmal, who had served the airport well for more than a decade, and many had vast amounts of money invested in stock. Other concessions had been granted directly to businessmen of standing by members of the Ruling family. Simply terminating contracts was not an option.

"It was made clear it was up to me to arrange a 'transition'," says McLoughlin. "I knew I was not going to be very popular."

While Aer Rianta worked on its proposal in Shannon, in Dubai the Department of Civil Aviation laid its own foundations for the new duty free facility.

Initial funding for the project came in the form of a Dhs 3 million ($820,000) loan from the National Bank of Dubai, guaranteed by the Government of Dubai. It was an investment that had, at its end, a specific desire. Dubai wanted to greatly increase its current throughput of passengers, which totalled around three million a year in 1983. The government wanted to tap into the transit market between East and West — their wish was that a duty free operation, similar to that successfully operating in Shannon, would attract new airlines and thus a whole new cache of transiting passengers. The duty free operation had to be not only first class but so attractive it would draw like a magnet and turn Dubai International into a 'must visit' destination.

So, with a firm brief and a tough timeline from Dubai's government, there was no time to waste for Aer Rianta. McLoughlin and Hanrahan's first job back in Shannon was to put together a team of ten duty free specialists, work on a blueprint, and head back to the Gulf…

"The clock was most definitely ticking," says Hanrahan.

*Among the eight Irishmen was (clockwise from top left) Colm McLoughlin,
John Sutcliffe, George Horan and Brendan O'Shea.*

Chapter Eight

Four Months

Old Time the clock-setter, that bald sexton, Time.
– William Shakespeare, English playwright

In September 1983, ten Irishmen from Aer Rianta landed at Dubai International Airport on a British Airways aircraft. These were the days before air bridges. An aircraft landed, opened its doors, awaited a passenger ramp, and disgorged its passengers onto the tarmac and into passably air-conditioned buses, which took them to the terminal.

McLoughlin had warned his eight colleagues, who were making their first trip to the Gulf, just what to expect; but when the doors of their aircraft opened, the nicely 'conditioned' interior atmosphere was sucked out and replaced with the airless summer heat. It was 45 degrees Celsius, and humidity was hovering around 100 per cent. Little could have prepared them for that first experience. "It was bloody hot!" says John Sutcliffe, one of the team members, wryly.

McLoughlin had drawn around him a task force of the brightest men in Aer Rianta. Alongside McLoughlin and Michael Hanrahan were John Sutcliffe, George Horan, Brendan O'Shea, Dave Hope, Michael Upton, Michael Cashin, Maurice Burke, and John O'Neill.

Hanrahan was project leader and McLoughlin his deputy. Horan was a shop floor merchandising expert, while Sutcliffe headed overall operations, O'Shea was a retail expert, while Hope was a time and motion-style operations man. Burke, Upton and Cashin were to set up the accounts operation with O'Neill the chief cashier.

They passed through the airport and into logistical problem number one. Dubai, as today, was full. In 1983 there was only a handful of five-star hotels in the emirate, compared to dozens by the end of 2008. "We were living in a mixture of places," says McLoughlin. "I was staying with a colleague of mine in an apartment in Deira Tower. One or two of our boys moved into the Le Meridien Hotel just across the road from the airport."

Then known as the Dubai International Hotel, this was considered one of the very best. With several bars, a nightclub, a plush gym, pool, tennis and squash courts, and sauna, the hotel was, at the height of the Gulf summer, an oasis of leisure and pleasure. Elsewhere, the ten Irishmen, many of whom enjoyed golf, heard that there was a round to be had on the UAE's first desert course, at the nearby Dubai Country Club. And they'd also heard that, around town, it was customary for visitors to sample the multicultural cuisine which Dubai's leading hotels and restaurants had to offer.

"I think I got one afternoon at the pool. That was it," recalls Horan. "We hit the ground running. I recall, by the December, I had only managed a couple of afternoons off. Most evenings when we left the office, I was so tired I didn't feel like socialising and literally went straight to bed when I got back to the hotel."

It was indeed all work and no play. Little did the team know that September, when they landed in Dubai, that this would be their daily routine for the next four months. Barely 12 hours after arriving in Dubai — hardly any time to recover from jetlag — the Aer Rianta team was back at the airport again for a briefing and visit to the facility they were to be transforming into a duty free. Orientation took 30 minutes, while meetings with some of the principals they would be working with lasted another hour. The enormity of the project they had taken on was staring them straight in the face.

A look at space which had been made available for the new facility — once a disused kitchen — led several to wonder if it were possible to create a sophisticated duty free, from scratch, in the slim period allowed. "We had decided to work towards opening just before Christmas, in order to catch the last few days of the festive rush," recalls Upton. "But this gave us barely more than 100 days."

"From day one, we worked from 7.30 in the morning through to the early hours of the following morning," McLoughlin remembers. "There wasn't time to get to know our surroundings — we had a massive challenge and a short time span to achieve it in."

The logistics included transportation. It took a week or more before cars were organised. "If we had to go and see a supplier over in Bur Dubai, the best way was to get a taxi to the Creek and cross on an *abra* [water taxi].

"We had to use taxis to go everywhere and often it was quicker to take a taxi along the Deira side of the Creek, jump on an *abra* to cross the water to Bur Dubai side, then pick up another cab! It took time but it was the efficient way to get around."

The group's combined experience, professionalism, and knowledge of the duty free industry, all gleaned at Shannon, were soon put to the test. The men worked as a team — temperament was banished and egos left on the doorstep.

"Our attitude was that we would work hard now — very hard — and after completing the project we could go back to Ireland, have a well-deserved rest, and get on with our lives and professions again," says Horan. "At least that was the plan."

Taking over some cramped, windowless, and, it is recalled, poorly air-conditioned offices to the rear of the old kitchen area, the team then got to work. Their immediate tasks were to identify the type of goods to go on sale — source them and place orders. It had been decided that the new facility would open with 24 shops. And, meanwhile, a concept had to be decided upon, interiors designed, colour schemes set in place, and the outlets built and fitted out.

But first McLoughlin was delegated one of the most politically difficult jobs he would face. The existing concession holders were to be visited — and he would inform them that their valuable outlets at the airport would be closing in December, never to reopen. "It would be fair to say that I was not the most popular man in Dubai," he admits.

But the Department of Civil Aviation eased the blow, offering that its new duty free would purchase all the stock the concessionaires carried. This would cost the new facility some $550,000 of its initial working capital.

As part of the package to placate airport retailers, Dubai Duty Free was compelled to absorb all their inventory, however bad.

(top) Gold was a risk for Dubai Duty Free with its limited cash reserves.

(left) Gangu Batra of Jashanmal National Company absorbed the blow of losing his company's stand at Dubai Airport, but went on to work with Dubai Duty Free for 25 years.

Four Months

Long-standing firms such as Jashanmal and Captain's Stores kept a lot of high-quality merchandise at the airport, which would fit nicely into Dubai Duty Free's planned inventory for its shelves. Other concessionaires, however, stocked items which, because of their 'down market' qualities, could never find their way on to the shelves of a brand-new, modern, duty free facility. But they were also purchased, although they never made it onto the shop floor for opening day and were later disposed of.

Purchasing stock in this way posed a certain amount of risk – not just because of the wastage that was to occur but also because one of the key goods was gold.

"Buying up all the existing stock was a goodwill gesture made by Mr Binhendi to rebuild relations," explains McLoughlin. "But some of the purchasing proved to be challenging – particularly the gold stocks. Because gold is a commodity which is always changing in price, we had to offer the merchants a price which would ensure they would make a profit on their original purchases. But we made sure that no-one was a loser in the buying game."

Aer Rianta also moved to keep relations and maintain a *status quo*, with McLoughlin stating that former concession-holders would, where possible, receive preferential status when Dubai Duty Free was ordering goods from the local market. It was a promise that was – and continues to be – fulfilled, and, 25 years on, several of those original concessionaires continue to supply the airport today.

"Losing our airport outlet was a blow at the time," admits Gangu Batra, CEO of Jashanmal National Company, which had held a concession at the airport since 1970. "But Colm made us a promise and he never broke his word. Although we have to be competitive in our pricing, we have been allowed to have a strong and mutually beneficial relationship with Dubai Duty Free."

Having smoothed ruffled feathers, plans moved from the drawing board and into reality. One priority was merchandise. As much as possible, and without compromising quality, there was an understandable desire – and logistical advantage – in sourcing goods locally.

"Brendan and I spent a lot of time down in the Dubai *souq* which was, at the time, the stronghold of Dubai's merchant community, and we soon realised our original conception of the merchant's community was rather off the mark. I remember taking an *abra* across the Creek from Deira to Bur Dubai and we walked and walked and walked," says McLoughlin. "We were searching for the original agents of internationally-recognised brand names.

Fly *Buy* Dubai

The iconic Dubai Creek abra was an important tool for Dubai Duty Free as its managers hopped between the emirate's various souks seeking suppliers.

In time, we discovered that everyone claimed to be an 'agent' for everything. For example, if we went in a tailor's shop and let it slip we were looking for wheelbarrows, they promised to have as many as we wanted, in whatever colour we wanted, by that afternoon. It was like unraveling a ball of string! Eventually we used a Chamber of Commerce directory, which helped us find out who the officially appointed agents were for this and that."

And there were other odd pitfalls in establishing a duty free facility 3,000 miles from their normal place of operation. Aer Rianta's experience, honed over the years, had taught them the type of merchandise which would be favourites in a duty free. And so they had brought with them a list of recommended merchandise based on their European experience. They knew that liquor, tobacco, and fragrances were top sellers. After all, they accounted for between 60 to 75 per cent of duty free sales throughout the world at that time. It was never questioned that they wouldn't reap the same success in Dubai.

Even before opening, however, the established European norms started to look somewhat out of place. The team quickly realised that in Dubai things were going to be different. The profile of a typical traveller who would use the Dubai Duty Free facility was a lot different from Shannon's. In Dubai, the traveller would be Asian and, instead of luxury goods to take back home, gold was preferred.

And so, unlike at Shannon where a large area of the duty free facility was set aside for crystalware — a top seller for them — in Dubai that large area was given over to gold, mainly *tola* bars and jewellery. Indeed, gold has been one of the best-sellers at Dubai Duty Free each year since the facility opened, and the *tola* bars are still massive favourites.

"When sourcing merchandise in the early days, we at least had the $550,000 worth of stocks from the existing concessionaires to build from and build into our inventory," Brendan O'Shea recalls. One of his major tasks as a retail expert was to assess the local market and bargain with traders for their best prices.

"The Irish are just as good at haggling as even the hardest Arab merchant. We secured some excellent deals," says McLoughlin proudly. "Thanks to the massive buying power of Dubai Duty Free, local traders have since received great support and hundreds of millions of dollars are pumped into the Dubai economy through Dubai Duty Free's buying policy," adds Sheikh Ahmed, President of Dubai Airports Company.

As O'Shea and his fellow Irishmen were building an inventory, a marketing campaign was also in the works. From the outset, Binhendi and McLoughlin were intent upon building a brand. "At that time, Dubai hardly registered internationally. There were only a few five-star hotels, but we had a long-term plan for greater prosperity and the duty free was in this plan," says Binhendi. "However, in 1983, our immediate aim was more about branding ourselves and creating our own identity."

To promote the new facility, McLoughlin brought in several local agencies to pitch their ideas for above-the-line and below-the-line concepts. There were a few good ideas, but nothing had caught neither his imagination nor Binhendi's.

"We had a few meetings, but by and large nothing really stood out," says McLoughlin. Binhendi adds: "I think we wanted something creative that jumped out and startled us. Nothing did at the beginning."

Cue the arrival of Anita Mehra. The daughter of one of the region's best known doctors and founder of Dubai's Iranian Hospital, Mehra had been visiting the emirate since the weeks after the formation of the United Arab Emirates, in 1971.

Fly *Buy* Dubai

She arrived full-time in 1983 and joined one of Dubai's better agencies during that period.

That same year she heard, through the PR grapevine, that the Department of Civil Aviation had been inviting a few agencies to pitch for an account for its new duty free. Her firm had not been invited, but as Dubai was then still a small city, everyone knew everyone — and their business. Placing a call to Binhendi was not difficult.

"So I called him up and said, 'I'm working with an advertising agency, can we pitch for the account?'" Mehra recalls.

There was a week remaining before a deadline by which Dubai Duty Free had to make a decision one way or the other. They were less than impressed with the materials they had received from the other bidders, so allowed this young upstart a crack at the account. "I told Anita, if they could put something together in one week, then I would he happy to meet them. Otherwise, it was out of the question," says Binhendi.

"So I said, 'Just give me one week and we'll put it together'," said Mehra. Mehra and her colleagues had just a few days, and a few sleepless nights, to conceptualise and produce a presentation for an account that could be about the biggest in Dubai at that time. At some point someone — and to this day, no-one recalls who — came up with a clever play on words.

"At the end of a week, we presented to Colm and Mohi (as we called Mr Binhendi) and I remember I was so nervous," recalls Mehra.

"Colm and Mohi grilled me — but when we did this concept we had brought up — 'Fly Buy Dubai' — they liked it a lot. After the presentation, maybe a couple of days later, I got a call and they said 'yes'. So I was the account executive for the Dubai Duty Free account until 1986, when I moved over to join them as a full-time member of the team."

'Fly Buy Dubai' perhaps summed up everything the facility would come to symbolise. As well as encompassing 'brand' Dubai, a feature which became increasingly important as the emirate grew to be a business and leisure destination in its own right, the phrase also encapsulated the concept of Dubai as an air transit hub, which it aspired to be.

"The identity of Dubai Duty Free would, I had supposed, be one of our legacies at the end of our four months in Dubai," says McLoughlin. "I hoped that we would leave behind something that would be sustainable. This would be a major part of it."

Elsewhere, anticipating their pending departure after a December opening, the team got to work preparing for the permanent management that would follow them. Procedures manuals had to be written for every

The 'Fly Buy Dubai' campaign has lasted a quarter of a century.

(right) Anita Mehra later joined Dubai Duty Free.

*The award winning 'Fly Buy Dubai' campaign would become synonymous with
Dubai Duty Free throughout its history and to the present day.*

Fly *Buy* Dubai

(top) Adverts in the Philippines press for Dubai Duty Free jobs received an enthusiastic response.

(left) Angelito Hernandez, President and Managing Director of IPAMS.

aspect of a complex retail operation — from purchasing and stock control to human resources management and after sales service, the list was endless. And while all this was going on, staff had to be recruited and trained, uniforms designed (the first outfits were designed in-house and made up by a local tailor), salary structures put in place, and accommodation for staff sourced and prepared for occupation.

The first batches of staff for the new complex were hired from India and the Philippines. McLoughlin and Hanrahan travelled to Bombay and Manila on initial recruitment drives. "We went principally with the Philippines, as the boys and girls from that country have such an excellent reputation for customer service," says McLoughlin. "It was a decision that served us well. Over the last quarter century we have employed some truly excellent people. Customer service was always one of our bywords, and this, in no short measure, has been thanks to the brilliant people we have employed on the shop floor."

The relationship between Dubai Duty Free and the Philippines began with the help of recruitment agency IPAMS, a company which continues to support Dubai Duty Free with top class employment candidates a quarter of a century later.

"I have encountered, or represented, few better employers than Dubai Duty Free, in terms of integrity and care of workers," says Angelito Hernandez, President and Managing Director of the company. "When opportunities are offered in Dubai, we are always flooded with applications, for people know the opportunities on offer are very tangible. It is not just a job, it is a career."

McLoughlin forged close ties with Hernandez and IPAMS, but on his initial trip to Manila in October 1983, he personally interviewed and selected hundreds of applicants.

"Of the 100 staff we opened with, 59 are still with Dubai Duty Free 25 years later, which is a testimony to the culture we tried to create," says McLoughlin. "We did not just recruit employees — we literally built a family whose dedication over the years was to pay great dividends."

The first batch of employees arrived from the Philippines just three weeks before the duty free was to open. A few days later, new recruits came from India, and then a second batch of Filipinos within a week of opening day.

Some staff were, of course, recruited locally between September and October of 1983, and they, along with some who had been working in the existing duty free shops, helped the new arrivals integrate into their new surrounds. But the very late arrival of the recruits from the Philippines and

India did create an urgent training problem.

"The staff we brought in for the frontline, to interface with the customers, were hand-picked for their personality, attitude, and savvy," says Horan.

So, with only a couple of weeks remaining before they were to be pressed into service, the new arrivals were taught grooming techniques, given coaching in English, taught the rudiments of a duty free enterprise, and imbibed with some product knowledge.

Training staff in the various currencies they might expect to use was another problem which, from the comforting surrounds of an office in Ireland when a blueprint for the new operation was being put in place, would never have occurred.

"Many of the first sales staff recruited had never seen any other currency than their own home country pesos or rupees," says McLoughlin. "We knew we would be working with a range of currencies at the duty free — predominantly US dollars, pounds sterling, and, of course, UAE dirhams. So, we went out to the money exchange in the *souq* and bought lots of different currencies so we could train the staff in currency values and how to give customers change."

The arrival of hundreds of staff also presented organisational challenges. They needed visas, transportation, housing, medical facilities, catering, and a plethora of other services. From scratch, the operation needed staff roster systems, in place for a never-ceasing 24/7 operation.

Elsewhere, one of the major problems the Irish team faced proved to be logistics. They were developing what was arguably the biggest retail logistical operation in the UAE at the time. Warehousing had to be sourced and manned, stock control systems put in place — in an era before such procedures could be done at the click of a computer mouse — delivery trucks purchased and delivered. Never before had the airport dealt with an ongoing stock management system, which would call for dozens of staff and a steady flow of truckloads of merchandise — much of it perishable or temperature-sensitive — to move in and out of the airport on a daily basis.

This would need a call upon Dubai Police, Customs department officials, and DCA staff to adopt radically different systems that were flexible, yet rigorous enough to maintain the integrity of airport security.

As one DCA official from the 1980s states: "Flexibility was not the byword of airport administration, anywhere in the Arab world, in those days. Although everyone was working together, it took new thinking to introduce a seachange in attitude and approach, in order to build into the airport the systems necessary for a successful duty free.

Four Months

Dubai Duty Free has achieved much thanks to its staff — and over the last 25 years the company has been underpinned by the quality of its employees.

Fly *Buy* Dubai

*Colm McLoughlin and George Horan were on a December 20 deadline
for the new Dubai Duty Free to open.*

These new systems were challenged by the circumstances. After considerable time devoted to finding a suitable facility, a warehouse was found in the area which today is Dubai Cargo Village. Logistically, in many countries in the northern hemisphere, not a problem. But in Dubai? Trucking supplies in hot weather was a major headache, especially if the stock being moved was chocolate or even cosmetics such as lipsticks. Heaps of lateral thinking was employed on an almost daily basis to get around a logistical nightmare.

Sometime during this six months, someone — and today no-one can quite remember who — came up with a mission statement. A mission statement is a brief of the purpose of a company, or other organisation. Companies sometimes find their mission statement useful simply for advertising; for others the intention is a genuine article of faith to keep members and users aware of the organisation's purpose.

Of course, back in 1983 a 'mission statement' was not the buzzword it is a generation on. Indeed, at the time it was not called a 'mission statement' but simply five principles against which Aer Rianta and Dubai Duty Free would measure themselves. The brief was to make Dubai Duty Free one of the best in the world. Customer service was an important part of the overall offering at Dubai Duty Free right from the start. With the concept that good customer service should be as important as profits, the following was promised:

High quality goods. A wide range of merchandise. Value for money. Convenience shopping. First class service.

"And we have never faltered from that," says George Horan. "I can say, absolutely, that these remain our cornerstone principles. They were never jargon, they were the cardinal 'rules' which we adhered to. That is why Dubai Duty Free is where it is today."

A quarter of a century ago, the Aer Rianta team had another promise — made to the Dubai government — to ensure that the new facility would play an integral part in the growth of Dubai on the world stage. From that first meeting between Binhendi, McLoughlin, and Hanrahan, there was a commitment made that they were going to turn the duty free facility into a multi-million dollar enterprise, attracting people from around the world and actually determining people's travel habits.

"Even today, to the layman, the thought of a passenger determining his travel habits according to where he could find the best, most comfortable airport, or the best value duty free, may seem hard to absorb," agrees Binhendi. "But then, if one could see how Dubai International Airport straddles the region as a global hub, then one can see that this is indeed the case.

"It was a concept that Sheikh Mohammed and the Dubai government believed in. We were charged with making that a reality. I never doubted for a moment, during those first four months, that we were not creating something that would drive this vision."

The vision, however, was becoming something of a personal nightmare for everyone involved. It was a flat-out situation, but none of the Aer Rianta team would have, in their wildest dreams, realised that the frantic work that went into the opening of the new facility would reap so many rewards. As the days flew by until December 20 — the date which had been decided for opening day — there wasn't even time to look out the window of their office — if there had been a window, that is! It was heads down and look in, and they didn't just tick off the days on the calendar as opening day drew nearer; they were literally ticking off the hours and cramming as much

Fly *Buy* Dubai

activity as they could into each action-packed 60 minutes.

The Aer Rianta boys who had formed such a close-knit team, literally eating, drinking, and sleeping Dubai Duty Free, brainstormed constantly, facing any adverse situation which they came up against, turning negatives into positives.

As October ran into November and November into December, there was no time for anyone to think about anything other than opening day. The date of December 20 was firmly set — a perfect time from a marketing viewpoint. Just five days before Christmas and a time when Dubai International Airport historically experiences one of its busiest times with passengers crisscrossing the globe to spend the festive season with family and friends. Transiting passengers were the target, but so too were the many expatriates living in the UAE who made an annual exodus for the holidays — and for the parents and friends who traditionally poured into the country at that time of year.

And so the countdown began. There was no time for the Aer Rianta team to think about families and friends back home preparing for the seasonal festivities; there was work to be done, and a copious amount at that.

"Those last few days were crazy. Some of the strangest of my life," says John Sutcliffe. "Everything came together, thanks to a lot of planning. But there were still many hurdles and late glitches that tested us all. The team from Aer Rianta all knew what we were doing, but for many, our own employees, people working at the airport, suppliers and others, this was new. So the whole operation was not only being led by us, but physically most of the work was being done by us. And it was a big, big undertaking."

In the days leading up to the opening, and as the wraps came off the various display counters, an elegance was revealed in the new duty free area. However, the main entrance to the facility, a new escalator, and a floor below the departures hall, were still being installed and tested.

The design and fitting out of the new facility was by renowned British companies: Fitch and Co, and Ruppel and Co, respectively. The decor featured warm pink marble on the floor, the perfect foil for the attractive glass display cabinets, and inviting shelving systems.

Concealed lighting added an attractive glow to the ambience. Signage was in golden yellow. It was all a far cry from the shopping facilities that customers had been accustomed to whilst browsing around in the past at Dubai Airport.

Rodney Fitch (of Fitch and Co) was a famous designer in Britain, with a reputation forged over a distinguished career spanning nearly 40 years. Fitch was Deputy Chairman of the London Institute, served as a member of the

Four Months

Council of the Royal College of Art, a Trustee of the Victoria and Albert Museum, and was later awarded a CBE in 1990 for his influence on the British design industry. Fitch was expensive, but forward-thinking, and emerging as a giant of the industry.

"Sheikh Mohammed looked (at) and approved the overall concepts. It represented a big, big transformation for the airport," says Binhendi. "He wanted the best."

As the countdown toward opening went on, hundreds of workers poured into the old kitchen, transforming it from an empty shell into an entity that was on par with anything else in the industry. It was impressive. *Very* impressive. But as the complex came together, what emerged was something even *more* impressive. It was not just a break with the past in Dubai Airport terms, but as good as anything in the duty free industry. It was an incredible start, and put down something of a marker for the industry of today.

As workers completed their respective tasks, Dubai Duty Free people moved in. Inevitably, for a project that was a first-of-a-kind, there had been delays. For example, proper access had not been available until around a week before the opening date. Therefore, as soon as people were able to move into the new facility, it was 'all hands on deck' as everyone was drafted in to stock the shelves and arrange items enticingly in cabinets and display areas — and tidy the areas up as they toiled!

"In those last few hours we did everything that was required to get the job done. I remember John Sutcliffe and I both washing the floors just minutes before we actually opened," says McLoughlin.

There was no time to feel homesick in those build-up to opening days — and as George Horan would say later: "Before we came to Dubai we didn't realise the enormity of the task ahead. At the beginning when we first set to work, we operated under difficult conditions with cramped windowless office space and limited air-conditioning despite the outside temperatures. But we were so engrossed in our respective tasks that we hardly gave any thought to our working environments.

"We were enthusiastic and determined to meet the challenges — we didn't even get on each other's nerves despite our working conditions which many people would probably not endure today. Looking back it was an exciting, pioneering, and very special time which none of us will ever forget."

With hours remaining before the opening of the re-branded Dubai Duty Free, everyone forgot their aching limbs and fatigue… and a sleepless night lay ahead.

Fly *Buy* Dubai

Four Months

In the last hours leading up to December 20, it was all hands on deck as staff fought to have the shop floor stocked and ready for business.

Titus Flavius Vespasianus, commonly known as Vespasian,
became Emperor of Rome on December 20, 69 AD.

Chapter Nine

December 20, 1983

Birth is the sudden opening of a window, through which you look out upon a stupendous prospect. For what has happened? A miracle. You have exchanged nothing for the possibility of everything.
– William MacNeile Dixon, British scholar

The day December 20 has played its role in the history of the world. On December 20 in 69 AD, Vespasian, formerly a general under Nero, entered Rome to claim the title of Emperor. And, on that same day in 1522, Suleiman the Magnificent accepted the surrender of the surviving Knights of Rhodes, who were allowed to evacuate. They eventually settled on Malta and became known as the Knights of Malta.

On the same December day in 1606 the Virginia Company loaded three ships with settlers and set sail to establish Jamestown, Virginia, the first permanent English settlement in the Americas.

The Welsh have also remembered this day since 1955, when Cardiff was proclaimed the capital city of Wales. In Spain, however, it is something of a black day because in 1973, Spanish Prime Minister Admiral Luis Carrero Blanco was assassinated by a car bomb attack in Madrid.

The weeks leading up to Dubai Duty Free's opening also saw a series of significant international events. In November, a NATO exercise had many Soviet officials believing they were seeing a first nuclear strike — it became the last scare of the Cold War. A few days later the first US cruise missiles arrived at Greenham Common airbase in England.

Then came an event that would push up the price of gold. This was hardly beneficial to Dubai Duty Free, which had guaranteed the highest market price to the former concession-holders at the airport when they purchased their stock. On November 26, 1983, the Brinks Mat robbery in London saw 6,800 gold bars worth nearly £26 million taken from a vault at Heathrow Airport. Only a fraction of the gold was recovered.

In politics around the world, military rule ended and democracy was restored in Argentina, while the Turkish region of Cyprus declared independence.

On a positive note — and a profitable one too for Dubai Duty Free — on December 2, 1983 Michael Jackson's music video *Thriller* was broadcast for the first time. It was to become the most famous music video of all time, resulting in millions of copies of the album of the same name being sold

Fly *Buy* Dubai

worldwide — tens of thousands of which have been sold through Dubai Duty Free from December 20, 1983 through to the present day.

December 20 is also the birth date of several internationally-renowned personalities and politicians, amongst them American automobile tyre pioneer Harvey Firestone (1868); Sir Robert Menzies, former Prime Minister of Australia (1894); Dr Mahathir Mohamad, the former Prime Minister of Malaysia (1925); British politician Sir Geoffrey Howe (1926); and oddball Israeli psychic Uri Geller (1946).

Historical and news websites generally accept that there were four 'celebrity' births on December 20, 1983: American actor Jonah Hill; Dutch model Lara Stone; and Mexican music star Adrián Varela. A fifth is not chronicled but it surely must be the most enduring. At around seven in the morning of December 20, 1983, Dubai Duty Free was officially 'born'. The opening of the new complex was unheralded. There was no official event, nor even ribbon-cutting. For the most part, the world's newspapers, including the local Dubai media, concentrated on international events.

In Britain two days earlier, a Provisional IRA car bomb had massacred six Christmas shoppers and injured 90 outside Harrods in London. On December 20, news was just filtering through that the original FIFA World Cup, the Jules Rimet Trophy, had been stolen from the headquarters of the Brazilian Football Confederation in Rio de Janeiro.

The IRA atrocity was plastered across front pages of local newspapers which appeared on the shelves at the newly-opened duty free. "After four months of intense work, most of us had given up reading newspapers or watching television. The 20-hour days we had been experiencing had almost detached us from the rest of the world," says one of the Aer Rianta team. "But the IRA bomb brought us all back to reality. It was a grim reminder of the troubles that dominated at home."

The night before opening had been a sleepless one for the ten Irishmen, and the majority of Dubai Duty Free's 100 staff. With the clock ticking down, there was little time for nerves, although everyone connected with the new enterprise recalls their trepidation.

"We were nervous," says McLoughlin. "We had so many niggling doubts: Had we bought enough stock of certain items? How were we to manage all the customers? There were technical issues too, simply because we were testing things for the first time: Would our cash registers break down? Would our credit system work? Were our currency conversion systems ready? Would we go bankrupt?"

"We were all apprehensive," says Binhendi. "A project can be backed up

December 20, 1983

(clockwise top left)) Dr Mahathir Mohammed, Jonah Hill and Uri Geller share birthdays with Dubai Duty Free, while on December 20, 1983, the Jules Rimet Trophy was stolen.

December 20, 1983

Nerves were
strained as the
company prepared to
open its shop floor.

by all the studies in the world, but you never really know if it will be a success until it's up and running."

On McLoughlin fell the biggest responsibility of a long night. After he and his compatriots had finished mopping, polishing, arranging, and tidying on the shop floor, he morphed into a somewhat reluctant bullion dealer. In addition to the gold Dubai Duty Free had inherited at a high price from the outgoing concession holders, they required even more stock in time for opening the following day. Leaving it until the last few hours, so that Dubai Duty Free could secure the best international gold price and not risk making a loss on their razor-thin margins, McLoughlin headed into the *souq* with his calculator.

"We needed to secure the best price per gram, because our agreement with the former gold vendor saw us buying his existing stock at a very inflated price," says McLoughlin. "We were trying to make both ends meet and balance everything by being deft in purchasing the rest of our gold stocks. We were constantly mindful that we had a very limited credit line

On the evening before opening $82,000 of gold was delivered to the shop floor in Colm McLoughlin's briefcase.

with the National Bank of Dubai."

After a couple of hours in the gold *souq*, bargaining and cajoling with wholesalers — many of whose businesses had been established in Dubai for a century or more and who knew how to drive a hard bargain — McLoughlin came up with the goods.

"I walked back into the duty free with $82,000 worth of gold in my briefcase and put it down on the counter," he says. "Frankly, it was a relief to hand it over."

Through the night, shelves were stocked, merchandise priced, and displays put together. Stock at Dubai Duty Free's nearby warehouse was gradually depleted as dozens of trucks shuttled both ways, filling up and dropping off goods.

"We werent in a blind panic. It was more of a well-ordered panic," recalls Horan.

Aer Rianta had promised December 20 for opening day and now there was considerable pressure to deliver. A delay at this stage, even by a day, would lead to repercussions in terms of confidence. As Binhendi observes: "A great many people were watching what was going on — some with enthusiasm, some with amazement and a few, I guess, thinking this was an endeavour destined for failure.

"Just as importantly, we had promised Sheikh Mohammed that this concept would be a success for Dubai. Sheikh Mohammed expected nothing less."

And so, with just minutes to go before the clock struck seven and final touches being completed on displays, McLoughlin and the team did a final sweep of the shop floor. Apart from a few minor changes here and there, and a notebook full of tasks that they would see to over coming days and weeks, Dubai Duty Free was ready.

When the green light was given, the escalator leading down from the passenger area to the duty free powered into action. After a few moments, and without realising that they were making history and ushering in a new era for Dubai, a crowd of passengers took the 15-second ride down the escalator. A few minutes later, a bottle of whiskey and a carton of cigarettes became the first-ever purchases in this brand-new world-class shopper's haven.

*Then Philippine First Lady Imelda Marcos remains one of Dubai Duty Free's
record customers spending $20,000 in a 25 minute shopping spree.*

Chapter Ten

$20 million

To me, the definition of focus is knowing exactly where you want to be
today, next week, next month, next year, then never deviating from
your plan. Once you can see, touch and feel your objective, all you
have to do is pull back and put all your strength behind it, and
you'll hit your target every time.
— *Bruce Jenner, American athlete*

In January 1984, less than a month after opening its doors, Dubai Duty
Free's first celebrity customer stepped quietly onto the escalator and down
into the Fitch-inspired retail utopia created therein. Her name was Imelda
Marcos — and in those days she was still a celebrity, although later that
status would be changed to one of notoriety.

During the 1980s she would be followed by the likes of big screen stars
Sylvester Stallone and Roger Moore, Brazilian soccer legend Zico, World
Heavyweight Champion Marvin Hagler, George Lucas of *Indiana Jones* and
Star Wars fame, and even Bono and The Edge, of Irish super-group U2.

Indeed, over the years since Dubai Duty Free opened its doors, a vast
number of celebrities have whiled away the hours between flights by
slipping out of Dubai Airport's VVIP suites and down into the shopping
haven. Many, like Stallone, were content to soak up some adulation from
startled passengers and Dubai Duty Free staff. Others bought a few items
almost *incognito*. Moore, perhaps best known for portraying two British
action heroes — Simon Templar in the television series *The Saint* from 1962
to 1969, and James '007' Bond in seven films from 1973 to 1985 — bagged
himself a pair of sunglasses, for example.

But it was that first-ever celebrity whose memory will remain a constant
in the sea of famous faces who have patronised the complex.

Imelda Marcos, First Lady of the Philippines, was nearing the end of her
second decade in Manila's Presidential Palace and, indeed, nearing the
height of her spending powers. Known as the 'Steel Butterfly', and later
ranked by an Australian magazine as 58 on its '100 Most Powerful Women in
the World' list, she was perhaps at her zenith.

In 1966, her husband, Ferdinand Marcos, had become the tenth President
of the Philippines. Together with Imelda, he would rule the Philippines as a
dictator from September 21, 1972 until he was ousted on February 25, 1986.

Imelda Marcos' extravagant lifestyle included sending a 'plane to pick up
Australian white sand for a new beach resort; and a property portfolio that

Fly *Buy* Dubai

included real estate in Manhattan, incorporating the $51 million Crown Building and the $60 million Herald Center. Her 175-piece art collection included works by Michelangelo, Botticelli, and Canaletto, while her shopping trips reportedly included five-million dollar buying sprees in New York, Rome, and Copenhagen during 1983 alone.

She responded to criticisms of her extravagance by claiming that it was her "duty to be some kind of light, a star to give [the poor] guidelines".

Whatever her ethics on life — and shopping — Imelda Marcos, larger than life, nonetheless created a stir as she made her grand entrance onto the Dubai Duty Free shop floor, complete with an entourage which included assistants, diplomatic staff, Dubai's Protocol Department officers, and what seemed like a whole force of local policemen!

Such tight security surrounding Imelda had been the norm since a day in December 1972 when an assailant had brazenly tried to stab her to death during an awards ceremony. The knife injuries on her hands and arms required 75 stitches. From that day onwards until her incarceration for corruption, wherever she went abroad, Imelda's personal security team was supported by a cadre of officers provided by her hosts.

With this vast entourage, and of course the world-famous face and trademark butterfly-sleeve dresses, Marcos' presence was felt wherever she went. All the Philippines Dubai Duty Free staff certainly knew her. So did many shoppers, those already in the shopping complex, and the dozens who followed her onto the shop floor.

It was like a rugby scrum, lots of pushing and shoving, as people tried to get close to see her, and the various security men trying hard to ensure no-one got close. Marcos greeted people and was very polite and friendly, certainly to the staff, many of whom were delighted to be meeting their First Lady — which was a chance in a lifetime. She said a few words to some, exchanged pleasantries, then her attention inevitably turned to shopping.

Her presence was almost a dream come true for Dubai Duty Free. It had been only a few months since representatives of Aer Rianta had huddled with Rodney Fitch, the renowned retail designer, to come up with a modern and inviting concept for their new facility. And now, just four weeks after opening, their vision was being endorsed by the world's most famous shopper.

Within 25 minutes, Imelda had clocked up $20,000 in purchases, all packed into a dozen bags carried by her assistants, before leaving the floor. Polite to a fault, she left $100 tips for 12 or so of the staff.

Hardly three years on, Ferdinand Marcos and his family fled to Hawaii

$20 million

Actor Roger Moore was another early visitor to Dubai Duty Free, purchasing a pair of sunglasses.

$20 million

Dubai Duty Free's tills were ringing nicely, but with first year projections of $20 million there was pressure to reach the high target set.

Fly *Buy* Dubai

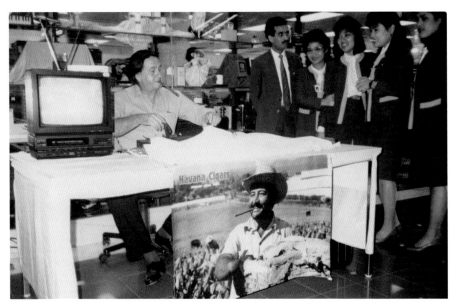

The shop floor proved busy, but although confidence was high so were the financial targets.

after his regime was toppled by a four-day People Power Revolution. In Malacañang Palace, Imelda left behind 15 mink coats, 508 gowns, 888 handbags, and 1,060 pairs of shoes. A few of those items had perhaps come from Dubai Duty Free...

The Imelda Marcos spending spree came at a very good time for Dubai Duty Free. A three million dirham overdraft at the National Bank of Dubai, good credit terms with many suppliers, and deft accountancy, were one thing. But in retail, cash flow is everything.

"From the moment we opened on December 20, 1983, we all had a great feeling. By the end of that day we had taken Dhs. 160,000 ($40,000) through the tills. It was a big relief," says McLoughlin.

While $40,000 at last provided the new enterprise with some positive cash flow, after four months of heavy expenditure, it was almost like a drop in the ocean — but it was a start. The team may have been euphoric, but they knew they had a mountain still to climb in terms of realising the financial investment that had gone into building the complex. It was pre-Christmas, a peak time for the world of retail, and for air travel. Yet $40,000 was only a fraction of the monumental $20 million that Aer Rianta had set as a first-year revenue projection.

"Back in Shannon, Michael Hanrahan and I had looked at the number of passengers Dubai International Airport was handling, and calculated the duty free norm for spend per passenger. That was how we arrived at our revenue projections," says McLoughlin. "We never lost confidence that we would reach this target, although for a first year it was admittedly ambitious."

"I personally never lost confidence," says Binhendi, whose responsibility it would have been should the enterprise have failed. "But that is not to say that everyone in Dubai was ebullient. There were, shall we say, some doubters."

The Aer Rianta team was due to leave at the end of February, handing over to a domestically-appointed management. But before then it was up to the ten Irishmen to improve, tweak, alter, modify, refine, and adjust just about everything, not only to get all in order before departure, but to ensure that whoever was to take over Dubai Duty Free would be on target to reaching that 'mountainous' $20 million target.

With the excitement and pressure of getting the complex opened successfully, there had been little time to think about a post-Aer Rianta era. Suddenly, with the Christmas rush over, one of the Irish ten aired a thought that made them wonder.

Fly *Buy* Dubai

The lure of the duty free escalator was proving strong, but the company's targets were high and delivering this would prove a challenge.

$20 million

Fly *Buy* Dubai

"It became obvious that it was rather late to begin training people to replace us," says George Horan. "There had been so much focus, given the limited timeframe to get up and running, that no-one had really stopped to think about a hand-over."

At the end of February Aer Rianta's six-month consultancy contract was up, and while the Department of Civil Aviation had not been overtly recruiting replacements for its temporary Irish contingent, some thought had gone into a post-Aer Rianta period.

"I had spotted Colm in Shannon and it was a specific request that he join the Aer Rianta group that came to Dubai," says Binhendi. "The more I saw of him and got to know him, the more I knew that he had the ideas, the personality and the drive to lead Dubai Duty Free."

Well before Dubai Duty Free even opened, Binhendi had floated an idea to his bosses that McLoughlin be offered — if Aer Rianta's consent could be obtained— a longer secondment. The idea was accepted and Binhendi prepared an offer of a two-year contract.

Over 15,000 products were on the shelves in Dubai Duty Free's first-ever shops. The stock ranged from music and video tapes, electronics, toys, sporting goods, ladies' apparel, gents' clothing, leatherwear, fragrances for men and women, clocks and watches, jewellery, gold, pearls, textiles, souvenirs from Dubai, confectionery, delicatessen items, international gifts, a children's shop, tobacco items, and liquor.

Indeed, the liquor and tobacco shop was a far cry from the original outlet, which had literally been a hole in the wall through which customers could peer and make their orders. Now, all leading brands of tobacco, cigars, and liquor were smartly arranged on shelves, and shoppers were able to make their purchases with ease. The shop floor team — stylishly clad in their uniforms of cream shirts or blouses, grey trousers or skirts, and navy blazers — looked the part.

"As I walked about the shop floor on that first day, there was no doubt in my mind that we couldn't let Colm go," Binhendi admits. "In the event, it was one of the best decisions I have ever made, either as Director-General of the Department of Civil Aviation."

And so, in early January, 1984, McLoughlin was called to Binhendi's office in the terminal building. He was made an offer and readily says it was one he couldn't refuse.

"I liked Mr Binhendi, both as a man and a boss. I also liked the ethos that filtered down from Sheikh Mohammed, that this had to be the best duty free offering the best value in the world," McLoughlin says.

$20 million

(top) Richard Kiel, who played the character Jaws is the James Bond films The Spy Who Loved Me and Moonraker, poses with some staff.

George Horan (right). Dubai Duty Free's staff in their first generation cream, grey and navy uniforms.

Fly *Buy* Dubai

In 1983, Dubai Duty Free's Persian and Arabic carpet shop was probably the only such outlet in the industry.

"Very quickly there was an understanding that we would have tremendous freedom in what we were doing and that nothing was impossible, but it should be done just right. We had been given a free reign to get the units and décor and consultants and designers that were necessary to achieve this.

"This ethos was portrayed through Mr Binhendi, because he was so very outward, dynamic… as was his boss Sheikh Mohammed, who was in charge of the airport — there was a dynamic duo at the summit of the operation."

The Department of Civil Aviation tabled an offer to McLoughlin. His services would be required on a two-year contract. He could handpick his own management from the Aer Rianta team, he would continue to have a free hand and, most importantly, as far as he was concerned, the Dubai government wanted him to forge on with the project with their full support.

"Colm had impressed everyone with his enthusiasm. Everybody who worked at the airport was proud, indeed the people of Dubai were proud of the new duty free. I guess no-one was surprised when it became known that an offer had been made for him to stay on," says Jamal Al Hai.

$20 million

*Mohi-Din Binhendi, Colm McLoughlin and Jamal Al Hai at
an early press conference.*

McLoughlin had worked for Aer Rianta for 14 years. He had left behind his wife Breeda, promising her he'd be back home in Ireland at the end of the six-month Dubai contract, and then they would resume their normal lives. Breeda McLoughlin had visited Dubai over the festive period and returned to the Emerald Isle expecting Colm to follow her home just two months later. His wife, his life, his job, his family and his very Irish roots were over 3,000 miles away in the west of Ireland...

Until this meeting with Binhendi , McLoughlin maintains that he had had no thoughts of staying on. But when the offer was made, his destiny was set.

"I had no doubt Dubai Duty Free would grow. When I was making up my mind whether to come here in the first place, I could see it becoming, you know, the Dubai we see today. The kind of attitude you encounter here is a little bit infectious."

He left Binhendi's office and, without saying anything of the offer, headed down to the Dubai Duty Free complex. It was mid-morning, a relatively quiet time on the shop floor. Flight restrictions into airports to the east and west dictate that mornings and evenings are peak periods in Dubai.

*In January 1984, Colm McLoughlin called his wife, Breeda, in Ireland to propose
making a permanent move to Dubai. He found his better-half enthusiastic.*

$20 million

Yet the shop floor was still humming. An Indian family hovered in the gold section, looking at *tola* bars and bracelets. In the tobacco section there were dozens of passengers filling baskets, while others browsed around what was, even at that time, an excellent selection of wines.

As he looked around, McLoughlin heard the clatter of tills, the laughter of children in the toy section, the chatter of shoppers as they perused.

"I instantly knew that this was home. That there was still a great deal to do," he says. "What was more, in this environment, working for these people, you had the opportunity to do it."

A little later the same day, back in the office, he was informed that a customer had stopped off at the duty free and purchased 80 gold chains and ten watches in under six minutes. Being the retailer that he is, this news really excited him and proved again to him that unbelievable possibilities lay ahead in Dubai.

That night, back at his hotel, McLoughlin placed a call to Ireland, for what he thought would be a tricky conversation with Breeda. As it turned out, it could not have been simpler. "I was shocked, for sure, but when Colm explained the opportunity, and said that he felt that this was what he wanted to do, there was no question," recalls Breeda. And so, a few months later, she arrived in the UAE.

But while McLoughlin had found his partner willing to accept change, his employer had been less enthusiastic. McLoughlin had asked Aer Rianta for a two-year leave of absence, but was turned down out of hand. He was needed back in Shannon.

Before him lay a choice: should he give up a solid, steady, and enjoyable job and pension, or chase a dream in a land so alien from his roots?

"Naaaa!" he says. "There was no choice to make."

With the shop floor now open, it was time for a longer-term strategy in terms of merchandising and management.

Chapter Eleven

Learning Curve

*If you hold a cat by the tail you learn things you
cannot learn any other way.*
— Mark Twain, American author

Colm McLoughlin was sure of two things. From the nine men who served with him on that first six-month consultancy from Ireland, two stood out. In the middle of February 1984 he invited John Sutcliffe to serve as his Deputy General Manager and George Horan to be Senior Shop Floor Controller. Like their future boss, the offer would come as something of a shock. In addition to leaving behind their roots in Ireland, both were presented with the scenario that they would have to cut their ties with Aer Rianta and the job security which that entailed.

"Colm was something of a mentor to me. I liked Dubai, but the chance to build this amazing new duty free under him was more powerful than the pull of home at that time," says Sutcliffe. "The five months I had been in the UAE had flashed by, as we were so busy, but the overriding impression I had was of the enormous possibility that Dubai had, and I think we all shared an excitement of the potential of the duty free."

Both men were, in the final analysis, prepared to take the chance. But of the three, Sutcliffe would leave later, in 1989.

"They were a formidable team," recalls Maurice Flanagan, who is today Executive Vice Chairman of Emirates Group but who was with Dnata when Dubai Duty Free was launched and became a close friend with McLoughlin over the years. "There were some skeptics at the time, as there was with the birth of Emirates, but of those who believed that the new duty free was a good idea, I doubt anyone would have thought for a moment that it would go on to be the remarkable success it has."

At the end of February 1984, seven of the ten Irishmen who had arrived in Dubai took a British Airways flight back to Heathrow, and then on to Shannon. For the three left behind, there was a sudden void.

"We had formed a tight clique over the months, sleeping, eating, working Dubai Duty Free," says Horan. "A camaraderie had been forged between us so there was more than a tinge of sadness when they left."

Together, McLoughlin, Sutcliffe, and Horan would be charged with moving Dubai's Duty Free during a period when it would need to evolve from its opening state, absorbing fresh market conditions and morphing into a more Gulf-orientated entity. The same month, the *Gulf Daily News* reported:

> '*...Travellers are drawn to an escalator that leads them down to a veritable Aladdin's Cave one floor below. Descending into this area of pink marble and twinkling lights there is a sense of excitement and expectation...*'

Local and international press was receptive towards Dubai Airport's initiative; indeed, comment was universally positive. And McLoughlin's management team never tired of watching the crowds as they walked around the tantalising displays. They watched — and they observed. "Those early days were a steep learning curve, where today, a quarter of a century later, it's just a continual learning curve," says Horan.

They kept a close eye on the items which were popular, analysed figures day in and day out, introduced new products, and expanded the range of brands. And all the while they were gauging customer response and constantly re-working the layout of the shop floor as and when they felt the need to draw attention to items or attract custom to certain areas.

The team soon learnt the tastes of different nationalities and catered for them accordingly. For example, in the early days of the operation, they discovered that Iranian men working in Kuwait, transiting through Dubai, favoured leather combat-style jackets! At the time the shop floor boasted a prominent suggestion box on nearly every counter. A surprising number of people suggested that this combat style of jacket be available, which set events in motion for Dubai Duty Free to gain one of its fastest-growing early sellers.

"We used to call them 'Iranian jackets', but oddly enough they were made in America. When we looked for that style, we discovered they were on sale in the local *souq* and many Iranian men wore them," says Horan. "We bought in a good number and they sold like hot cakes."

More stock changes were made when it was discovered that Bangladeshi women, who made up a surprisingly high demographic of shoppers, wanted colourful saris and fine textiles to take home to family and friends.

More unusually — at least in comparison with Shannon that is — they discovered that travellers to other Middle Eastern countries and to Asian destinations liked to take fresh fruit with them. Their favourites were apples, oranges, pineapples, mangoes, grapes — and bananas! In fact bananas were such a popular item that the duty free was literally selling them by the crateful. Fresh fruits don't normally figure in the 'must buy' items in the

Learning Curve

'Travellers are drawn to an escalator that leads them down to a veritable Aladdin's Cave' was how one publication described Dubai Duty Free.

(right) Bananas and other fresh fruits were a surprisingly hot selling line, a peculiarity of the Dubai marketplace.

Sari textiles became an early hit for Dubai Duty Free. (top) The Ladies Fashion outlet in the first shop floor. (centre) Aishwarya Rai posing in front of the Taj Mahal. (bottom) And the sari has gone on to grow in popularity beyond Asian women, as this 2007 shot of ladies tennis star Maria Kirilenko shows.

Dubai Duty Free quickly learned that the Middle Eastern market was, in many ways, far removed from Ireland. Major sellers included powdered milk brand Nido (top) and loose tea (left).

world's duty free shops — but Dubai, with its eclectic mix of nationalities passing through its airport, discovered it had to cater for a diverse range of tastes and expectancies.

The Dubai Duty Free team scoured the local markets for the freshest of produce. But it has to be kept in mind at this juncture that neither Dubai, nor the UAE for that matter, grew such items locally. The whole of the GCC region during the '80s was very reliant on imported foodstuffs and, at the time, the range of fresh fruit and vegetables was not as prolific as it is today. To satisfy demands, fruits had to be sourced from overseas and flown in to sell at the duty free.

And something which certainly didn't make it on to the stock control sheets at Shannon was tins of Nido milk powder or Tang orange drink powder — but they ran off the shelves in Dubai. This demand was driven by the Sub-Continent market, where these brands were unavailable.

Another highly-popular item was loose tea leaves. There is a story, which has gone down in the annals of Dubai Duty Free's history, about a customer travelling home to India: he filled a pillowcase with his favourite brand of loose tea but suffered quite a bit of spillage during his flight. In a letter to Dubai Duty Free management from his destination, he suggested that a new way should be found for packing tea leaves.

Indeed, customer feedback is something that Dubai Duty Free has thrived on since day one. From the outset, the plan was that customer service should be as important as profits, and this, coupled with constantly re-evaluating every facet of the facility, has kept Dubai Duty Free ahead of the game in what has become a highly competitive industry. And so the loose tea leaves were packaged accordingly and another bestseller entered the record books.

But while Iranian jackets, saris, and fruit were successful adoptions, the market took an age to absorb Dubai Duty Free's initial Waterford crystal stock. Recalling how Shannon duty free had helped to turn the fortunes of this fine Irish-made crystal into a huge success story, the Irish team at Dubai Duty Free at first anticipated similar success. They were to be proven wrong initially, but through a determined marketing thrust over a period of time, they succeeded in seeing the Waterford pieces start to move off the shelves. This proved yet again that with Dubai they were dealing with a slightly different type of consumer.

The more recent history of Waterford crystal, and how Shannon duty free turned it into a huge worldwide enterprise, is an interesting study on the power of a duty free enterprise on the global stage. In 1947, a Czech immigrant in Ireland established a glass works in the city of Waterford. It

Fly *Buy* Dubai

gained recognition and began producing designs which reflected the cultural roots of Ireland, using local influences and names to describe its patterns, which went on to include ranges entitled Adare, Alana, Colleen, Kincora, Lismore, Maeve, Tramore, and many more.

Thanks to gaining an outstanding reputation over the ensuing years, and, in no short measure due to name-recognition developed through — and as a result of — Shannon, Waterford's exquisite crystal chandeliers today hang in well-known buildings including Windsor Castle and Westminster Abbey.

Hence the reason that a large selection of Waterford crystal had been imported by Aer Rianta and prominently displayed with the expectation that it would sell as well in the Middle East as it did in Shannon. But the Irishmen soon learnt not to over-estimate an already proven norm.

"In complete contrast to Shannon and indeed much of Europe, Waterford crystal did very badly," Sutcliffe said resignedly. "But we weren't to be beaten; with refinement we managed to increase turnover markedly."

Back in the early 1980s, tourism in the Middle East was confined mostly to Egypt, and to a lesser extent Jordan. In the Gulf, the tourism market was getting itself together but it was spasmodic. Bahrain at the time was leading the field as it had already created a certain sophistication having promoted tourism since the mid-70s. The first real tourism drive began in Dubai in late 1984 when the emirate had only two dedicated beachside tourist hotels. However, the city also boasted several internationally-recognised business hotels including the Sheraton, Hyatt, Hilton, and InterContinental, and they were well-patronised by the hordes of businessmen who were flocking into Dubai in search of new opportunities and contracts.

On the flip side of the coin, the beach hotels then were patronised rather more by the domestic industry than tourists. And for holidaymakers — and indeed expatriates who made regular visits to their homeland — there were few mementos of Dubai to take back to family and friends.

The Dubai government, under the visionary leadership of Ruler Sheikh Rashid, had determinedly gone after economic diversification. Almost as soon as the emirate became an oil exporter, this had manifested itself through heavy industries. Consumer goods and perishables, however, were still mostly imported. Souvenirs of the emirate were unknown other than a few items such as brass coffee pots, hubble bubble (*hookah*, or *shisha*) pipes, and miniature silver dhows set on wooden plinths, so there was a drastic need to identify and produce new items. In fact, the Dubai Duty Free policy, from the outset, was to identify and support local small industries and entrepreneurs.

"There were no instructions, as such, from anybody to include souvenirs

Learning Curve

Photographed with Colm McLoughlin, an early visitor to Dubai Duty Free was 7' 2" Kareem Abdul-Jabbar. Considered to be one of the greatest NBA players of all time and winner of a record six MVP awards. It is not recalled if Dubai Duty Free stocked anything in his size.

(top) Jabbar, with ball, in NBA action.

in our stock inventory, but Dubai was our home base and we had to include something which would reflect the country. In those days souvenirs in places such as duty frees was called 'Destination Merchandising'. We had done a good job sourcing items, but a lot of the products were not made in the UAE, although we represented the UAE," says McLoughlin. "We went to great efforts to source products that were made in the emirates — all seven of them."

While Dubai Duty Free cannot claim a giant success along the lines of Shannon airport's duty free catapulting Waterford crystal onto the world stage, it has since supported lots of local producers and helped turn their fortunes.

"Products bearing the 'Made in the UAE' label generate tens of millions of dollars in turnover every year, and this filters down to boost many industries, create jobs, and wealth," says Sheikh Ahmed. "We have been conscious of the need for Dubai Duty Free to support the nation. I am happy to say that businesses in the Northern Emirates, Abu Dhabi, and, of course, Dubai, have all benefited from excellent exposure to the millions of passengers who shop at Dubai Duty Free each year."

From a few earthenware pots and postcard-makers in the early days, over the last quarter-century the range of UAE-made goods has gone on to include a very popular range of locally- and regionally-grown dates, replica artifacts and antiques, books on local subjects and personalities, and a host of other items with an Arabic flavour, including the distinctive local perfumes.

"Twenty years ago, there was limited interest in Arabic fragrances, but today they're a hot ticket item," says Sean Staunton, Manager, Operations. "On the duty free shop floor, anywhere in the world, products get the floor space that their profitability deserves. That is the hard-nosed reality of retail. In Dubai Duty Free today, you can see the amount of space allocated, and the premium position given, to specialist UAE merchandise. It is a growing and significant portion of the business."

The early months of 1984 were all about tweaking. The Irishmen had the deep knowledge of their industry but were constantly re-appraising knowledge of their specific market. 'Adopt, Adapt, and Improve' is the motto of the Round Table, but it equally summed up the work that Dubai Duty Free's management were undertaking at that time.

"Only after a few months did I begin to believe we were getting it absolutely right," says Horan. "The principles of our job were the same, only the application was different in this part of the world."

(top) Dubai Duty Free was at the vanguard of Dubai's fledgling destination merchandising industry.

(right) Arabic perfumes, with their strong scents and intricate bottles, were well received by foreign consumers.

Fly *Buy* Dubai

And over these months of 'Adopt, Adapt, and Improve' Dubai Duty Free refined itself, the turnover reflecting their success. After a few months with figures hovering below expected returns, threatening the operation to miss its $20 million first-year target, daily turnover started to improve, suggesting they were getting it right.

"There was never any pressure on them," says Binhendi. "In fact, when Aer Rianta projected such a turnover in the beginning, there were plenty of sceptics and few believers. Viewed from today's perspective, and a mammoth $1 billion turnover, $20 million seems like small change, but at the time it was a huge, huge figure. Indeed, I doubt the airport earned $100,000 a year under the old concession system."

As Binhendi points out, in Dubai there are two elements to satisfy: while the sceptics were beginning to be won over, with Dubai Duty Free looking increasingly busy, the one to impress was the man who had championed the airport and believed in the duty free concept. Sheikh Mohammed is not a man impressed easily, and demands from others the same high level of performance he demands from himself.

During the summer of 1984 McLoughlin received a call in his office from Binhendi. Sheikh Mohammed had requested the Irishman to see him at the palace.

"So I duly presented myself somewhat apprehensively. Sheikh Mohammed then turned to his advisor, Brigadier Michael Barclay, and said, 'Barclay, tell him...' I held my breath wondering what was coming next, when Brigadier Barclay related a story. He had been on a 'plane coming from America and sitting beside him was a lady. They got chatting, and when the Brigadier told her he worked in Dubai, the lady had said: 'Oh, is that where the famous Duty Free is?'"

Barclay duly related this encounter to Sheikh Mohammed when he returned to Dubai, and his story was received with enthusiasm. The future Ruler of Dubai was, even then, intent on establishing the emirate as an international entity. The likes of Emirates, Godolphin, Jumeirah, Dubai Airports, Nakheel, and other brands, which would contribute significantly to building the Dubai brand, were still to come. Dubai Duty Free may just have been finding its feet at the time, but seemingly it had begun to find its mark on the global stage.

"See," said Sheikh Mohammed, tongue in cheek, to those assembled in his *Majlis*, "Dubai is famous. Duty Free is famous!"

He knew that the process of building Dubai was just beginning, but this early result showed how it could be done.

Learning Curve

Sheikh Mohammed with British Prime Minister Margaret Thatcher. Even then he was concerned with Dubai's image and impact around the world.

"Sheikh Mohammed went on to say what a terrific operation we were running, that the business was doing great, and if I ever needed anything I should go to him directly," says McLoughlin, "but I never have. We always got the utmost support."

A few days later, on June 22, 1984, McLoughlin, Sutcliffe, and Horan were presented with their first half-year figures. Against all expectations, Dubai Duty Free was matching the sort of turnover that would be required to meet its ambitious first-year target.

Nice is one of the leading resorts on the French Riviera — and the unlikely scene of one of Dubai Duty Free's most remarkable successes.

Chapter Twelve

Frank Capra was right

"I wasn't expecting it *[to win a Grammy]...*
I'm such a newcomer among all these people."
— *Christina Aguilera, American singer*

Flying into the Provence-Alpes-Côte d'Azur, via the Nice Côte d'Azur Airport, Breeda McLoughlin could perhaps have been forgiven for a sense of anticipation in 1985.

Located on the Mediterranean coast in the South of France, between Marseille in France and Genoa in Italy, Nice is a leading resort on the French Riviera. There was a great deal to do and see. Nice is the second most popular French city among tourists, after Paris. Visitors normally head for the Quai des Etats-Unis and Promenade des Anglais — 'Walk of the English' — a celebrated promenade along the Mediterranean. Many head for the Saint Nicolas Orthodox Cathedral, or the astonishing architecture and history of Place Garibaldi, named after Giuseppe Garibaldi, hero of Italian unification. Like any Mediterranean city, Nice has squares, which allow people to gather, to organise shows, performances, or public displays, or just to chill on a terrace. Of these, the guides say, Place Masséna is the loveliest.

The same guides recommend a plethora of restaurants, for Nice is famed for its cuisine, which blends local resources such as olive oil, anchovies, fruit, and vegetables, but also resources from more remote regions, in particular those from Northern Europe.

Perhaps most of all, the wife of the Dubai Duty Free Managing Director may have anticipated the weather. She had moved to the Gulf, where she would now reside. Dubai was still at its balmy best, the end of the winter season bringing fresh, crisp mornings. But as the months had passed, these fresh mornings had given away to spiraling heat and, worse still for a newcomer, by summer the mercury-busting temperatures were accompanied by, at times, oppressive humidity.

By contrast, after three months of high summer in Dubai, Breeda noted a Mediterranean climate. Summers started quite late because of a notable season lag. Hot temperatures become common in August, which is the warmest month with daytime highs frequently reaching 35°C, a good 10 degrees lower than Dubai, not even allowing for the fact that most days the coast was swept by a cool and pleasant sea breeze.

But, as Breeda was to discover, her invitation to Nice came at a price.

Fly *Buy* Dubai

Founded in 1984, the Tax Free World Association (TFWA) is a non-profit-making international organisation related to the duty free and travel retail industries. Quickly it had become the world's largest duty free and travel retail association. TFWA pursues four main activities: Exhibitions, Conferences, Research and Corporate Development. TFWA's exhibitions quickly became major events in the industry calendar, which is why Cannes, in 1985, sat at the pinnacle of the industry's year. The Tax Free World Association attracted some 3,000 visitors a day even then, while the social highpoint of the gathering was the industries' Frontier awards ceremony.

"Nice happened toward the end of what had been a very good time," says Sutcliffe. "Turnover was rising, our reputation was growing, and certainly the feedback I was getting, from people I knew within the industry itself, was very positive indeed."

Already Dubai Duty Free had claimed a couple of awards, from Ricoh and Kodak, both in recognition of outstanding sales. This inspired the Dubai team to enter for the first ever *Frontier* magazine awards in 1985. The UK-based magazine has remained, since its inception, the world's leading publication for the trade, and, it could be said, has grown alongside Dubai Duty Free. The *Frontier* magazine awards would go on to be considered the industry's 'Oscars'. The event was held in Nice, while in future they would be staged in Cannes.

"I don't think there was an expectation that Dubai Duty Free would win in 1985. For goodness sake, we were hardly more than a year old and were setting ourselves up to go head-to-head with the best and the brightest in the industry," says Anita Mehra. This is a view shared by McLoughlin, who adds: "It was speculative, to say the least, but by entering ourselves in the Frontier awards our intention was more to draw attention to who we were and what we were doing."

Academy Award-winning Italian-American film director Frank Capra stated at the 1936 Academy Awards ceremony that: "The Oscar is the most valuable, but least expensive, item of world-wide public relations ever invented by any industry."

Admittedly Nice was on a far smaller scale, at an event which those outside of the industry failed to register, but it nevertheless held true for duty free. With only seven awards on offer, the high-profile and highly sought-after award winners joined an elite club by which the travel retail and duty free industries benchmark their overall performances.

The panel of six judges, drawn from the duty free industry worldwide, looked at all the nominees. Before flying to France, McLoughlin had been

Frank Capra was right

informed that Dubai had been short listed for 'Airport Duty Free Operator of the Year' along with Dufrital, which ran Milan's Linate International Airport, and Maya-Free at Jomo Kenyatta International in Nairobi.

"Frankly, a top three finish was far better than I expected, and, although we did deserve it, I think everyone here understood that we were too new to be serious contenders", says Horan.

Arriving in Nice, the McLoughlins and their small team got to work on the serious business of networking at the exhibition. It was then that they really came to understand the enormity of the task of establishing Dubai — despite its shortlisting.

"I had Breeda giving out leaflets throughout the exhibition. Bless her, she thought she was going on a short holiday to the Côte d'Azur, and instead she was working flat out," says McLoughlin.

The small Dubai team had arrived with an agenda to meet and secure new suppliers, forge contacts with other duty frees, interface with companies bringing new technologies and methods to the industry, and generally promote Dubai Duty Free and Dubai itself.

Oscar winning director Frank Capra considered the Oscars' value as being in the publicity they generated.

(top) New Orleans, Louisiana. Definitely nowhere near Dubai.

(left) Breeda McLoughlin was pressed into service for the company during the memorable TFWE.

Frank Capra was right

"I remember producing, with Colm, a small leaflet on Dubai, explaining where it was, talking about our vibrant economy, tourism, and the airport. It was, to our knowledge, the first promotional leaflet on Dubai ever produced," says Mehra. "That was only in 1984. How far we have come..."

"Breeda is not employed by Dubai Duty Free but she attended many things in the early days and was ready when it came to representing Dubai Duty Free," says McLoughlin. "I recall Breeda going around and distributing brochures for me, and because in those days people didn't know where Dubai was, she would look back and see them put it in a bin.

"People would ask me, 'That is in Saudi, isn't it?'" says Breeda.

Back in 1980s the hard work of making a name remained to be done. McLoughlin recalls a trade fair in Britain where he was discussing pricing machines with a saleswoman. After a brief discussion on the product McLoughlin was convinced and prepared to order a handful of these, with the provision that there was a service agent not too far away should they break.

"She went blank when I mentioned Dubai and, clearly having no clue where this was, said that the nearest service agent was in Louisiana!" says McLoughlin.

When the Irishman explained where Dubai actually was this did not help, because, as he recalls, in general there was a reluctance to supply 'somewhere in Saudi Arabia'. Many people, frankly, explained that they could not supply goods as they doubted they would get paid.

"Today, we get cornered by people selling things. Then, people did not want to know us," says Horan.

The lack of name recognition did not help with suppliers. McLoughlin, Sutcliffe, and Horan all cite examples of manufacturers who refused to supply Dubai, several dismissing the emirate as a place in Saudi Arabia. One French perfume company, which today sells hundreds of thousands of bottles of its products off Dubai's shelves, took many months to decide if they were willing to supply stock.

Toward the end of the TFWA event, the serious business of preceding days was set aside as more than 400 international travel, duty-free retailers and suppliers attended the *Frontier* awards in Nice. The black tie bash was a time to relax. For most of the tens of thousands of tourists on the Côte d'Azur that evening, it was a chance for sightseeing, fine dining, romantic strolls, or taking in many of the region's cultural landmarks. The duty free industry, dominated by self-confessed anoraks, enjoys nothing more than an evening filled with duty free talk.

Fly *Buy* Dubai

Dubai Duty Free had a table, of course, but in those days, as a newcomer, was banished to the remote ends of the ballroom. It did not matter. Dubai Duty Free had been short-listed for several awards, and for this virgin enterprise, even if not claiming any of the Oscars on offer — which was, they concede today, a remote possibility — it was an opportunity to have those there sit up and see that the tiny Gulf emirate was now well and truly on the map.

The evening started well. Dubai Duty Free faced stiff competition in a category for Best Marketing Campaign (Operator). It was pitched alongside Amsterdam's Schiphol Airport — long recognised as being one of the finest facilities in the world — the British Airport Authority, Duty Free Shoppers Singapore, and the International Association of Airport Duty Free Suppliers. To appear alongside such internationally-recognised heavyweights in the industry was a coup in itself. Dubai Duty Free didn't win, but came away justly satisfied with a 'highly commended' certificate.

"I thought to myself how Mr Binhendi would be happy with that," says McLoughlin. "It showed that we were already competing when measured against the best in the world."

Half an hour later, after some other awards had been handed out, came the big one: Airport Duty Free Operator of the Year.

Close by Dubai's table was one belonging to Maya-Free, which ran Jomo Kenyatta International in Nairobi. They looked pleased with themselves. But toward the centre of the room, on a well-positioned table, were the much-touted stars of the night. Dufrital ran the duty free at Milan-Linate International Airport. They were the home favorites. European. Big. Established.

The 'star' of the evening was Jacques Médecin, at the height of his powers while serving as mayor of the city of Nice from 1966 to 1990. Médecin was there to hand out the 'Oscars'. On stage, he hovered near the Airport Duty Free Operator of the Year trophy.

"That was about as close, honestly, as I thought I would get to the trophy," says McLoughlin.

The Irishman almost fell off his seat when the compere, after a brief moment of silence designed to heighten the suspense that had fallen across the room, announced that Dubai Duty Free had claimed the evening's biggest prize.

Dubai's managing director found himself next to Médecin on stage, and for once was lost for words.

"I could not believe it. Dubai had scooped the biggest prize in the

Frank Capra was right

(top) Colm McLoughlin receives the Frontier Award from Jacques Médecin.

(right) On winning an Oscar in 1965, Bob Hope reported seeing his peers green with envy.

*Sheikh Ahmed bin Saeed Al Maktoum, who led the Dubai Duty Free project,
with the Oscar for Airport Duty Free Operator of the Year.*

Frank Capra was right

industry without completing even two full years of business," says McLoughlin. "It was a testimony to the scope of Sheikh Mohammed's vision, of Mr Binhendi's abilities, the brilliance of the team who were seconded from Aer Rianta and, most importantly, the hard work of all our staff. From the beginning we created a culture where we succeeded and failed together. That win was their success."

McLoughlin shies away from Bob Hope's famous 1965 quote that, when winning an Academy Award, "For the first time, you can actually see the losers turn green." Yet he concedes Dubai Duty Free's success took the industry by storm. It was, perhaps, the moment that Dubai became an industry leader.

The judges praised Dubai Duty Free for its 'understanding of the needs of its customers, as reflected in the shop layout and promotional activities'.

Médecin, who had liked the look of Dufrital, from nearby Milan, was courteous but perhaps remote given that he too knew little of these upstarts from Dubai. But just as this evening marked the beginning for Dubai Duty Free, which would go on to far greater things, this period also coincided with the gradual demise of the mayor himself. A charismatic Gaullist, he was undone by his personal and political friendship with Jean-Marie Le Pen and, not long after the 1985 evening, was accused of corruption following an exposé of judicial and police corruption by British novelist Graham Greene. He fled France in 1990.

As for Dubai, that first award — or 'Oscar' — still holds pride of place in a massive display cabinet at Dubai International Airport. Indeed, as the airport and subsequently its duty free facility has expanded over the years, so too has the display cabinet increased in size to accommodate all the awards which have been bestowed on various departments over the years.

Those involved with the duty free were in a state of euphoria.

"Most of us found out about the *Frontier* Awards success the following day," says Jamal Al Hai. "My personal response was of happiness for Colm and his team, who had brought so much to the job. But then one thinks of the wider angle. It was Dubai Airport's first major international success. Without exaggeration, with this we sat astride the world stage. With a great deal of work, by so many people, this would become commonplace later, but in 1985 this was the beginning of Dubai receiving international recognition."

The Oscar statuette was transported from France to Dubai within 24 hours of the dinner in Nice. First to be presented with them was Binhendi, who quickly ensured that Sheikh Mohammed, father of the Dubai Duty Free project, had seen the statuette and heard about the success.

Fly *Buy* Dubai

"Sheikh Mohammed's attitude was that such international recognition was good for Dubai as a whole, and that Dubai Duty Free must be doing well to have achieved such a notable result so early in its life," says Binhendi.

Back on the shop floor, McLoughlin ensured that staff had an opportunity to see the trophy for themselves, while Mehra and her PR team organised interviews and photo shoots, churned out press releases, and briefed journalists. As Frank Capra had observed, free publicity was too good an opportunity to miss.

Dubai Duty Free needed to crow. And loud. These were the days when the company's marketing budget amounted to a few advertisements in local newspapers and magazines. Domestically there was no other market, and the budgets certainly did not exist to embark upon campaigns in regional and international media. The brand was, if born at all, in its infancy.

On a domestic front, it was an opportunity that was too good to miss. Dubai Duty Free's management resolved to use the win to generate awareness. Someone came up with the idea of a swanky gala dinner, with a guest list that included Dubai's elite.

"I remember we had days to organise the dinner," says Mehra.

Dubai Duty Free emulated the awards night in Nice with its very own 'Oscars' night in Dubai just a few weeks later. Those in attendance included leading dignitaries from both the Airport and the government, ambassadors, leading VIPs and CEOs from the city's commercial and industrial companies, the media, and a fair amount of celebrities too. Over 300 people gathered in the Crystal Ballroom at Dubai's Hyatt Regency Hotel. Determined to put a stamp on the evening, McLoughlin heard that The Hollies were already in town.

"I remember heading across town with cash, as the deal was cash," says McLoughlin. "But we needed a headliner. At the time it was one of the highest profile events ever staged in Dubai."

An English beat group heavily influenced by the Everly Brothers, The Hollies were known for rich three-part harmonies rivaling those of The Beach Boys, ringing guitars, infectious melodies, jazz-oriented backbeats, and a squeaky-clean image. On stage, they belted out a back catalogue of US and UK Top Ten hits that included 'Here I Go Again', 'I'm Alive', 'Stop Stop Stop', 'Carrie Anne', and the iconic 'He Ain't Heavy, He's My Brother'.

If Nice had established Dubai Duty Free in the industry, that evening at the Hyatt Regency Hotel cemented the company's reputation in its domestic market. But if anyone thought Dubai Duty Free had peaked, they were in for a rude awakening.

Frank Capra was right

(top) Sheikh Ahmed and Jamal Al Hai (right) preside over a cake cutting at Dubai's Oscar Night celebration.

(right) Mohi-Din Binhendi with the Oscar.

Frank Capra was right

Dubai Duty Free's 'Oscar Night' at the Hyatt Hotel in 1985. (inset) The Hollies were tapped to entertain Dubai's good and great at a celebration of the success in Nice.

The DUTY FREE Capital of the World!

The next time you fly East or West, make a scheduled transit stop at
Dubai International Airport. Take this excellent opportunity to stop and
shop at Dubai Duty Free Shopping Complex, the World's No.1 for best value shopping.
Our amazing choice of prestige DUTY FREE products ranging from perfumes,
cosmetics, electronics, fashion wear to gold, pearls and even furs, at the world's lowest
bargain prices, are the best buys you will ever make.
And our elegantly designed DUTY FREE SHOPPING COMPLEX will be
an added delight to your shopping stop at Dubai International Airport.

The world's best value Airport DUTY FREE Shopping

Triple Award Winning
DUTY FREE

DUBAI INTERNATIONAL AIRPORT

DUTY FREE SHOPPING COMPLEX

*In the wake of a surprise success in Nice, Dubai Duty Free was able to
promote its status as the best duty free shop in the world.*

Chapter Thirteen

Tax Haven

You must pay taxes.
But there's no law that says you gotta leave a tip.
— Morgan Stanley advertisement

Looking back, the timing of Dubai Duty Free's launch had not been that impressive. The Gulf was beset by the Iran-Iraq War, which rumbled on from September 1980 to August 1988. By its end, an estimated million people had died, military and civilian, while neither protagonist had gained any advantage. Instead, the belligerence of both sides cost their respective nations dearly, and depressed the rest of the Gulf and Middle East. The Gulf States, which were themselves on the perimeter of a grim, never-ceasing war, found their economies depressed and stagnated. When the so-called Tanker War erupted, during which both sides indiscriminately mined international shipping lanes, the situation only got worse.

For Dubai International Airport the 1970s had been a relative boom time. Each year saw double-digit growth in traffic movements, steep increases in passenger arrivals, and optimism. The 1980s, set against the backdrop of Baghdad's and Tehran's intransigence, saw stagnation.

"Stagnation was seen as good, a miracle even," says Binhendi, who, as Director General of the Department of Civil Aviation, saw his colleagues in the region in a panic as their own figures slid. "At times we slashed airport fees for carriers. We just kept competitive, offered good service, and assured our international partners as much as possible of the safety of Dubai."

The war could not go on forever, and for Dubai this lean period in growth was utilised for consolidation. The Ruler, Sheikh Rashid, brought online vast infrastructure projects such as Jebel Ali Port, which would pave the way for Dubai to surge ahead at the end of the conflict, when a post-war market adjustment saw the region boom.

For Dubai's civil aviation sector, which had been placed under Sheikh Mohammed's control in 1977, there were similar developments during the 1980s despite the shadow of the war. While growth flat-lined, the emirate began to initiate the projects that would see it emerge as a global aviation hub in the years after a ceasefire between Iran and Iraq.

Dubai Duty Free may have been serving an airport that was not growing as well as it should. But that did not stop it emerging nonetheless. In 1986 Dubai Duty Free had won two more *Frontier* Awards — one for The Best

Tax Haven

Colm McLoughlin (centre), George Horan (left) and John Sutcliffe (right), pose with Dubai Duty Free's trio of Frontier Awards and some of the company's shop floor staffers.

*In 1986 Colm McLoughlin was himself honoured with an 'Oscar',
named as Duty Free Person of the Year.*

Tax Haven

Marketing Campaign by an Operator, and one distinction for Colm McLoughlin himself, named Duty Free Person of the Year. The Irish Trinity, as the team of McLoughlin, Sutcliffe, and Horan were fast becoming known, now had a trio of identical trophies to be proud of. Or, as McLoughlin has been known to say in his inimitable way, displaying typical Irish laid-back humour: "The judges said a lot of nice things about us and we now have a matching set of three trophies."

As Dubai was moving into the second half of the 1980s, it had become recognised internationally as a major business hub in the Middle East. Its growth plan for the next decades was rolled out by the government as a strategic plan for economic diversification. Aware that reliance on oil as the mainstay of the economy was foolhardy (Dubai has always been acutely aware that its oil reserves would not last forever and even by the mid-'80s knew that it was beginning to dwindle) the government started to actively encourage new industries such as distribution, banking and finance, and manufacturing. Importantly, the twin industries of aviation and tourism had already been identified as being potentially strong revenue-earners for the emirate.

To enhance the future of the International Airport, the Dubai government launched Emirates — 'the international airline of the UAE' — in October, 1985. His Highness Sheikh Ahmed bin Saeed Al Maktoum, President of the Department of Civil Aviation, had been appointed Chairman of the new airline, and his business plan called for a fast-expanding network which would help increase the number of passengers using the Airport's facilities. It has become a well-known fact of aviation history — not just regionally but internationally — that the marriage between the airline, the airport, and the duty free in Dubai has been an incredible success and the envy of other countries, many of whom have aspired to emulate the triple winning formula.

At the head of the enterprise, Sheikh Ahmed would prove an extraordinary success. Aged 23, having completed studies in the US, he emerged as a public servant in 1985. During the early months of planning for the launch of an airline for Dubai, Maurice Flanagan was introduced to the young sheikh during a meeting at Sheikh Mohammed's Zabeel Palace.

"This is Sheikh Ahmed," said Sheikh Mohammed. "He will be Chairman of Emirates. You will report to him."

With this 15-word introduction, Sheikh Mohammed recruited for the industry a man who would go on to be dubbed the 'aviation Sheikh' and be feted as one of the brightest young leaders in the industry. At the time of the launch of Emirates, Sheikh Ahmed was appointed as Chairman of the Department of Civil Aviation. Under this remit, Sheikh Ahmed was essentially the new boss of Dubai Duty Free.

"Sheikh Ahmed was a very perceptive man. Although he never wished to be involved in the day-to-day affairs of the duty free, his retention of details always astounded me," says McLoughlin. "As with Emirates, over the years Sheikh Ahmed has become an impressive leader, with a tremendous all-round knowledge of the industry. I doubt if aviation in Dubai would have been anywhere it is today without such a leader.

"He had managed the airport, duty free, and Emirates very effectively."

Certainly all three went hand-in-hand — with duty free facilities being an unusually powerful factor for airlines signing up for landing rights in the Emirate. Indeed, in the *Business Traveller* magazine's Best Airports awards category of 1987, an unparalleled 85 per cent of respondents visiting Dubai Airport cited its duty free shopping facilities as a reason for doing so. The fact that the operation's shops sold the most competitive duty free goods and

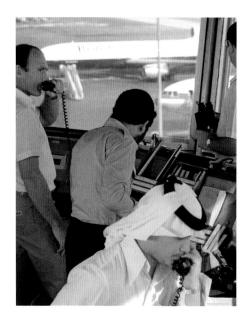

On several occasions there were scuffles on board aircraft when transiting passengers were informed they were not going to disembark into the Dubai International Airport terminal.

Tax Haven

the airport encouraged passengers in transit to disembark, contributed greatly to its international recognition and continually-growing success. In an interview with *Business Traveller* in 1988, Binhendi recalled an incident when transit passengers actually fought with the cabin crew because they were not allowed off the flight! Now, no-one would want there to be mutiny on board any aircraft parked on their apron, but it did point to the fact that people were transiting through Dubai specifically to pick up hoards of shopping.

Dubai Duty Free was also noted as marketing its duty free as a service to its passengers and not as a means of making vast profits — a laudable maneuver which certainly in the long run has resulted in incredible benefits and worldwide recognition. Binhendi said at that time: "The difference is that the shops here are run by the airport authority. By comparison, most other airports run duty free on a concession basis and so too commercialism comes into it. We are killing ourselves to give passengers the best duty free in the world."

This period also saw Dubai Duty Free killing themselves to make sure a domestic and international audience knew that they were the best duty free in the world. Aside from domestic advertising and the post-Nice gala dinner, perhaps the most high-profile sponsorship of the first year was when Dubai Duty Free was main sponsor of a ski team demonstration in Dubai Creek. Twenty-four thousand people lined the creek to see 25 American water skiers pull off some hairy stunts.

This was followed by support for a costume ball at the Metropolitan Hotel. Perhaps the most memorable early event, or not, as the case may be, was a poetry contest for Dubai schools.

"We became the official judges on that event. I remember going down to a school one Friday afternoon to judge one poetry competition," says McLoughlin. "I was taken aback when I arrived; there must have been 5,000 school children and I sat there from one o'clock in the afternoon till eleven in the evening. It was a marathon."

Poetry aside, as turnover increased, so did a desire to spend on Dubai Duty Free the brand. In order to do so, they needed a team. McLoughlin did not need to look far to find the leader of that team.

"My first son, Cyrus, was born in January 1986, so I took two months off work," says Anita Mehra, who had won the Dubai Duty Free account for her firm , and been the primary manager of the account since the summer of 1984. "When I wanted to go back to work, Colm offered me the chance to come in as Marketing Officer. It did not need much thought."

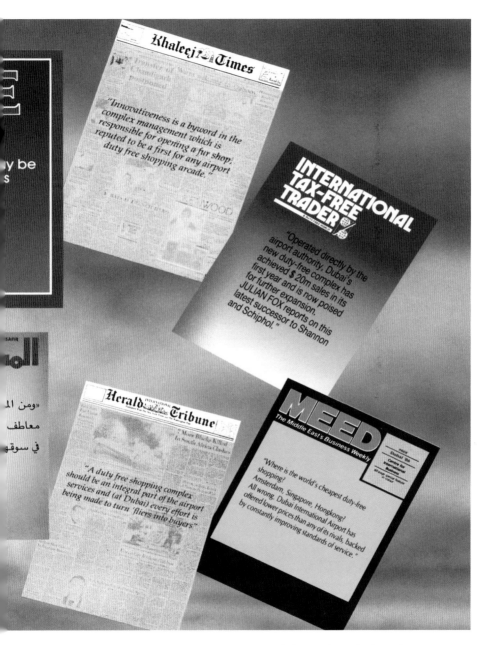

*Some of the media comment generated during the early days of
Dubai Duty Free operations.*

Fly *Buy* Dubai

Amid poetry, water skiing, a kids' ice hockey tournament in the Middle East's only ice rink, in Dubai, and other small events, *Frontier* Awards and an emerging reputation were creating a buzz of interest. The *International Herald Tribune* said, in November 1985:

> *'There are not many duty free shops in the world where you can buy almost anything from a de-luxe combat jacket to a bar of gold. But that's part of the choice offered at the duty free shopping complex in Dubai International Airport. The duty free shops there are now among the fastest growing at any airport in the world'.*

Time magazine commented: 'Amsterdam may be cheap but Dubai is even better value.' *The Wall Street Journal* meanwhile wrote: 'One of the most important facilities recently opened at Dubai International Airport is its lavish duty-free shopping complex which last Fall won the award for the World's Number One Airport Duty Free Operator. It started operating in December, 1983 and is now one of the most elaborate duty free stores in the world…'

"The international comment was invaluable, but we knew that we had to do more," says Sutcliffe. Binhendi adds: "Colm came with a proposal. There was an industry standard that a few percent of turnover was the allotted budget for marketing. He wanted to go well beyond this. He wanted us to have a brand."

Dubai Duty Free's marketing and promotions budget, as a percentage, was roughly double the industry norm. Worldwide, just about every significant player in the industry worked on a two per cent cut. Dubai opted for four. Years before the Department of Tourism and Commerce Marketing, even before Emirates, spending to create a viable name for Dubai, and a brand, was accepted as being desirable.

"It's always been higher because we thought promoting our brand and ourselves and our duty free was very important," says McLoughlin. "I think our policy paid off."

Dubai Duty Free's marketing budget for 1986, its second year of operations, had been set at slightly over $1 million, four per cent of its estimated turnover. The award-winning 'Fly Buy Dubai' campaign would gobble up a swathe of this, leaving little for the sort of high-profile sponsorships that Dubai Duty Free would later become famous for. But this did change as Dubai International Airport itself metamorphosed. Again, the catalyst was Sheikh Ahmed.

Sheikh Ahmed's involvement in Dubai's aviation sector added fresh impetus and marked the beginning of a new era.

Fly *Buy* Dubai

His arrival would see a greater sense of urgency in developing the airport.

"It's not just me, but anyone will tell you that Sheikh Ahmed is a great boss, someone who gets things done," says Binhendi . "His most impressive attribute is decision-making. He absorbs information, considers things, and then makes a quick decision."

Under Sheikh Ahmed's leadership it was not just the duty free which was attracting passengers in the late '80s — it was also the fact that they were either arriving into or transiting through an exceptional operation which had just undertaken an overhaul to the benefit of everyone from airlines to passengers. By 1988 a new $35 million arrivals terminal had taken pressure off the original terminal which was turned into a facility specifically for departure and transit passengers. The revamped facilities compared most favourably with the best that Europe's or the Far East's major airports could offer. Moreover, Dubai's Department of Civil Aviation had introduced new training processes for all its staff no matter at which level they were

Dubai Airport's competitiveness meant that the facility's air traffic controllers were now managing far busier skies over the emirate.

employed. This training was not only gearing staff into the implementation of new technology — for the world of aviation was then going through incredible advancements — it was also levelled at people skills and encouraging a more service-minded attitude for all. This worked from senior management down. The DCA also took immense steps in ensuring that passengers would enjoy a speedy turnaround from arrival to exit of the airport. This involved harnessing all the support they could muster from immigration and customs authorities as these departments were outside the airport's control.

To ensure that everyone met each other halfway was indeed an incredible feat, and so arriving passengers and, to a lesser extent, departing passengers too began to enjoy a more user-friendly airport where they did not have to experience long waits either in arrivals or departures.

Working and solving problems together, between all the collective authorities, has indeed contributed to Dubai International Airport's overall success. Airlines enjoyed using Dubai International because of its economical landing and airport handling fees. In the late '80s they were only a sixth of the world's average, and in 1988 had only risen three per cent over three years whereas other airport authorities over the world had increased their fees tenfold. Even more importantly, Dubai's 'Open Skies' policy — one of the world's most liberal — allowed all airlines the freedom to come and go at any time of the day or night. There was — and still is — no 'slot' on time restrictions, and there are full traffic rights. To this end, Dubai became a favoured stopping-off point for flights to and from the East and West, allowing transit stops for long-haul flights unable to land at their destinations during noise-restricted hours.

Generously competitive landing fees at Dubai Airport contributed to the increase of international airlines using Dubai International, and an aggressive marketing campaign selling the airport to the world led to carriers literally lining up to be able to use Dubai's facilities. And while Dubai International Airport benefited, so too did Emirates. Landing rights were secured and reciprocal arrangements made; thus, the airline was able to grow and fly to new destinations. And, at the end of it all, Dubai Duty Free became a winner too.

However it must be said at this juncture that Dubai International Airport did not give preferential treatment to its own homegrown airline, Emirates. Unlike other national carriers in the world, Emirates stood in line with all the rest.

Binhendi said in 1988: "We will assist Emirates, of course, but we won't suspend our Open Skies policy. Emirates will have to fight for market share like all the other airlines."

By the end of 1988, Open Skies had enticed 51 airlines to service 87 destinations from Dubai, turning the emirate into an aviation crossroads of the Gulf — a status previously long-held by Bahrain.

In 1988, of the four million passengers then handled annually at Dubai, some two million were merely in transit — and using the duty free facility to pass the time between flights. The cash tills were ringing on overtime, for sure.

It meant too that Dubai's population — small as it was in those days in comparison to today — was enjoying the world's greatest choice of airline services. Keen prices were paid for tickets as the free trading emirate believed in flexible pricing. It was again a win-win situation for Dubai International — for no other emirate in the UAE which boasted an airport at that time could come close to Dubai's international influence on a commercial basis.

Emirates was forced to hone its commercial success without the protectionist elements that underpinned many other international airlines. In the same way, the Dubai government and Department of Civil Aviation sought a duty free that was competitive on the world stage. Dubai Duty free was, essentially, a monopoly, and could have been left to grind out a profit, squeezing its shoppers. But there was a larger concern for Dubai.

Until the late-1980s, Dubai had benefited from the fact that aircraft required a refueling stop. But the advent of new long-haul aircraft, capable of completing non-stop services, meant that stopovers in the Gulf were in danger of being rendered unnecessary.

The Dubai Hub, to remain a Hub against this backdrop, needed to be ultra-competitive. The Department of Civil Aviation maintains arguably the most competitive pricing structure of any airport in the world. Dnata, charged with ground handling, was winning plaudits, and a third element, Dubai Duty free, had to remain on top of its game in order to ensure that international passengers remained attracted.

"We succeeded on all three counts," observes Binhendi.

Tax Haven

*Increasing passenger numbers and flight movements showed that
Dubai International Airport was becoming a regional hub.*

*Snooker, the sport of gentlemen, would dominate Dubai Duty Free's
marketing efforts during the company's early years.*

Chapter Fourteen

Soggy Bread

Money is a headache, and money is the cure.
— *Everett Mámor, French author*

On December 20, 1983, Dubai Duty Free opened with a handy $44,000 in takings. With this began the inexorable climb upwards. Stock was refined, new lines introduced, displays improved, price structures honed. By the end of 1986 duty free revenues hit the $32 million mark — and were still growing.

In 1987, Dubai Duty Free opened an Arrivals Duty Free facility. Selling a fair selection of goods, excluding, in the early years of its operation, liquor, it was an instant success and has continued to be a busy 24-hour operation, expanding in both size and range of goods since. The new shop was the first Arrivals facility of its kind in the Middle East and, said McLoughlin at the time: "Even the big airports in Europe don't have duty free shops catering to arriving passengers. This is because of an EEC agreement."

In Dubai, however, there was no such red tape.

"We took it to Mr Binhendi, who took it to Sheikh Ahmed," says George Horan. "As is Sheikh Ahmed's way, he recognised the value of the idea and immediately gave the green light."

In the spring of 1987 Duty Free opened three new outlets, landside, to serve people who were visiting the airport to see off departing passengers or welcoming those arriving. These two new additions to Dubai Duty Free's portfolio enhanced takings that were already in the ascendancy. The original shop floor was, hardly 30 months into its life, operating very successfully. That first day $44,000 had increased to around $200,000 a day, almost five times the growth, from the same retail space.

"Profit has never been our single, overriding motive," said McLoughlin. "Keeping passengers happy is, and always has been, a major consideration — and the Arrivals shop was primarily set up for passenger convenience."

Passenger convenience, however, also had the advantage of allowing more passengers to spend more. By 1987 the airport was handling an increasing number of passengers, thanks to the inauguration of that new arrivals terminal. From 3.77 million in 1986, traffic was growing at a phenomenal rate, crossing the five million mark in 1990.

Each morning, McLoughlin would arrive in his office and review the previous day's sales figures. By the summer of 1987, with the main duty free performing well, arrivals and landside shops open, there was a trend toward a breakthrough.

"I doubt anyone could have imagined a seven-figure daily turnover, back in 1984. It was an excellent performance, the result of hard work on the part of the management and staff of the duty free," says Sheikh Ahmed.

Perhaps one million dirhams ($275,000) was somewhat symbolic. One million dollars a day, which took 15 more years to reach was, arguably, a bigger event in world terms. But it would be trite not to recognise the enormity of such an event. Those involved in Dubai Duty Free were keeping a close eye on sales figures in 1987.

"I had half an eye on it," says George Horan. "So did most of the management. It was tantalisingly close for a long time."

Then, on October 13 and 14, 1987, the figure fell just short. It was clear that, given a general upward trend, the glass ceiling was about to be breached. On the morning of October 16, McLoughlin arrived at work. On his desk was the daily report, produced by the Finance Department.

"It was on October 15, 1987 that the day's sales topped Dhs. 1 million for the first time ever. Looking back, I was more excited then, than on the day we broke the million dollar mark. But it was a marvelous milestone," says McLoughlin.

Perhaps understated by the Managing Director, especially considering the figures. Dubai Duty Free was opened with a Dhs. 3 million line of credit with the National Bank of Dubai (rapidly eaten up and depleted pre-opening). On this single day, Dubai Duty Free turned over the equivalent of a third of that that investment. October 15's turnover represented a tenfold increase on opening day. It is also worth noting that, allowing for inflation, $275,000 today is the equivalent of $750,000 today.

With turnover increasing, the job of developing the Dubai Duty Free brand, and promoting Dubai, became higher on the agenda, simply because there was now a budget to support such an enterprise. From an emirate-wide schools poetry contest and a water-skiing exhibition in those very early days, backed up by the successful 'Fly Buy Dubai' campaign, Dubai Duty Free was making baby steps forward. Now it was time for a jump forward.

They backed the Gulf Water-Ski Championships in 1986. It was the beginning of an incredible alliance with sporting events, and it was through this that brand Dubai Duty Free gained more visibility locally, regionally, and internationally. Soon, the company's logo was appearing at a variety of sporting venues around Dubai — local golfers in particular benefiting from the Duty Free sponsorship.

Soggy Bread

By 1987, the company had set its sights farther. There was a surprising dabble with show jumping. The All England Jumping Course at Hickstead is the leading outdoor show jumping venue in England. Hickstead's Derby meeting, in June, is a four-day, action-packed event attracting up to 20,000 spectators.

Arguably the highlight of the meeting is the British Jumping Derby, a 1,195-metre course with tricky jumps including the aptly-named Devil's Dyke — three fences in short succession with a water-filled ditch in the middle and the difficult Derby Bank, a jump with 3ft 5in rails on top and a 10ft 6in slope down the front. The 1986 meeting was won by German star Paul Schockemöhle, three times European Champion, on his formidable mount Deister. It was Schockemöhle's third Hickstead Derby success.

Showjumping was just a one-off, but equestrian pursuits would become long-term. Perhaps it was natural that thoroughbred racing would become a feature of Dubai Duty Free's strategy. By the second half of the 1980s, the Maktoum family were enjoying sustained success on the racecourses of the world. Sheikh Mohammed — in particular — had emerged as Britain's

In October 1987 Dubai Duty Free turned over one million dirhams in a day for the first time. Allowing for inflation, that is $750,000 today.

Fly *Buy* Dubai

2008 marks the 21st consecutive year that Dubai Duty Free has sponsored horse racing around the world.

Soggy Bread

champion owner, for the first time, in 1985. Through the likes of such horses as Oh So Sharp, Pebbles, Ajdal, and English and Irish Oaks-winner Unite, his maroon and white colours were, arguably, Dubai's major public relations asset worldwide during this period. Sheikh Mohammed had enjoyed successes in America, noticeably through Pebbles, in the Breeders' Cup, and Deceit Dancer. Sheikh Maktoum had won the Irish Derby with Shareef Dancer, his fourth classic success in Europe in three seasons. Sheikh Hamdan had claimed the Melbourne Cup with At Talaq, while 1987 was the year that the youngest of the four brothers, Sheikh Ahmed bin Rashid Al Maktoum, would emerge as a major owner with his ultra classy Mtoto. Horses owned by the brothers from Dubai won four of the five British classics in 1985.

"I can honestly say that we have never, ever been instructed to sponsor anything," says McLoughlin. "On a few occasions it has been suggested that we look at things — and as such have been happy to support them. But it has never been a case of outside interference.

"Horse racing, which appeals to our local base, has always offered tremendous value for money in terms of exposure. We have sponsored top class racing in several European countries."

Dubai Duty Free's introduction to racing came at France's famed Longchamp in 1987. At the heart of the Bois de Boulogne, Longchamp is one of the most prestigious racecourses in the world. The first-ever race was run at Longchamp on April 27, 1857 in front of a massive crowd, including Emperor Napoleon III. Today, among the track's multitude of big events are the Grand Prix de Paris and Prix de l'Arc de Triomphe. The Arc weekend is Europe's biggest two-day combined purse.

Sponsoring at Longchamp during the summer of 1987 proved to be the first of over 20 consecutive seasons when Dubai Duty Free would back a growing portfolio of the best thoroughbred races in Europe.

But even as Dubai Duty Free's management team were organising their summers around the organisation requirements for Hickstead and Longchamp, work was underway that would see Dubai Duty Free bring top class sports to their home base.

Early in 1987 an introduction to the World Professional Billiards and Snooker Association, also known as World Snooker, had set in motion discussions to bring top class snooker to the UAE.

Billiards had been a popular activity among British Army officers stationed in India, and variations on the more traditional billiard games were devised. One variation, devised in the officers' mess in Jabalpur during 1874 or 1875, was to add coloured balls to the reds and black which were used for pool. The word 'snooker' also has military origins, being a slang term for first-year cadets or inexperienced personnel. One version of events states that Colonel Sir Neville Chamberlain of the Devonshire regiment was playing this new game when his opponent failed to pot a ball and Chamberlain called him a "snooker".

In 1969 the BBC commissioned the snooker tournament *Pot Black* to demonstrate the potential of colour television, with the green table and multi-coloured balls being ideal for showing off the advantages of colour broadcasting. The TV series became a ratings success, and the game quickly became a mainstream sport.

World Snooker oversaw a sport that was beginning to broaden its appeal from its base. In the mid-1980s there was a gradual push toward organising tournaments away from these regions.

Top professional snooker players played on a ranking circuit, which ranked points, earned by players through their performances over the previous two seasons, to determine a world ranking. The most important event in professional snooker is the World Championship, followed by ranking tournaments and then invitational tournaments, to which most of the top players are invited. The most important tournament category is The Masters.

"We liked it. The staging costs were reasonable, and it was high profile," says Anita Mehra. "Snooker was at its zenith as a spectator sport at the time. It was big."

Steve Davis was a genuine sports star, having transcended his sport. By the time of Dubai's interest in snooker he had won the World Championship in 1981, 1983, 1984, and 1987, the first four of six eventual titles. Ironically, one of his most memorable matches was one he lost: the 1985 World Championship final against Dennis Taylor, when a nail-biting finale drew 18.5 million viewers, a record post-midnight audience on British television and a record audience for BBC2.

"When you looked at names like Steve Davis, who would be part of a Dubai event, these were household names, top, international names," says Gof Malone, a senior journalist in the Gulf city during that period.

Just as Dubai Duty Free the brand emerged abroad, at Hickstead and Longchamp, in the winter of 1988, hardly more than three years after the facility opened, Dubai Duty Free made its first big splash at home.

In Dubai, years before the emirate began organising these big, world class events for which it has become renowned, this would be a major undertaking. Snooker was big business. Along with the players came WAGS

Soggy Bread

Colm McLoughlin, John Sutcliffe and Anita Mehra
with the world's top eight snooker players.

(Wives and Girlfriends), families, agents, assorted hangers-on, officials, dozens of journalists, and fans. These were days before Dubai World Cups, Tennis Opens, Golf Opens, and other huge sporting events. And Dubai Duty Free, which had taken on this burden, was charged with making sure Dubai was able to organise what was, at the time, such a big event.

"There was a downside, for sure," says Binhendi. "Snooker drew a lot of media. If we dropped the ball and drew bad publicity because of that, it would have been disastrous."

A committee was given the job of steering the event. Just because of the newness of the exercise, it was a project that tested everyone. It was a massive undertaking just because it was the first time that all the administrative elements of an international sporting event were drawn together. Immigration and airport administration for the hundreds of arrivals and departures, Dubai Television as host broadcaster (it was one of the very first international events they handled), Al Nasr Leisureland, the venue, Dubai Police, a handful of hotels, hospitality, marketing, and so on.

From the side of World Snooker, an expansion into Dubai was important

Soggy Bread

Steve Davis, the greatest cueman of his generation, makes a break during the Dubai Duty Free Masters.

Fly *Buy* Dubai

as few tournaments were outside their traditional base markets at the time. For the Dubai Masters, eight of the world's best players were invited.

"We did not really know Dubai that first year," says Steve Davis. "But the organisers were keen and well-drilled. As players, we were always going to support any effort to spread the roots of snooker, but I think most were attracted by the way it was done. We appreciated their enthusiasm."

Davis headlined the eight big names who flew to Dubai, accompanied by the likes of former World Champions Terry Griffiths, Dennis Taylor, the charismatic Jimmy 'Whirlwind' White, and Joe Johnson, well-known as the surprise winner of the 1986 World Championship.

That first year, according to Bharat Godkhindi, deputy general manager of marketing and projects, was when Dubai set out to set the bar high in terms of handling competitors.

"Everything was to be Rolls-Royce, " he says. "Nothing was done on the cheap. The players were to be handled in a top level manner, ensuring that they spoke highly of Dubai and this, in itself, generated publicity."

With some trepidation on the part of Dubai Duty Free, the box office opened at Al Nasr ten days before these well-paid snooker stars were due to arrive. Godkhindi, Mehra and their public relations department had been drip-feeding stories into the local media for weeks. The media eat up such stories, understandably, as alongside coverage of international sporting events there was little top-notch sport to report upon.

"Even at that stage, in 1988, Dubai Duty Free was churning out press releases that were being snapped up by the media. Pre-event coverage was phenomenal," says Cherian Thomas, then assistant sports editor at *Khaleej Times*, one of Dubai's leading daily broadsheets. "There was huge coverage of the event, even in the Arabic press which was not as snooker-friendly as the English media. But the roll-out of material did ratchet up public expectation." But would public expectation be enough? The box office opened at Al Nasr Leisureland within eight days of Davis and his cohorts arriving in the city. Dubai Duty Free could afford to lose money should no tickets be sold, but the embarrassment of an empty venue would have been tantamount to abject failure.

"I recall some trepidation," says George Horan. "We believed that snooker would be hit here, and our research showed that people said they would attend, but that meant nothing if we did not manage to persuade them to *actually* buy tickets and show up."

Despite the media, there were now queues at Al Nasr Leisureland. The Box Office saw a steady stream of visitors, but not the flood that all

Soggy Bread

Stephen Hendry embarks upon some bargain hunting while on a visit to the Dubai Duty Free shop floor.

promoters dream about. That most indomitable of boxing promoters, Don King, had stated that: "If you cast your bread upon the water and you have faith, you'll get back cash. If you don't have faith, you'll get soggy bread."

Thousands of tickets had gone on sale for the entire tournament. As the days ran on toward the Dubai Duty Free Masters, sales were less than brisk. The media campaign continued to unfold, with less than startling Box Office results. While Dubai Duty Free was not in the events business as a money-making exercise, and never would be, the cash or soggy bread analogy was nevertheless valid. And while, today, no-one will admit to any troubled, sleepless nights, there must have been concerns that Dubai's first major sporting event would play to empty seats.

Then, something happened.

"Just 48 hours before the opening ceremony there was a sudden surge," says Mehra. "There were queues at the box office."

As sessions were being sold out, Mehra, Godkhindi and their fellow managers suddenly encountered a phenomenon that they would become accustomed to in later years as Dubai Duty Free expanded its portfolio.

Soggy Bread

England's Neal Foulds won the Dubai Duty Free Masters,
the first professional snooker event staged in the UAE.

Fly *Buy* Dubai

The event would go on to become one of the highlights of the global snooker calendar, attracting some of the game's luminaries, such as Steve Davis (above) and (left) Alex Higgins and James Wattana.

Soggy Bread

"Right before an event you become very popular and suddenly have a lot more friends," chuckles Horan. In Middle Eastern vernacular, suddenly people who normally only had a nodding acquaintance with management of Dubai Duty Free were exercising their *Wasta* — an Arabic term that can best be translated into English as 'clout', 'connections', 'influence', or 'pull' — in order to procure rare tickets.

Wasta would be the only way to get tickets for most sessions of the 1988 Dubai Duty Free Masters. By the time that the eight players were flying into the emirate ahead of the tournament, Box Office simply had no tickets left.

As the six days of the Masters unfolded, Davis, as fans came to expect, reached the final. He was at the peak of his considerable powers, and was breathtaking to watch. His opponent, however, was something of a surprise. Neal Foulds, 25 years old, not only reached that final but, in a gripping match, watched by a sell-out 500-strong crowd, edged out Davis 5 to 4.

"That first event really put Dubai on the map in snooker terms. We were received so well and looked after. The response of the public was warm," says Foulds. "Of course, I am a bit biased as I won, but from that year Dubai became one of the events that all professionals wanted to play."

"Professional snooker was something new here and created a lot of excitement," says Sheikh Ahmed. "But what I was happy about particularly was the way that the event was managed. It was very professional. Today, Dubai has a reputation for this, but the Masters was a first.

"In a way, the benchmark set by this event was the template against which subsequent events in Dubai set themselves, and from which event management in Dubai grew. The Masters pioneered this high standard."

Dubai Duty Free was at the cusp of this new-found approach to promoting Dubai. Sheikh Ahmed gave his assent to a plan that would see 1988's exhibition tournament morph into a ranking event.

"It was never going to be a one-off, as long as we got it right. We were committed to creating a top-ranking event," says Mehra.

The Classic, which ran for the following six years from 1989, brought such luminaries from the world of green baize and wooden cues as Steve Davis, Stephen Hendry, and John Parrott, to Dubai. Years before Dubai Duty Free created headlines by putting the world's top two ranked tennis players on a helipad, the world would become accustomed to snooker stars in the desert.

"We were there to think out of the box, in order not only to boost the Dubai Duty Free brand, but to promote Dubai," says McLoughlin. "That underscored everything we did."

With Dubai International Airport undergoing a major expansion, Dubai Duty Free hit upon a new promotional concept that would sweep the industry.

Chapter Fifteen

Quite a Surprise

Depend on the rabbit's foot if you will,
but remember it didn't work for the rabbit.
— R. E. Shay, British author

Dubai had a way of doing things that, often, harked back to its roots. In 1980, the Ruler, Sheikh Rashid bin Saeed Al Maktoum, suffered a stroke. He would never return to his robust former self. But for a decade he remained in power, overseeing the efforts of his sons to carry the emirate — and the UAE — forward. In many ways, his essence remained prevalent.

One of Sheikh Rashid's most humbling traits was his simple Bedouin manner when it came to doing business.

In 1958 he had bulldozed across imperialist efforts to derail the plan and forged ahead with an airport for Dubai. In typical fashion he committed himself to major contracts with a handshake. In the summer of 1959, on a short holiday to Britain, he broke off his private engagements to meet with representatives of IAL (International Aeradio Limited), when he agreed to purchase equipment to the value of £17,000. The deal was sealed with a handshake.

"Sheikh Rashid did things with a handshake. This was his manner. He considered that a handshake was a contract between both parties," says Abdullah Saleh, a *Majlis* stalwart. "Sheikh Rashid launched deals worth hundreds of millions with a handshake, and then expected things to move from there. Of course, foreign companies struggled with this, but a handshake was Sheikh Rashid's commitment. He never broke his commitments."

IAL, having worked with the Dubai Ruler on a number of different issues, knew that his handshake was as good as a written contract with the Ruler. But it nevertheless caused consternation in the company's London headquarters.

A report from the records of the British administration in Dubai during that period stated: 'While he was in London, the Ruler asked the company to order technical equipment to the value of £17,000; this they have now done. There is no formal agreement, between the company and the Ruler, but the company have sent him a copy of the record of their conversations in London which they hope he will sign as a form of contract...'

Trust, Sheikh Rashid believed, mattered as much as bits of paper. And

Fly *Buy* Dubai

while in the modern world, this is a concept that gets harder and harder to accept, Sheikh Rashid's way of doing business seems somewhat romantic and harks back to an era of nobility and decency. The essence of a gentleman's agreement is that it relies upon the honor of the parties for its fulfillment, rather than being in any way enforceable. The term has come to sound distinctly old-fashioned, because of its implicit assumption that both parties will be gentlemen.

Even in Dubai, where Sheikh Rashid's era was reaching its end, such implicit trust could not be maintained indefinitely. Yet there are examples that remain, even until the present day.

At the beginning of 1984, Colm McLoughlin, John Sutcliffe, and George Horan had left Aer Rianta and joined Dubai Duty Free. Simply because they were being lured away from the stability of long-standing jobs, and their homeland, they had been given two-year agreements. By the spring of 1986 these ended.

"I've never had another, until the present day," says McLoughlin. "When you deal with Sheikh Ahmed you know you are dealing with a gentleman."

Sheikh Rashid's brother, head of the Department of Civil Aviation, continued in the same vein, although when it comes to building multi-billion dollar airports and purchasing billions of dollars of aircraft for Emirates the airline, contracts are tied down extremely tightly.

But the head of Dubai Duty Free and his team never looked over their shoulders. McLoughlin's lack of contract has not prevented him from looking to the long term. By the end of 1988 he was nearly two years out of contract and the future was very much on his mind. Dubai Duty Free had completed its first major sporting event, an extraordinary sell-out success, and was showing another steep increase in turnover. On December 20, 1988, revenue for the previous 12-month period was announced at $55 million, almost a four-fold increase over 1984, Dubai Duty Free's first full year of trading.

"It was an excellent result, but one which created uncertainty more than being a source of back-slapping," says Horan. "Such a huge volume of trade, through a relatively small trading space."

"Within the real estate we had at our disposal, it was clear that our growth could not go much further," says McLoughlin. "The airport was getting busier. We could do better. Of that there was no doubt."

There was also statistical evidence to support McLoughlin's claim that they could do better. The growth in Dubai Duty Free's business had come to a difficult political backdrop. Undoubtedly, with a world recession raging,

Quite a Surprise

Sheikh Ahmed bin Saeed Al Maktoum's leadership has drawn much positive comment from acrosss the organisations he heads.

the 1980s were tough years for aviation. In the Gulf the situation was exacerbated by the Iran-Iraq War. Almost flat-lining aircraft movement statistics told their own story in Dubai. This was cannon fodder for the doom-mongers and soothsayers who preached conservatism above all else.

In 1983, there were 36,000 scheduled civil aviation traffic movements. By Dubai's standards, a growth to barely 40,000 in 1989 was flat-lining, especially when one factored in the increase provided by the launch of Dubai's own airline in 1985.

"We heard the soothsayers," says Mohammed Ahli, Director General of Dubai Civil Aviation Authority. "But Dubai never lost its direction and its positive approach. I don't remember any meetings where people were sitting around questioning the future. The only questions being bandied around were how we could move forward better, faster, more efficiently and in better shape."

"We wanted to be the best in the world," says Sheikh Ahmed.

For Dubai Duty Free, if the lean years of civil aviation had seen such a

Quite a Surprise

The Dubai Duty Free shop floor was set for a major expansion.

Fly *Buy* Dubai

With the end of the Iran-Iraq War hopes were high that Dubai would boom. Dubai Duty Free was ready to capitalise thanks to things like staff training (top), which would allow the company to serve the increasing number of passengers who would now pass through Dubai International Airport.

huge increase in turnover, it was clear that things would only get better. The drag-down effect that the Iran-Iraq War had on the Gulf as a whole was palpable. Iranian official figures would later state that the conflict cost the Islamic Republic $500 billion. Iraq's loss would be estimated to be in excess of that figure. The two protagonists would lose an estimated one trillion dollars due to their folly, not to mention a million lives lost.

The cost to the region was far higher. Oil prices were dragged down by OPEC over-production. But a far bigger impact was made by enormous capital flight, when money rapidly flowed out of the region because of a war that disturbed investors and caused them to lose confidence in the Gulf's economic strength.

On July 18, 1988, there was finally a concerned move to end the simmering conflict. The Iranian government sent a letter to UN Secretary-General Javier Pérez de Cuéllar, which stated: 'The Islamic Republic of Iran, because of the importance it attaches to the lives of human beings and the establishment of justice and regional and international peace and security, accepts Security Council Resolution 598.' Two days later, peace broke out on the front lines between the two countries.

What peace would mean to the Gulf was clear. For Dubai International Airport it was even clearer. The war had artificially restricted growth during most of the 1980s. Most of the 1990s would see a boom.

In Dubai, after a war of attrition itself due to surging turnover during its early formative years, Dubai Duty Free was now looking to establish the retail and organisational capacity that would allow the business to prosper further.

Firefighting the logistical supply chain problems and taking on more staff was one thing. Getting to grips with the situation was quite another. As things stood, a dearth of space meant only so much could be done. This had included a series of re-designs for the perfumery and leather goods outlets, and an elegant pink décor for a new-look perfumery.

"It was at this point that we also got serious in terms of procedures," says Ramesh Cidambi. "We began a rolling programme that would see stock-holding and purchasing procedures gradually become computerised."

Staff training programmes were sharpened and became a more pronounced part of the sales effort. Plans for a new administration complex included in-house training facilities, ongoing for staff regardless of their level within the organisation.

With so much effort going on, revenue grew accordingly, but it was recognised that it could only go so far.

Fly *Buy* Dubai

But as Dubai International began to handle more than four million passengers a year, a decision needed to be made on direction. The management of Dubai Airport and Dubai Duty Free needed to take a decision on what would affect the long-term approach to duty free in the emirate. Was there an appetite to see how far the thing could grow, or was the airport happy with its lot?

"When we looked at the situation during that period, there was a clear case for further investment, and to give Dubai Duty Free more scope for growth," says Sheikh Ahmed.

By the end of 1988, with Sheikh Ahmed's ascent, planning forged ahead on a complete overhaul — a huge new area of shop floor, separate administration offices, and a huge new warehouse.

With Terminal 2 completed, major works were already underway on Terminal 1, where consultants Gibb Petermuller had been tasked with a conversion and upgrade.

"We are stripping out virtually everything. That is what makes it such a complicated job," said John Hely, Gibb Petermuller's project manager. "The original building is structurally sound, so no significant remedial work is called for."

In August 1988, $11 million was allocated for six more parking aprons, adding to the 21 already in place, a new computerised radar system, and a new fuelling system for aircraft. The latter would see underground pipes used instead of conventional tankers.

"It is not just a matter of belief in aviation. We have belief in the industry, but also complete confidence that we have in place the people who can fulfill the promise of Dubai," says Sheikh Ahmed. "And this consistent factor had meant that when we have looked to the future, any plans we conceived were always carried forward with a belief in what we were doing."

For months Dubai Duty Free's management went into a huddle, working with architects, designers, and consultants.

"In 1983 it was a case of doing the best we could do, within the set of circumstances we were presented with," says McLoughlin. "This was a different proposition. Sheikh Ahmed was behind us and the Department of Civil Aviation was committed to providing us, within reason, with what we required to grow."

First, they required more floor space. Within the confines of the existing airport there was only one obvious solution. They earmarked the office area adjacent to the duty free shopping complex. This represented a natural point

Quite a Surprise

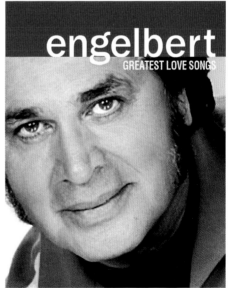

Visiting the shop floor in 1988 was Engelbert Humperdinck, who rose to international fame during the 1960s and 1970s with hits such as 'Can't Take My Eyes Off You', 'Release Me', 'Quando, Quando, Quando'.

of growth, yet itself posed a question. Where would McLoughlin, his managers, and the whole administrative team go?

Being based away from the airport was not an option. Sheikh Ahmed came up with the answer — that they build an administrative complex on to Terminal 1.

"But we had a tiny window," says Sutcliffe. "In order to start work on the shop floor, the administration had to be moved. Therefore the office complex was effectively holding us up from expansion."

With typical Dubai verve, Sheikh Ahmed's answer was to cut out any time-wasting. Even while architects were doing their stuff, he had begun clearing the area where building work would later occur. His office helped cut through red tape in clearing building regulations and obtaining necessary permissions. The tendering process was short and sweet. Work quickly got underway.

"It was quite remarkable. Even for Dubai," says Peter Hill.

At the end of 1988, with designs for the administrative block still on the design boards, Sheikh Ahmed had ordered that a new duty free shopping complex must be ready by December 20, 1989 — Dubai Duty Free's sixth anniversary.

"Sheikh Ahmed does not mess about," chuckles Maurice Flanagan, who a couple of years earlier had been given six months to start an airline. "He gives you all the support you need and expects that you will get on with the job."

The project would, if successful, give Dubai Duty Free an additional 70 per cent of retail space. But achieving that would not be without its price.

"There were a lot of sleepless nights," says Mehra.

While continuing to trade, 24 hours a day, the management of Dubai Duty Free would plan, design, and execute a new administration and shop floor, move their offices as seamlessly as possible, recruit and train several hundred new staff, and put in place systems that would cope with what was anticipated to be a surge of business. Not to mention running perennially-demanding events like Dubai Duty Free's racing portfolio abroad and the snooker at home.

First came the office block. Contractors accepted the job with tight time requirements and singeing financial penalties for delays. From ground-breaking, they were given just four months to hand over the project.

While this site was a hive of activity, McLoughlin was looking to revamp his shop floor. In 1983, the celebrated genius of Rodney Fitch had developed Dubai Duty Free's first shop floor. Fitch made statements like: "The history

Quite a Surprise

Celebrated design genius Rodney Fitch worked on the company's first expansion.
Later he would receive a CBE from Queen Elizabeth.

of flight doesn't define the human experience, nor does the Industrial Revolution, but the business of shopping started when we were cavemen. The hunting and gathering form has now evolved into four million square foot malls, which is only another form of hunting and gathering."

Fitch's genius earned him a CBE from Queen Elizabeth, but after hardly more than half a decade serving Dubai Duty Free it was time for a new take and a new direction.

In the Middle Ages, market halls were constructed, essentially just covered marketplaces. It took hundreds of years before the first shops in a modern sense were built, usually supplying one type of article or services, such as a baker, a tailor, or a cobbler. It was only in the 19th century that arcades were invented, a street of several different shops, roofed over. Nearly 200 years later, the industry moved at an incredible pace.

Five years on, Dubai Duty Free would turn to Welshman Tom Ellery, noted in the retail industry for his exquisite and striking visual displays. The word 'genius' was bandied about, and whether or not he could really be considered among the world's greatest thinkers, Einstein-esque, it was

Fly *Buy* Dubai

*'Uncle' Tom Ellery (left)
cut his retail teeth on the
shop floor at Harrods
(top) and went on to
impact Dubai Duty Free
during the 1990s.*

nevertheless true that the Austrian chemist could never have sold confectionery like the Welshman.

"Ellery was at the very top of the game in the early 1980s," says branding expert Claude Ghaoui. "His ideas were gold. Wherever he worked, revenue grew."

The biggest names on the high street, across Europe, in North America, and even in the Far East, in places like Singapore and Japan, clamoured for Ellery's time. He was, in short, well beyond the Middle East market of the early 1980s. But that did not stop Colm McLoughlin.

"I remember I called him from home," recalls McLoughlin. "I was surprised to get through, but he was a nice guy and we talked briefly."

Then Ellery let fly with his fees.

"I almost dropped the telephone," laughs McLoughlin. "But we wanted his talents on board."

The Dubai Duty Free supremo quickly pulled his thoughts together and, without missing too much of a beat, replied: "Well, if that is all you charge…" Within days, Ellery had signed on as a consultant for Dubai Duty Free. It was a business relationship made in heaven. The Welshman got to work on a redesign on the shop floor, bringing a wealth of global experience to the job.

He was cutting-edge, absorbed with ideas and concepts drawn from the many countries in which he had worked. This was a period when Ellery worked on every continent and had taken major contracts and consultancies in dozens of the world's major shopping capitals.

Yet for all his high-priced reputation, the veteran retailer was no *prima donna*. Just as Dubai Duty Free's Irish management had had to adopt and adapt in order to hone the shop floor in 1983, he was wise enough not to impose his own ideas upon Dubai. He took in the existing sales operation, walked the *souq* downtown, in order to absorb the character and 'pulse' of the local market. Then he flew back to London and got to work.

By the time of Ellery's departure for home, building work was now underway on an administrative block on one end of Terminal 1. Although this was, in construction terms, a rush job, in Dubai Duty Free terms the offices from where the duty free would be run were endowed with far more space than their cramped predecessor, and enough room for a decade or more of growth. Things like training and briefing rooms, a proper canteen, defined areas for each department, and items that one would consider the norm, had all been absent or greatly limited in the small old office area. The new block would allow for these 'luxuries' and endow Dubai Duty Free with growing room as it expanded further.

Foundations were completed, piling work was nearly finished, and hundreds of labourers were beginning to gather on-site each morning as the actual building began to take shape, when Ellery started to report back from Wales.

"Ellery's work represented the best in the business. It was clear from the outset that our association with him was going to be an outstanding success," says Horan, who, as shop floor manager, was going to be working closer than anyone with Ellery's concepts.

While the world's best retail concepts were being designed — with a Dubai spin, in a Welsh studio, half a world away — the management team of Dubai Duty Free was preparing to pick up sticks and move several hundred metres across Dubai International Airport. In just 120 days the administrative building shot up, a remarkable effort, even by Dubai standards. Dubai Duty Free had no time for an easy, phased programme that would see departments morph over to their plush new offices.

"It was like a military operation," says George Horan. "The same day that the building was handed over there were people moving in."

Elsewhere, workers were ready to move in — aiming to strip the old office block of anything that could be salvaged, and then break up the rest. Double-quick.

"Such was the importance of the sixth anniversary, and our expansion, that we hoped to have a VVIP from the Ruling Family of Dubai officiate at the grand opening of the new, improved shop," says McLoughlin. "That meant that there was added pressure to ensure that we were ready on time. By December 20."

With a matter of weeks remaining, work was now underway on a swathe of new floor space, made available as the old offices were removed, while a rolling programme was underway to refit all of the existing sales area. Only good planning prevented chaos breaking out.

"There was constant pressure, as the work had to be completed on time, but also because we had to ensure that the shop floor was interrupted as little as possible," says Antony Joseph, a Dubai Duty Free pioneer.

On December 20, 1989, Sheikh Mohammed cut the ribbon on the new, vastly improved Dubai Duty Free. He toured the site with Sheikh Ahmed and Colm McLoughlin, finding his way among the usual throng of shoppers. Amidst a kerfuffle of jostling press photographers and reporters, staff and shoppers getting close in order to get a view, and Sheikh Mohammed's own entourage, his arrival created quite a stir.

Quite a Surprise

Indeed, the following morning's news coverage in the Arabic and English media was full of the visit. Sheikh Mohammed's hour in Dubai Duty Free was front page news. Which, in a way, caused another big story to be deflected from public view. Annual figures of $76.4 million for 1989 represented a $10 million increase over 1988.

"Given the circumstances, with so many people engaged in the shifting of our administration, so much behind-the-scenes work and disruptions to the shop floor, this represented another tremendous result," says Horan. "And there were grounds for optimism that we were now going to embark upon a period of more greatly enhanced results.

"And, of course, there was a new element."

Amid the upheaval of the previous 12 months, McLoughlin, Horan, Mehra, and others had set out to come up with a new promotion for the new Dubai Duty Free they were building. It needed something different, something big, something sexy.

Nearly two decades on, no-one is entirely sure of where their big idea came from. There are many claimants.

"I remember Mr Binhendi suggesting that we raffle a private 'plane as a

Initial suggestions were that Dubai Duty Free offer a private jet in order to mark its new expansion.

*Sheikh Mohammed inaugurates the new Dubai Duty Free expansion, watched by
Sheikh Ahmed, Mohi-Din Binhendi and Colm McLoughlin.*

one-off, with tickets at maybe $10,000 each, to celebrate the opening," says McLoughlin. "That was the starting point."

Raffling a small aircraft was unusual, but also impractical, and costly. Not many of Dubai International Airport's customers would consider investing $10,000 in a ticket. Dubai Duty Free would have created a millionaire's draw that may have generated some publicity.

"We said, 'People can't park an airplane in their garage', and with that in mind, the idea panned out into the concept that was launched," says Mehra.

The concept that they were searching for needed to have far wider appeal.

"Someone came up with a luxury car," says McLoughlin. "I'm not sure who, but from there the whole thing fell into place."

By the middle of 1989 a proposal went to Sheikh Ahmed for his approval. On December 20, 1989, there was another reason to celebrate the opening of the expanded shop floor. Having cleared many administrative and organisational hurdles, the opening of the revamped Dubai Duty Free coincided with what, in hindsight, was a watershed for the industry.

One thousand tickets each at priced at Dhs. 500 — approximately $139 — were put up for sale. The prize was a Bentley Mulsanne. With a name that alluded to Bentley's famous racing history, which included five victories at the 24 Hours of Le Mans — the Mulsanne Straight is a stretch of the Le Mans course where cars reach their highest speeds — the Mulsanne car epitomised the very spirit of Bentley, renowned for performance and complete comfort. Only 970 examples of this model were produced, between 1987 and 1992.

Built by the original Rolls-Royce company, the Mulsanne was a Rolls-Royce in everything but name — but with much more scintillating performance — and ten years after the introduction of the Mulsanne Turbo, Bentley would outsell its Rolls-Royce stablemates two-to-one.

As Mehra describes it, the car had a very "Oooooh!" factor among customers. Placed prominently near the base of the escalator that led down to Dubai Duty Free, it was not a car that one could pass by without a second glance… or a third. Dubai Duty Free was forced to employ a security guard, just to ensure that the Mulsanne's many fans were kept at bay. This was an excellent investment according to Sheikh Ahmed, from whom this particular model of car was borrowed, for display purposes.

With plenty of "Oooooh!" behind it, thus began the 'Finest Surprise', a promotion that would become one of the longest-running promotions of its kind in the world, and widely considered as the most successful in the history of duty free. Indeed, so successful that it is estimated that upwards of 50 airport duty frees around the world have adopted the concept.

Quite a Surprise

"We knew it was going to be big — and make a splash," says Mehra. "So Colm had the go-ahead to push Finest Surprise more than we ever had anything before."

This included advertisements in the *Herald Tribune* and *Wall Street Journal* in the USA, and *The Times* in London. This sparked instant results for Dubai. In an era before the Internet got hold, Dubai Duty Free's telephone started ringing off the hook.

"I remember getting calls saying, 'We're going to transit to Dubai can you please book or reserve tickets for us?' It was mad," recalls Mehra.

McLoughlin was soon reporting to Sheikh Ahmed a flood of evidence that people were amending their flights to take in Dubai International Airport as a transit point in order to snap up raffle tickets.

Within ten days of the launch of what was supposed to be a one-off draw, unsold numbers of the 1,000 tickets were dwindling.

"As this was a first, it was impossible to anticipate," says Horan. "But it was only days before someone raised the question, at a management meeting, of what to do next and whether Finest Surprise should be repeated."

The limited edition Bentley Mulsanne was the car of aristocracy. For Dubai Duty Free it had the Oooooh factor they were seeking.

Extraordinary scenes in Dubai Duty Free as the winning ticket for the first Finest Surprise car is drawn. A Lebanese businessman won the Bentley.

Fly *Buy* Dubai

"Judging from the success we were seeing, there was no question that Finest Surprise should roll into a second car, and even more, should demand remain," says McLoughlin. "Sheikh Ahmed was open to suggestions."

Less than two weeks after Finest Surprise tickets went on sale, Dubai Duty Free staff started organising a second. And just in time. There was one full day when tickets for the first draw had run out. Dubai Duty Free managers faced vociferous complaints.

"I recall one man who demanded we find him a ticket, insisting to me that he had changed his travel plans and added several hours on his overall journey time, in order to pass through Dubai International," says Anita Mehra.

In the 7,306 days stretching between December 20, 1989 and December 20, 2008, this remains the only day when tickets for Finest Surprise were not available for sale on Dubai Duty Free's shop floor.

Some weeks later, with the 1,000 tickets sold, Sheikh Ahmed would get his car back, and Dubai Duty Free would purchase another. This would be delivered to Lebanon. Businessman Simon Simonian took a call at his home in Beirut.

"I was incredulous," he says. "To be honest, I thought it was a joke, someone was winding me up."

Whereas one may have thought McLoughlin would have been the first to telephone Lebanon, the call was made by a staffer in the Marketing Department of Dubai Duty Free, a tradition that remains until the present day.

"They do the work. It is for them to make that life-changing call," he says. "I know it is a telephone call that people like to place, as telling someone of that level of fortune is a rush for sure."

The promotion, and the name of Simonian, caught the attention of the world's media. The promotion itself made no actual money for Dubai Duty Free due to its high overheads. Of the $100,000 in revenue generated by each car, this is plowed back into purchasing the prize, marketing, administering and organising the competition, and flying winners to Dubai to be handed the keys of their new car, along with shipping the car to their home countries.

But the sheer weight of publicity just in the period from the unveiling of Finest Surprise until the draw, and Simonian's jubilant receipt of the car, was worth half a year's marketing budget in itself.

Since then, over 1,300 people from over 70 countries have won the car of their dreams — ordinary people, from office boys and building site labourers to bankers and doctors.

Quite a Surprise

Since 1989 the shop floor has been permanently graced with luxury cars — closing in on 1,500 of them.

The promotion has, over the years, attracted many thousands of visitors to Dubai for they see that the odds of winning at only 1,000 to one are a lucrative proposition. It has become common to find people joining together in syndicates to purchase a Finest Surprise ticket. For many recipients — syndicates and individuals — this has offered the opportunity to set themselves up in some far corner of the world and be independently wealthy.

"Some of my fondest memories of my time in Dubai have been of the consortiums who have won cars, and seen the financial equivalent change their lives," says McLoughlin. "There comes to mind a group of labourers from India who pooled what was, for them, a great deal of money. The windfall that the win represented allowed them to return home permanently, set themselves up and their children."

There is no age restriction for purchases, and many people passing through Dubai Duty Free have purchased tickets in the names of their children. It has not been unusual for Colm McLoughlin or a member of his management team to be presenting the keys of a shiny new top-of-the-range

Fly *Buy* Dubai

Rolls-Royce, BMW, Lamborghini, Ferrari, or Porsche to a babe in arms. The operation has one specific stipulation — regardless of whether the ticket was bought by one person in the name of another, it is the person whose name that appears on the ticket who receives the keys.

While retaining the magic formula of 1,000 tickets at Dhs. 500, the success of the Finest Surprise saw it slowly expanding. Soon, multiple cars were offered in the Departures, offering entrants a choice of the car they hoped to win. Another car was offered in Arrivals. Later, Finest Surprise tickets have been occasionally offered outside the Duty Free shop floor. Such has been the promotion's popularity and worldwide attraction, the operation has set up parallel draws at leading local and international events with which Dubai Duty Free is associated. These include the biennial Dubai Air Show, the annual Dubai World Cup horse race meeting, the Dubai Tennis Championships, the annual Arabian Travel Market, and leading external events such as horse racing which are Dubai Duty Free-sponsored.

The first time a Finest Surprise draw was held overseas saw McLoughlin and his team headed for the famous horse races at Newbury in England. The

Dubai Duty Free's international advertising promoted Finest Surprise around the globe.

draw was for an MG sports car worth (at the time) £25,000. The vehicle was a collector's item as it was part of a re-launched edition for the famous sports car marque.

Dubai Duty Free had to apply for permission to hold the raffle, and everything was done in accordance with the UK's Lotteries and Gaming Act.

"We will only do such draws in overseas territories if we are involved with sponsorship or part sponsorship of an event, in order to make the event more attractive," said McLoughlin at the time.

The Finest Surprise promotion was a unique concept in 1989, succeeding in attracting the public's imagination from the very beginning. "Dubai Duty Free has marketed this promotion worldwide and, to its credit, there is still a huge demand from the public looking to win a dream car," commented Sheikh Ahmed. Added McLoughlin, who is invariably on hand to draw the winning ticket and, later to present the keys for the luxury vehicle: "The initial response to Finest Surprise was incredible and we quickly realised this promotion could become synonymous with Dubai Duty Free."

Today, on average, there are two draws a month for two cars, with tickets available to incoming, transiting, outgoing, and online buyers. The cars are a focal point on the shop floor at Dubai Duty Free, providing an additional incentive for people to buy tickets before they fly.

Mehra recalls: "It first hit me that we had really made something of Dubai Duty Free one day when I was on a flight going to Japan. I overheard a conversation between two people, with one saying to the other: 'Do you want to re-transit in Dubai, so we can buy a draw ticket?'"

"For me, that was my moment, when I felt we were making an impact, both for Dubai and the duty free. People who knew nothing about Dubai were talking about Dubai Duty Free. That was when I grasped the impact that we were making — and of course grasped the enormity of the Finest Surprise.

Colm McLoughlin and his deputy John Sutcliffe on the shop floor. Sutcliffe was to move to new pastures.

Chapter Sixteen

Changing of the Guard

Over a long distance, you learn about the strength of your horse.
Over a long time, you learn about the character of your friend.
— *Chinese Proverb*

Tipperary-born John Sutcliffe had been part of the original Aer Rianta team which set up and opened Dubai Duty Free in December 1983. His indomitable spirit and enthusiasm in those early set-up weeks provided much of the fillip which kept the team going through long days and, often as not, even longer nights.

"They were tough times in terms of work, but we had a team spirit. John had a lot to do with that," says George Horan.

But an outward lightness of spirit belied a tough ambition. With Aer Rianta, Sutcliffe was a senior internal auditor having joined the company in 1977. His early days in finance with two American companies in Ireland — construction giant Bechtel and the pharmaceutical group Merck, Sharpe and Dohme — had helped develop his career. The American discipline is highly communication- and participation-focused — which he readily agrees are two large parts of his managerial make-up today.

Nearing the end of Aer Rianta's six-month contract, Civil Aviation Director-General Mohi-Din Binhendi had requested from McLoughlin that he and several of his compatriots continue to fill the top three positions in the newly opened company. Of the eight Irishmen seconded to Dubai, two stood out. McLoughlin wished to have Sutcliffe as his deputy, and keep George Horan's expertise on the shop floor as manager.

"It was clear that John and George would be vital to our success," says McLoughlin, ignoring a potential one-liner that he did not have a Paul or Ringo in his team.

"It was a huge opportunity. In Colm, I would learn from the best. In Dubai we had an opportunity to forge something truly remarkable," says Sutcliffe, reminiscing back a quarter of a century.

With Horan also on-board, Aer Rianta were approached about releasing the trio for a longer-term secondment. When this was denied, it was time for some soul-searching. Staying on after the initial six-month contract was over, and becoming an employee of Dubai Duty Free, needed more than a little heart-searching. In the end all three went with their gut feeling that they were going to be a part of forging something new.

Fly *Buy* Dubai

Having weighed up the odds for moving to Dubai, or staying with Aer Rianta, Sutcliffe felt the former would offer a good managerial position early in his career. It meant resigning — but as fate would have it, his subsequent career path has taken him down the Aer Rianta road again.

As Deputy General Manager at Dubai Duty Free, Sutcliffe also became more involved in the retailing side of the operation — and discovered he had a flair for it.

"All of a sudden I came across something that gave me a freshness in my work," he says. "We were a good team in Dubai. Colm had the retail knowledge, I had the back office experience. In some ways we were similar and we were both strong-headed, which may have caused a few flash points over the years."

It is a recollection shared by McLoughlin, who recalls: "John and I shared a few heated discussions over the years. But it was one of the best working relationships I ever had — and of course working together closely during those early years we managed to achieve quite a bit."

"And we became good friends," says Sutcliffe.

Sutcliffe blossomed. He even had his own Irish folk music programme on a local radio station that quickly picked up an enthusiastic following.

"I look back to those years in Dubai with an enormous sense of nostalgia. They were good days. I was surrounded by good people, in a great place to live, and we all loved our work," says Sutcliffe.

Sutcliffe is recalled by former workmates as a team player and a popular personality.

"He was well liked. Even under pressure John could make people laugh," says Anita Mehra. "He was good with people below him. All the staff loved him,"' says Bharat Jhaveri, a Dubai Duty Free pioneer.

"He was such a warm personality — like Colm," says Binhendi. "But when the situation required, he rolled up his sleeves and got the job done."

Sutcliffe had appeared as normal during the late months of 1989. The full management team was under pressure in the countdown to Dubai Duty Free opening its major expansion of floor space — and launching Finest Surprises. It was a period when McLoughlin continued to rely upon his number two.

"The thing about John was his eagerness," says McLoughlin. "You would mention something to him and he would always say 'Leave it to me' and you knew that you could rely on it getting done."

On December 20, 1989, after the formal celebrations that marked the opening of Dubai Duty Free's expansion, after the VVIPs had left and media drifted away, McLoughlin got back to his office and a mound of paperwork.

Changing of the Guard

John Sutcliffe (second left) at a Dubai Duty Free social event with
Jeff and Claire Iredale, Jen Walton, Frankie Elgood, Ian Walton and Kevin Morrissey.

A knock on his office door would mark the end of one of the two men's most productive working relationships. Sutcliffe informed his friend and mentor that he was preparing to tender his resignation.

"I was surprised, yes. It was a shock," says McLoughlin. "But when I looked at it, John was an ambitious young man thirsting for advancement and challenge."

Sutcliffe had been given an opportunity he found difficult to refuse. His old bosses at Aer Rianta had approached and invited him to rejoin them to head up the fledgling Moscow Duty Free business for its 1990 opening. It was an amazing opportunity to be in charge of an entire business and sit in the big chair. As a career move it was an exciting challenge.

"Although it was tough at times, the responsibility gave me a lot of self-confidence. I had no time to think about the difficult conditions because we were getting on with the job," Sutcliffe told Martin Moodie in an interview for *The World Rover*. "By the time I left after two years and three months, I felt I could run General Motors. We had the problems of warehousing and generating merchandise to market. It was like being thrown in at the deep

Fly *Buy* Dubai

Despite the turmoil being felt in the region, Dubai Duty Free's tills had got busier and Colm McLoughlin had been called upon to receive a growing number of regional and international awards.

end — but it was a great experience," he says.

And an experience which was to stand him in good stead for the next chapter in his career story, for in 1992 he was winging his way back to the Gulf again — this time to Bahrain, where Aer Rianta had re-opened and was running a new-look Bahrain Duty Free.

When his mind strays back to the exciting time when he was involved in Dubai Duty Free, Sutcliffe says: "I played my part in helping it grow from nothing to one of the world's greatest businesses and that's an achievement I'm proud of.

"As Irish people we take pride in our achievements in this part of the world. There are Colm, George, Brendan O'Shea, and our own current or past involvement in Bahrain, Lebanon, Syria, Kuwait, Oman, Egypt, Cyprus, and Qatar. It's a serious footprint for a small island like Ireland to make."

In many ways, Aer Rianta's tempting away of the Deputy General Manager of Dubai Duty Free could not come at a worse time. While the 1980s had proven moribund years in economic terms for the Gulf, due to the UAE's biggest and most militaristic neighbours waging a fruitless war against each other, the Iran-Iraq War was now over. While the Gulf's economy had stuttered along, Dubai Duty Free had been doing quite nicely. Born into a war situation, some three years into the war, Dubai Duty Free had come of age while Tehran and Baghdad had still been pursuing their folly.

The war had finally ended officially on August 20, 1988. During Dubai Duty Free's first full post-war trading year, in 1989, a further $10 million had been added. An average of an extra $27,000 per day.

If this represented a jump, as the region recovered from a war that cost an estimated one trillion dollars (just between the two protagonists) and claimed a million lives, 1990 would be a year of phenomenal change for Dubai Duty Free.

"The year 1990 represented something of a fresh start," says Binhendi. "Colm and his team had brought the thing around full circle since the opening. After the few early years, 1990 was when I expected everything to click."

On the very first day that Dubai Duty Free began trading with its larger-shop floor, one of the stalwarts of the team was now preparing to go his own way. Was it a blow?

"Personally it was," admits McLoughlin. "John was my friend.

"Professionally, he did what was right for him and I applauded his ambition."

In 1990, Dubai Duty Free backed the World Karate Championships which were being staged in the emirates.

Pictured with a Frontier Award, George Horan was ready made to step into the Deputy General Manager's position.

Changing of the Guard

Of course, the blow was eased by having a readymade replacement in the wings.

The third member of the so-called 'Irish Trinity' that managed Dubai Duty Free was Horan. He was the quietest, least ebullient of the trio. Yet on his watch as Shop Floor Manager the operation had managed to grow its business at an alarming rate.

"The excitement of seeing the business grow was — and still is — fantastic. There had been a lot of evolution and change and nothing was static, there was a continuous process of improvement," he says, referring to both the duty free in 1989 and the Emirate in general.

McLoughlin knew "in a heartbeat" who would be Sutcliffe's successor.

But things might have been a little different if Horan hadn't decided to make a life-changing decision. He had been part of Brendan O'Regan's original Sales and Catering Company, which became Aer Rianta. It was the early '70s and Horan, working in the finance department and recently married, found things a little tight existing on only one salary. So he and his wife Carmel decided to set up a little business which, if it began to grow, would allow Horan to quit his day job and concentrate on developing it into a bigger entity. The couple then diversified from their original business concept — a supermarket — into selling boats and, after a while, added sailing accessories to their inventory.

Business was good and Horan was ready to resign. He told his boss of his intentions but was persuaded to take some time out and consider his options before making a final decision. It was possibly the best advice he had ever been given.

During his time away he was able to be more objective and soon realised that running his own business wasn't as glamorous as he had originally thought — and there was a lot of physical labour involved too. Eventually the Horans would sell their thriving business to a former oilman who had made his money working in Abu Dhabi and was looking to settle down back home.

Horan stayed in the duty free business — and was quickly rewarded with an opportunity for a six-month stint in Dubai setting up a duty free operation as part of the Aer Rianta consultancy team. He took it.

Horan recalls the days preceding his departure for the Gulf: "Our knowledge of Dubai at that time was primitive. We had heard all sorts of stories about it. The doctor who gave us our injections before we left had been in the Gulf with the British Army and he gave us every jab imaginable, telling us we were going into some kind of hellhole…!"

Fly *Buy* Dubai

Clearly it wasn't. And some six years later Horan was offered a promotion that would change his life again. For a time, Horan combined duties as Deputy General Manager and Shop Floor Manager. But holding down what had been essentially two jobs proved a problem. A renowned perfectionist, the shop floor hummed with efficiency and he was on top of everything. Now, for long periods, the man in charge was absent.

"As shop floor manager you are on the floor most of the day. Everything catches your eye. This is what the job is. It has to be perfect," he says. "When I became DGM I still got to the floor every day — and still do — but there was not enough time to be as thorough as I liked."

By now it was 1990. The shop floor was rocking. Dubai International Airport was on course for a record-breaking year which would end with a near 15 per cent increase in civilian scheduled traffic movements.

The economy in Dubai and the UAE was going through a corrective period. Market forces were naturally adjusting to allow for the stagnation of an eight-year war. Tourism was returning. The airport, in which the Dubai government had continued to invest heavily during this lean period, was ready to become the region's aviation hub. A plethora of new airlines and new services were being inaugurated. Passenger numbers were rocketing.

And the tens of thousands of new passengers were more than catered for by the airport's new and revamped duty free operation.

The spring and summer of 1990 were record-breaking periods. Turnover topped $300,000 in a day for the first time. This represented more than $200 a minute, 24 hours a day. Rising takings led at least some members of senior management to privately opine that Dubai Duty Free would crash through the $100 million barrier for the year. Easily.

"It was, frankly, an exciting time. There was boundless potential," says Horan. "We had come out of the war period and people in the UAE were on such a high. Sheikh Ahmed and the Dubai government had done such a fantastic job in having the airport ready to absorb and cater for the boom that — if you will pardon the pun — the sky was really the limit."

Then it all came crashing down.

George and Carmel Horan on the occasion of George being
inducted as a Keeper of the Quaich.

With the end of the Iran-Iraq War Dubai Duty Free was positioned to grow at an extraordinary rate. But regional troubles were again set to impact.

Chapter Seventeen

Facing Crisis

There never was a good war or a bad peace.
— *Benjamin Franklin, American statesman*

The late 1980s had been a period of strident growth for Dubai International Airport. By 1990, the Department of Civil Aviation was preparing to launch its 'cargo village' and an aviation college. Dubai Duty Free had surged ahead. Emirates (the airline) was reporting one of its busiest periods, opening a record five new destinations that year, which would take the carrier from its original three to 21.

"In aviation terms, by 1990 things were on a high. There was fast-paced development, backed by a government that believed in the industry, and in Dubai's own place within it," says Maurice Flanagan. "Exciting times were ahead of us.

"Travelling around the world, you got a feel that people were recognising that something was going on. The Emirates brand was just emerging, while Dubai Duty Free was already something of an icon."

Throughout the 1980s the Dubai government had invested. It boasted by far the most developed infrastructure in the region, including projects such as Jebel Ali Port, Dubai Dry Docks, Dubai International Airport, the Dubai World Trade Centre, a modern telecommunications system, and good roads. With its lack of red tape, Dubai was ideally positioned to evolve further as the commercial hub of the Gulf.

In the early part of the year, the airport had published annual results. These showed a big jump in aircraft movements in 1989, now averaging 183 a day. And 1990 was showing potential to be far better. KLM had significantly increased its scheduled services to Dubai, along with British Airways, while new services were inaugurated with TAROM (Romania's national carrier), Interflug of East Germany, Balkan Airlines of Bulgaria, Libyan Arab Airlines and — somewhat ironically — Iraqi Airways.

In 1990, Iraq, only just out of its war with Iran, began railing against its erstwhile ally Kuwait. Kuwait had loaned Iraq $14 billion to help finance the war, which Baghdad could not afford to repay. Iraq accused Kuwait of slant-drilling across the border into Iraq's Rumaila oil field.

Either way, the decision to go to war was perhaps premeditated for a long time. According to author Gregory Gause in his book *International Relations of the Middle East*, Iraqi sources now state that Saddam Hussein's decision to attack his neighbour was made months before the actual invasion.

Despite emerging tensions, a general belief that Hussein was sabre-rattling, plus a tiredness over the general volatility of the Middle Eastern political scene, meant that, for a time, life went on as normal.

"That first quarter of 1990 was thrilling," says Mohammed Tayyeb, a Pioneer. "The shop floor was packed 24 hours a day. We were going from strength to strength in turnover terms."

Things were so busy, in fact, that Dubai Duty Free's management took a decision to bring forward several rounds of foreign recruitment. Adverts appeared in several newspapers in the Philippines. Several hundred places in Dubai were potentially up for grabs.

"By now the word had got out," says Angelito Hernandez, President and Managing Director of IPAMS, which handled Dubai Duty Free's recruitment in the country. "Word goes round surprisingly quickly on which companies, which countries, and which regions are good employers. Dubai Duty Free was always a good employer, from the very start. They look after their people. When staff come home on leave they talk, tell relatives and friends. Pretty quickly the market picks up different trends and people seeking jobs abroad know who the best employers are."

In early 1990, more than a thousand applications were received for every place available.

Yet even while the process of evaluating potential new staff was underway at IPAMS HQ in Manila, arriving before these new applicants in the Gulf were dozens of people engaged in quite different work. Several governments from around the world were sending envoys, most heading to Baghdad in an effort to persuade Hussein of his course toward another war.

As early as January a US War College report stated that: 'Baghdad should not be expected to deliberately provoke military confrontations with anyone. Its best interests now and in the immediate future are served by peace'.

No-one was able to convince the President of Iraq.

By July, what had seemed like sabre-rattling had morphed into a full-blown crisis. Iraq was moving troops in the general direction of its border with Kuwait. Even while Hussein was being besieged in his palaces by mediators, he was, it seemed, preparing for some form of action against Kuwait.

The countdown to yet another war was underway.

"The summer is traditionally a busy period for us. It is a time when an abundance of expatriates and their families head for their own countries on leave," says Sheikh Ahmed.

The 1990 period was so busy, the company brought forward several rounds of recruitment.

(right) Several potential recruits undertake a primary exam at the offices of IPAMS in Manila.

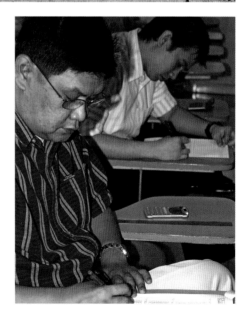

241

Fly *Buy* Dubai

Indeed, the airport was busy, perhaps busier than normal. But the usual traffic patterns were not in evidence. Instead of vacationers heading for cooler climes, the airport was full of families heading into uncertainty. Many would not return for months. Aircraft were arriving more than half-empty, while tickets out of the region were at a premium.

And, given the uncertainty, the luxuries presented on the shop floor of Dubai Duty Free were less commanding of attention.

"The summer bounce never happened. People were getting out under a cloud of uncertainty. This definitely affected purchasing power, as they were tightening their fiscal belts due to the uncertainty," says Malcolm Corrigan, a Jersey-based financial analyst and Gulf expert.

Back in Manila, IPAMS was finding potential candidates for jobs in the Gulf dropping out at an alarming rate.

"It was understandable," says Hernandez. "Although these were premium jobs, needed by people who had families they needed to feed, there were not many who would wish to fly into what the media was saying was going to soon be a war zone."

Iraqi President Saddam Hussein embarked upon a futile war.

Facing Crisis

As applicants for new positions were drying up, Dubai Duty Free was suspending its new wave of recruitment. Indeed, with waves of expatriates leaving the Gulf for their home countries, ahead of what looked like a certain war, McLoughlin was ready to be even-handed with his own team.

"We were well over eight hundred kilometres from the Iraq-Kuwait border. Everyone recognised that," says McLoughlin. "Yet with the media stating that war was inevitable, and the unpredictability of the situation, we had to be fair to our own people."

At the beginning of July, McLoughlin signed off on a staff memo that made it clear that Dubai Duty Free employees could take their annual leave then. Should they wish, while the situation continued as it did, or grew worse, they could stay away from their jobs for an extended period utilising future leave or, if necessary, leave of absence. Their jobs would remain open.

"There was no way anyone would be forced to work when they feared the situation," he says. "That would have been like slavery. I would never coerce anyone into staying if they were unhappy."

Instead management went on the offensive with an information campaign, letting staff know the distances involved, plans for their safety, and ensuring that they were briefed upon the developing crisis.

"Mr McLoughlin, Mr Horan and the other managers were very fair in their handling of the war. They were also visible on the shop floor, speaking to people. It was very reassuring, particularly for the many staff who had not been in Dubai and away from their homes for a long time," says Pascal Fernandes, a pioneer. "For many of my colleagues, who had not worked through a crisis such as this, the pictures we saw on the BBC and CNN could be very frightening."

To the eternal credit of the Dubai Duty Free team, not one of the staff came forward and asked for the additional facilities on offer, although many did take their leave earlier in order to return home during the blackest period.

"During this time, and even after the invasion, our staff arrived back in Dubai from their vacations on time," says Sayed Saifoddin, another pioneer. "No-one took a leave of absence and I cannot think of one case where we had a problem. Our staff were mature, took well-thought-out, rational decisions, and behaved in a very noble manner."

On a wider level, however, Dubai as a whole needed to make its own way.

"There were some serious decisions to be made," says Sheikh Ahmed. "We increased consultations with the government, brought in our own security assessors, and most of all used a commonsense approach."

(top, right to left) Mohi-Din Binhendi, Colm McLoughlin and Anita Mehra. Management took a conscious decision to be visible for staff on the shop floor throughout the crisis, as a source reassurance.

(left) The war was a disaster for the whole region.

Facing Crisis

By mid-July, it seems, Hussein concluded that the United States and the rest of the outside world would not physically interfere to defend Kuwait. A flurry of last-minute diplomatic efforts seemed to be failing.

Sheikh Ahmed met every day with his most senior management in order to formulate a battle plan. As far as Dubai Duty Free went, it was a matter of doing the best they could for their staff and operations, while their turnover slipped as the region's expatriates put distance between themselves and a potential war zone.

"All management leave was cancelled, and the managements of the airport and Emirates were meeting to assess different scenarios and deciding how this would be dealt with," says Sheikh Ahmed. "The UAE and Dubai governments had their input, although I believed, like most people, that something would give and that a full-blown crisis could be avoided."

Sheikh Ahmed recalls a particular meeting, on August 1. The meeting heard that everything was in place should Kuwait come under attack. They also heard that an attack was imminent.

"We did not really need to relay this to the staff, as every television channel was saying the same thing," says McLoughlin. "But George, Anita, Mohi, myself and other managers decided that we needed to be extra visible among the staff. I guess we felt that we could be a reassuring influence, that if we were around and behaving normally, then everything was as normal."

On the border between Kuwait and Iraq, four elite Iraqi Republican Guard divisions and Iraqi Army special forces units equivalent to a full division were now amassed awaiting the word. The situation looked ominous.

"We were ready, but even while last-ditch diplomacy was being reported, there was still a belief that the worst would not happen, although there was a certain nervousness," says Sheikh Ahmed.

On August 1, Flight EK 825, an Emirates Airbus A310-300, lifted off from Kuwait International Airport bound for Dubai. The flight was full, as had been every flight out of Kuwait for several weeks as Kuwaiti and expatriate families fled what seemed to be impending danger. On board were all Emirates' employees in Kuwait and their families.

On August 2, at 0200 hours, Iraq launched an invasion with more than 100,000 soldiers and 700 tanks. Within just hours Kuwait City was taken, along with the airports and two airbases. Iraq established a puppet provisional government and Hussein threatened to turn Kuwait city into a "graveyard" if any country dared to attempt a "take-over by force".

Within hours the United Nations Security Council, in emergency session, had called for the "immediate and unconditional" withdrawal of Iraqi forces from Kuwait. British Prime Minister Margaret Thatcher branded the invasion "absolutely unacceptable", while American President George Bush condemned the attack as "a naked act of aggression".

By the time Iraqi troops ground to a halt not far from the Kuwait-Saudi Arabian border, Hussein's tanks were still far from Dubai.

"In addition to everything else, I remember cursing him (Saddam) for ruining what was going to be a record year for us," says Horan. "After the Iran-Iraq War lost the people of the Gulf so much, Iraq was now at it again, so soon after the last disaster... no regard for life and no regard for the impact of his actions."

After months of swirling, divisive uncertainty, however, Hussein had now laid down his cards. Now it was up to the international community to respond.

August 1 and 2, 1990 represent two of the worst days of turnover in the history of Dubai Duty Free — matched only by September 11, 2001 and its immediate aftermath. And while Kuwait City is 856 kilometres from Dubai, the impression gained from the media did not help. The Gulf War was the most widely-televised war of modern times. As the international response was shaped and eventually struck back, people all over the world were able to watch, almost in real time, pictures of missiles hitting their targets and fighters taking off from aircraft carriers.

"It was impressive television, but did not help with international perception. We were safe and knew it and a long way away from any troubles," says Mohammed Al Ahli.

There had been a rush on tickets in pre-war weeks, as families sought to go home. But after August 2 this went into freefall, several sources reporting in the local media that air ticket bookings had dropped 90 per cent. Kenya Airways, which had recently introduced a third weekly Boeing 707 to Nairobi, had reported cabin load factors in the high 90s throughout the year. By late August, post-invasion, it was hovering at near 50 per cent.

"At times, the shop floor was, although not a morgue, dreadfully quiet compared to normal," says Horan.

McLoughlin, Horan, Godkhindi, Mehra and others were all now co-opted into Dubai's public relations war. Business as normal was the theme. Using the international media, always so ready to cover the anomaly of Middle Eastern progressiveness the emirate represented, from the head of government down it was time to get out and preach the message of Dubai's peaceful continuity. Aviation, which represented the door of the emirate, was

Facing Crisis

(top) Dubai International Airport was shockingly quiet.

(right) Colm McLoughlin was a part of the public relations war, using his voice to help correct misinformation.

Facing Crisis

The Kuwait crisis hit Dubai Duty Free so badly that at times there were virtually no shoppers.

Fly *Buy* Dubai

Dubai was 848 kilometers from Kuwait City. But the liberation of the country would affect Dubai and the UAE badly.

of course of high importance in this regard. Sheikh Ahmed and the 'Big Guns' of Emirates, Dubai Duty Free, and Dnata, were rolled out to provide firepower to that message.

"We repeated the mantra that, in Dubai, it was business as usual," says McLoughlin. "Dubai is 848 kilometres away from Kuwait City."

Rounds of interviews were arranged, and despite loosening revenue streams, Dubai Duty Free embarked on an advertising campaign. It went against the grain of corporate communications practice, but the Dubai brand, championed by its duty free, its airline and others, would not be allowed to suffer.

"We were pro-active, not re-active," says Mehra. "Colm was at perhaps his most visible in the last 25 years, like Sheikh Ahmed and Maurice Flanagan, using their media recognition to trumpet Dubai's continuity."

Sheikh Ahmed took a broadly similar fight to the insurance companies, who were engaged in what amounted to price-gouging. Mohammed Ahli, Director of Operations at the airport, added: "Insurance firms are making a big fuss by declaring this entire area as a dangerous zone. Either they have seen this as an opportunity to make some more money — or they are ignorant of the geographical locations of the Gulf states."

Despite the PR splurge on Dubai's side, the region suffered a long and uncomfortable late summer. For Dubai Duty Free the balmy days of $300,000-a-day turnover were now a memory. Early-year predictions that the operation would smash through the $100 million turnover ceiling were history.

"We were suffering," says McLoughlin. "The passengers were just not there. Those that were traveling were being ultra-cautious in their spending — quite natural given the uncertainty."

On television, pictures showed a global coalition coming together. The UAE threw its weight behind an emerging United States-led, United Nations-sanctioned political and military coalition to oust the Iraqis and restore Kuwait's rightful rulers to power.

It was a massive undertaking encompassing military forces from Afghanistan, Argentina, Australia, Bangladesh, Belgium, Canada, Czechoslovakia, Denmark, Egypt, France, Germany, Greece, Holland, Honduras, Hungary, Italy, Morocco, New Zealand, Niger, Norway, Pakistan, Poland, Portugal, Senegal, South Korea, Spain, Syria, Turkey, and the United Kingdom, along with all the GCC states.

Yet war remained a last resort to free Kuwait and the UAE, especially President Sheikh Zayed bin Sultan Al Nahyan, led efforts to find a diplomatic solution. His Minister of Defence, Sheikh Mohammed, had a dual task, to help seek a diplomatic solution and also prepare his forces for the last resort. On September 2, following a meeting with British Foreign Secretary Douglas Hurd, Sheikh Mohammed reiterated the UAE's position, and answered criticism from a small number of states in the Arab world about the involvement of foreign forces in the crisis:

'Once the reason for these foreign armed forces being stationed in the Gulf is removed, they will withdraw. But the international community had made a commitment to defend the sovereignty of Kuwait. Freeing Kuwait will be the only end to this troubling scenario.

Let me be perfectly clear. The UAE is participating fully and strenuously in the search for a political solution to this crisis. We wish to guarantee an immediate withdrawal of Iraqi armed forces from Kuwait, after which the UAE will work to see the beginnings of a new phase of stability and cooperation within this region.'

Fly *Buy* Dubai

While diplomats fought a diplomatic war to end the crisis, McLoughlin, his Dubai Duty Free management colleagues, and others in Dubai's aviation industry were left to fight the prevailing tide of events. Even the most ignorant of foreign observers could have not avoided the fact that Dubai was well over 800 kilometres from Kuwait City.

Yet Iraq's response to the growing international coalition — firing Scud missiles — did not help the climate of fear.

"We had to recognise that, at some point, probably within months, this would be over, and do our best to ride out the storm around us," says Paul Chakramakil, another pioneer. "Being a duty free operation our prices were low anyway, we were not like a mall where we could engage in a round of cost-cutting in order to attract customers. There simply weren't that volume of customers out there."

Thanks to the dramatic takings of the first half of the year, on December 20, 1990, amid the crisis, Dubai Duty Free announced a record turnover of $95 million. This represented an increase of over $21 million over the previous 12-month period.

"We were delighted by this," says Sheikh Ahmed. "Amid all the

Despite the troubles, Dubai Duty Free ended 1990 with just short of $100 million in goods sold.

Facing Crisis

newspaper stories of gloom and despondency, Dubai Duty Free was able to show a defiant, and huge, increase. The media carried the story with banner headlines, which made contrasting reading with all the bad stories."

While there was a feeling of jubilation, it was tinged with disappointment at what may have been. Due to the crisis it would be two years before Dubai Duty Free would clear the glass ceiling of $100 million. Yet even while the media was full of stories of Dubai Duty Free's record year, its management was going into stealth mode. While not compromising on medium-term plans, in the short-term there was a need to put unnecessary spending on hold. Company hospitality — such as staff parties — was put on hold, sponsorships were held back, advertising focus was honed, and promotions were, in some cases, delayed. Recruitment was frozen for six months, while investment in IT was eased back.

While it was "not time to batten down the hatches", as Horan puts it, it was time to take a medium-term view. Just in case the pending Gulf War would drag out, Dubai Duty Free needed to assume that its revenues would continue to be as sluggish as they were.

Throughout the latter part of 1990 and into the early days of 1991, the UAE continued its diplomatic offensive without any sign of a shift in Iraq's position. On January 6, ahead of gathering clouds of war, Hussein promised "the Mother of all Battles". Meanwhile, in Kuwait, his troops were behaving like common thieves and looting on an almost unprecedented scale.

On January 11, US Secretary of State James Baker flew into Abu Dhabi to meet with President Sheikh Zayed, Sheikh Mohammed bin Rashid Al Maktoum, and other senior officials. The situation, he explained, looked hopeless and, unless Hussein had a sudden change of heart, war seemed inevitable. Around 770,000 allied troops were assembled on the Arabian Peninsula at this time. The UAE contributed thousands of men on the ground while its navy and air force were integrated into the coalition.

The coalition struck on January 16, unleashing a bombing campaign of unsurpassed intensity in an effort to weaken the Iraqi positions in Kuwait and reduce the chances of allied casualties. On February 22, after Hussein had ignored the last deadline set by US President George Bush for him to pull out of Kuwait, an intense ground offensive began. US Lieutenant-General Tom Kelly would later observe that "Iraq went from the fourth-largest army in the world to the second-largest army in Iraq in 100 hours."

Hussein had sacrificed his people just to make a point. Of Iraq's 545,000 troops in Kuwait, an official estimate produced by the United States stated that more than 100,000 Iraqi soldiers died, 300,000 were wounded, 150,000

*As UAE Minister of Defence, Sheikh Mohammed bin Rashid Al Maktoum
was heavily involved in the crisis.*

had deserted, and 60,000 were taken prisoner.

On February 26, four days after the allied ground offensive began, Baghdad Radio announced that Saddam Hussein had ordered his troops out of Kuwait under the terms of a Soviet Union-brokered peace plan. The coalition forces had already swept to the outskirts of Kuwait City and they charged through southern Iraq in an unexpectedly easy campaign with minimal loss of life.

On March 4, Sheikh Mohammed issued a statement that gave insight into his underlining beliefs, that would underpin the future of Dubai and the UAE. It included the passage:

> 'The United Arab Emirates will continue to stand for peace... steadfast in her support for her friends. The Emirates remain a cosmopolitan meeting place, where differing cultures and religions reside in peace. It is this model of tolerance that we hope to export to the rest of the world...'

With Kuwait free, it was time for the rest of the region to pick up the pieces from Hussein's folly. The Gulf would take months to get back to normal.

"We knew it was up to us. So we got on with it," says McLoughlin.

The great Sheikh Rashid is greeted by Sheikh Mohammed upon his return to the country following a foreign visit.

Chapter Eighteen

Legends All

A leader is a dealer in hope.
— *Napoleon Bonaparte, French statesman*

In 1983, ten Irishmen had landed in Dubai on a brief secondment to forge a duty free shopping facility. Ireland's links with Dubai were somewhat tenuous and remote. Perhaps the best known were a few flat racing classics won in Ireland by the sons of the Ruler of the distant emirate.

Most of the ten looked into their temporary home. They learned about the open economy, the relaxed atmosphere, and the congenial lifestyle. There was an almost total lack of crime, religious tolerance, and a refreshing sense of community. Some learned of the progressive government that was deft, red tape-free, and progressive in its approach. Most learned of a man named Sheikh Rashid.

After a stroke in 1980, the father of Dubai had never fully returned to public life, although his influence continued to be felt. In 1983 he was a background figure. His sons had moved smoothly into the roles for which they had been prepared. A seamless transition of power had been good for Dubai. Yet Sheikh Rashid's influence remained.

"You could not avoid him," says Horan. "When his name cropped up, nationals spoke of him in hushed, reverent tones."

"Coming from a society where there was a certain amount of skepticism when it came to political figures, it was something strange to hear such reverence," says McLoughlin. "But the more you learned about Sheikh Rashid, and the history of the Maktoum family, the more you understood."

Napoleon Bonaparte had said that: 'A leader is a dealer in hope'. And more than any Gulf leader in his generation, Sheikh Rashid brought hope. Before oil had ushered in an era of development, he had saved Dubai from the morass of poverty and hopelessness. His legacy was enormous.

"I never met him," says McLoughlin. "But you could not help but love the man."

Outside of the UAE, obscured by the Kuwait crisis, there was far too little recognition of the end of an era. On October 7, 1990, Sheikh Rashid passed away. Over ensuing days foreign leaders flowed through Dubai International Airport in order to pay their respects, while the UAE embarked upon a 40-day mourning period. In London, *The Independent* reported his passing calling him 'the merchant prince'. The *Daily Telegraph* in London published a lengthy obituary. The newspaper stated: '...he led his pocket-sized Gulf emirate to an unprecedented prosperity based not only on oil but also trade.' Another stated: 'He leaves behind a Dubai that far outclasses any other Middle Eastern city as a place to live and do business and that bears comparison with Hong Kong and Singapore.' Agency France-Presse observed that Sheikh Rashid moulded Dubai into 'a strong candidate to take over Hong Kong's position in world trade in the 21st century'.

It was also startling how far Dubai had come. Sheikh Rashid had become Ruler in 1958. Few people had even heard of the former Trucial States. When Sheikh Rashid passed away, the United Nations Security Council staged a one-minute silence to mark the death of the father of Dubai.

As is Islamic custom, the following day Sheikh Rashid was buried. Tens of thousands of people lined the streets. Over the next few days, Sheikh Rashid's sons shook the hands, and accepted the respects of, thousands of visitors to the palace.

"Although you did not know him directly, you felt as though you knew Sheikh Rashid," says Horan. "His numerous achievements, his vision, his care for his people. He was like a father of the city. His death hung like a weight over us."

"Without someone like him, Dubai would not have been what it was," adds Mehra. "In the year he died the emirate had a duty free that was turning over something in the region of $300,000 on a good day — at an airport that had not even existed when he became ruler."

"I doubt that the government of Dubai had revenue of $300,000 when Sheikh Rashid acceded as Ruler," says Sheikh Ahmed, brother of the deceased legend. "He built his vision through sheer force of will."

"I remember, sometime in the mid-1960s, Sheikh Rashid purchased his first private aircraft. He was travelling somewhere, so we went to see him off," says George Chapman, a Briton who has lived in Dubai for over six decades. "Gesturing to the aircraft, he turned to me, winked, showed me his playful smile, and said, 'I'm sure you never thought I would have one of these.'

"That was Sheikh Rashid. The trappings of power were a means to an end. And that was development. He was justifiably proud of his airport."

In the death of Sheikh Rashid it was, as he had planned, a matter of continuity. Sheikh Maktoum bin Rashid Al Maktoum would become Ruler of Dubai, also inheriting the posts of UAE Vice-President and Prime Minister. Sheikh Mohammed, as he had done since 1977, would continue to steer the development of aviation in the emirate.

Legends All

(top) Sheikh Rashid greets French President Valéry Giscard d'Estaing.

(right) Sheikh Rashid and Sheikh Mohammed inspect a guard of honour.

Fly *Buy* Dubai

"The continuity of leadership was important for Dubai," says Mohi-Din Binhendi. "And it was apparent in Dubai's response to the crisis in the Gulf. Just as Sheikh Rashid had a long-term view of everything, his sons shared this trait. It was about continuity."

Continuity was something that Dubai Duty Free had struggled and succeeded in maintaining during the dark days of invasion of the Gulf War. In 1988, England's Neal Foulds had claimed the Dubai Masters, a non-ranking snooker event and one of the first top class sporting events in the UAE. A year later, the newly branded Dubai Duty Free Classic had risen in value to £200,000 in prize money and boasted world ranking points for participants. Word of player experiences in Dubai during the Dubai Masters had clearly got around the professional snooker circuit. There were 32 places on the 'plane to Dubai on offer when a three-day qualification tournament got underway in Blackpool, in the northwest of England. The 128 entries in Blackpool included 18 of the world's top 25 players.

"From the beginning our policy was to show players true Arabian hospitality, a slice of the care and attention to detail that Dubai was becoming famous for," says Mehra. "Whatever the ranking of the player, when they came to Dubai they were treated like VIPs. And even the stars of world snooker, like Steve Davis and Stephen Hendry, would return to Britain wowing over the level of care they were shown in the UAE."

It was a policy that would reap three-fold benefits. Firstly, the Dubai Duty Free Classic would continue to attract the finest players in the sport. Secondly, it would set a benchmark that sportsmen and women the world over would come to acknowledge as the best — even the likes of Tiger Woods, Frankie Dettori, or Roger Federer. Thirdly, when the chips were down, as they soon would be, Dubai was not just another venue for a tournament, it was a place that endured in the minds of most.

In 1989 Hendry had defeated Welsh veteran Doug Mountjoy in the inaugural final of the Dubai Duty Free Classic, in doing so scooping a £40,000 purse. A list of 32 that included John Parrott, Tony Drago, and James Wattana, along with the fiery Alex Higgins, again proved a sell-out at the venue for many sessions.

Higgins was quoted during his stormy career, saying that: "Snooker has gone down the tubes. It has been run by friends of friends who couldn't organise a raffle." He certainly did not believe this was the case about Dubai, and, when playing, was a regular feature in Dubai qualifying tournaments."

In 1989, the 32 were again feted like champions, ushered through the

Legends All

Stephen Hendry with Bharat and Radhika Godkhindi. Bharat is one of the prime movers in the Dubai Duty Free Classic and later the Dubai Tennis Championships.

airport like world leaders, given the run of their five-star hotel, and whisked around Dubai in a fleet of cars laid on by Dubai Duty Free .

"I love coming to Dubai," said Hendry in a press conference that year. "This is one of the high points of the season."

The result was again the same. Entries into the Dubai qualification tournament in 1990 flooded in, including all the sport's big names. In addition to the hospitality, they were gunning for one of the richest purses of tournament money in the sport, around £215,000. The previous year had attracted welcome publicity for Dubai, millions of dollars of television and newspaper coverage.

"We sat down to look at what would make Dubai bigger in terms of publicity," says Horan. "Then someone came up with the car."

It was, in a way, a risk. Dubai Duty Free would offer a Mercedes 500SL, or a BMW 850i, worth around £90,000, to any player achieving snooker's ultimate score. In snooker, a break is the total score achieved on a single visit to the table. A century break — 100 points — is considered top class. But the

Fly *Buy* Dubai

Perhaps the most famed point in Dubai's association with snooker came when world champions Steve Davis and Stephen Hendry ventured into the desert for a publicity shoot.

Fly *Buy* Dubai

Championship winner John Parrott (centre) and runner-up Tony Knowles (second right) show off their trophies following the 1991 Dubai Snooker Classic.

highest break possible without the benefit of an opponent's foul is 147, encompassing all 15 reds with 15 blacks for 120 points, then all six colours for a further 27 points.

The first official maximum 147 had been achieved by the legendary Joe Davis in 1955. The next came 11 years later, in 1966, but there had been 11 during the 1980s.

"It was a big, big thing at the time. Outside of the Snooker World Championship, our tournament pioneered the concept of a huge prize for someone achieving that state of perfection," says Mehra.

The World Number 4, John Parrott, commented at the time: "I can't believe it. It's a fantastic gesture by Dubai Duty Free and is as generous an offer as has ever been made in snooker. If I am lucky enough to make it to the finals, I'd be tempted to go for the maximum. I've achieved it about six times in practice. But if I did it in Dubai I wouldn't mind driving the car all the way back to Liverpool."

No-one ever managed to achieve a 147 in the Classic during its six-year life. Yet the publicity scored by the huge prize proved to be worth millions

for the event and the emirate, in terms of coverage.

"There were a few tense moments," chuckles McLoughlin. "Throughout this period we had the world's very best players in Dubai. Several got close."

The publicity surrounding the 1990 tournament threatened to turn negative after Iraqi troops marched into Kuwait City. The war began on August 2, roughly three months before the Dubai Duty Free Classic was due to begin. The obvious reaction was to cancel, especially as it would be natural for some of the 32 Dubai-bound players to get the jitters. No Classic at all may have been better than one devoid of its big names.

"It took five minutes to decide that there was no way we were going to cancel the Classic," says McLoughlin. "Sheikh Ahmed wanted business-as-usual. This is what we were telling the media and trying to portray. There was a crisis more than 800 kilometres away. Dubai, however, was open for business."

Dubai Duty Free went on the offensive, Mehra flying to London on a mission to brief anyone within the sport who would listen. The World Professional Billiards and Snooker Association was not renowned for its deft

Fly *Buy* Dubai

Sheikh Ahmed greets Stephen Hendry ahead of the Dubai Snooker Classic final in 1989.
The Scot won the event and claimed a £40,000 purse.

footwork; faced with losing one of its most prestigious and valuable events outside of the World Championship, UK Championship, the Snooker Grand Prix, and The Masters, the WPBSA took on board Dubai's arguments.

"Thanks to the reputation of the tournament among the players, the trust that had been built, when we talked about the realities of the situation, the players listened," says Mehra. "It is a testimony to the sport that not one of the players who qualified for Dubai cried off."

While the military build-up continued in the Gulf, eventually going on to reach some 770,000 personnel, on September 16 and 17, six weeks after the invasion occurred, a full complement of 64 players took part in a two-day qualifier in Stoke-on-Trent in England. All 16 who came through this test went on to strut their stuff in the UAE.

"Simply because the tournament went ahead, as it should, Dubai showed that life went on. We gained huge publicity. The Gulf was full of newsmen and correspondents, all of whom had nothing to report on but a grinding military build-up," says McLoughlin. "Suddenly there was this world class snooker tournament going on. In addition to the sports pages, there was vast coverage on news pages around the world."

Stephen Hendry eventually claimed the tournament for a second consecutive year, one of three Dubai wins in six years. But the big winner in 1990 — aside from Dubai itself — was a player not even in the tournament. Masood Akil, an Emirati working for Barclay's Bank, had been given the opportunity to face six-times world champion Steve Davis in a three-frame exhibition match at Dubai International Hotel. The match was billed as an informal affair on the sidelines of serious tournament business at Al Nasr Leisureland. As for Akil, he would be a lamb for the slaughter. Surely.

Yet, after winning the first frame and losing the next, Akil took advantage of a couple of uncharacteristic errors by the Englishman to win the deciding frame 62-37.

"I don't know who was most shocked; Davis, the crowd, or Akil himself," says McLoughlin. "But credit to Steve Davis, he took it well."

In a way, in their reasonable and well-adjusted response to the crisis, the world's best snooker players should have paved the way for the world's golf players.

The history of the Dubai Desert Classic stretches back to 1986 when Sheikh Mohammed gave approval for the innovative concept of developing a grass golf course in the desert. Until this point the UAE's golfers were restricted to playing on oiled sand, putting on 'browns' rather than greens.

"We improvised — and you got used to it after a while," says McLoughlin, himself a keen golfer and former Captain at the Dubai Creek Golf and Yacht Club and Emirates Golf Club.

Bringing a grass golf course to the Gulf would prove a logistical challenge, needing project managers to overcome a variety of technological demands in order to ensure that they met with Sheikh Mohammed's requirements. He dictated that the course was not just a first, but that it was world class, and that it would be capable of hosting a tournament of the world's best golfers.

Just two years after he approved plans, the Emirates Golf Club was opened. Carved from the desert, the course — with its lush fairways and large quick greens — used natural terrain to provide a formidable test of golf. 'The Desert Miracle' was the name given to Emirates Golf Club.

Designer Karl Litten's main aim was to preserve as much of the land's natural character, numerous patches of desert, and the natural vegetation that is consistent with this terrain and will gobble up wayward shots. The

Fly *Buy* Dubai

par-72 Majlis Championship Course, spanning more than 7,100 yards, gives a par four dog-leg, with a challenging signature eighth hole that demands a determined drive on this ascending turf. All great golfers, including Ian Woosnam and Tiger Woods, would lose tournaments by punching shots into the lake.

In 1988 the concept of a world class golf tournament for Dubai was unveiled, a European PGA Tour event. While Emirates Airline was the title sponsor, it was something that Dubai Duty Free was keen to support.

"We were there from the start as it was obvious that Sheikh Mohammed's vision would make this one of the world's great events. And this was the way it has worked out," says McLoughlin. "I remember that first Dubai Desert Classic, in 1989, it was a major coup for Dubai and really led the way for the current internationalisation of world golf."

In January 1989, on an unforgettable evening, England's Mark James calmly rolled in his putt on the final hole at the newly-built Emirates Golf Club to secure a unique slice of sporting history as the inaugural winner of the Dubai Desert Classic.

"We committed to that event and would remain supporters of it until the present day," says McLoughlin. "But our commitment to the sport — and Dubai's place within it — only grew."

In January 1990, Ryder Cup-winning Irishman Eamonn Darcy had lifted the famous trophy, a giant, glittering Arabian coffee pot. From the humble beginning of 1989, on a course that was carved out from a piece of barren desert, the tournament was growing way beyond expectations and was already considered one of the most prestigious events on the European PGA Tour. Just as Dubai Duty Free had helped snooker by establishing one of the world's best player-hospitality standards, the organisers of the Dubai Desert Classic feted its entrants like no other event, the Majors included.

"I always look forward to playing in Dubai because the conditions are first class and the hospitality is excellent," says Scottish star Colin Montgomerie.

Yet for all its lure, the stars of the sport balked in 1991. The Gulf crisis dominated newscasts all over the world, but months after snooker's finest turned out for their event in Dubai, the greens of the Emirates Golf Club remained sadly quiet in January 1991.

The Classic would bounce back a year later, when five times Major winner 'Seve' Ballesteros added star power to the event, in a year when the charismatic Spaniard would go on to win the European Tour Order of Merit.

Legends All

(top) Dubai Duty Free would become one of golf's biggest corporate supporters in Dubai.

(right) Salah Tahlak, Colm McLoughlin and former Formula One world champion and keen golfer Nigel Mansell.

Fly *Buy* Dubai

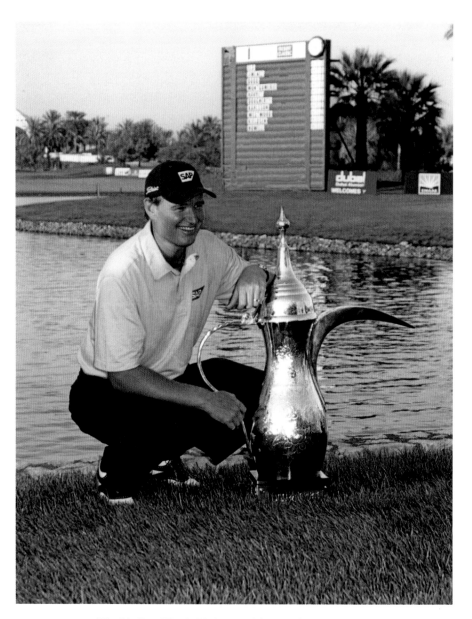

*'The Big Easy' Ernie Els is one of the sport's greats to have
landed the Dubai Desert Classic, in 1994, 2002 and 2005.*

But even that one-year hiatus could not prevent the impetus that golf now had.

"Golf is a very important part of our marketing strategy," says Sinead El Sibai.

With the Classic still in its portfolio, Dubai Duty Free went on to operate and host the annual duty free industry-linked Dubai Golf World Cup, which attracts international duty free and aviation industry representatives. The company has long been an active supporter of the UAE Junior Development Programme and a sponsor of the Dubai Duty Free UAE Nationals Cup, Dubai Duty Free Golf Cup, and the Dubai Duty Free Seniors Cup.

Backing the evolution of UAE nationals within the sport is something that McLoughlin takes seriously.

"I love the Classic. It is a great event. Dubai the brand has been forged by bringing the best sports stars in the world here. When we see Frankie Dettori here, or Tiger Woods, or Roger Federer, their presence generates such media that it all helps to ensure Dubai is known globally," says McLoughlin. "Yet we take seriously our responsibility to ensure that Emiratis are also emerging in the international sporting stage.

"Look at the impact during the Athens Olympics when Sheikh Ahmed Al Maktoum became the first Olympic medallist from the UAE, with gold in the shooting."

In just a few years, the UAE Junior Development Programme and Dubai Duty Free UAE Nationals Cup have helped kick-start the sport among Emiratis and drive up standards, or rather drive down handicaps.

"One day, in the not-too-distant future, we will see Emirati players on the professional circuit," says McLoughlin. "When that happens, we will be proud to say that Dubai Duty Free played its part."

Football legend George Best (front row, second left) turned out in Dubai Duty Free kit in 1988 – another publicity coup for the company. (inset) In Northern Ireland colours during his playing days.

In 1990 — amid a regional conflict — Dubai Duty Free scooped another Frontier Award.

Chapter Nineteen

Come Out Fighting

*The Irish don't know what they want and are prepared to
fight to the death to get it.*
— *Sidney Littlewood, Irish legalitarian*

Operation Desert Shield began on August 7, 1990 when US troops were moved into Saudi Arabia. Eventually, the alliance boasted 956,600 personnel, 1,820 aircraft, 3,318 tanks, 8 aircraft carriers, 2 battleships, 20 cruisers, 20 destroyers, and 5 submarines.

The crisis had served to derail Dubai Duty Free's seemingly invincible march toward breaking the $100 billion barrier for turnover, in 1990. The media had jumped on end-of-year results to hail $95,155,555 of turnover, an extraordinary success given the half-year of misery that Saddam Hussein had heaped on the region. But in Dubai Duty Free headquarters there was concern, and an acute understanding, that the Gulf War had not even begun. A rocky 1991 lay ahead.

"On the face of it 1990 was a good year. $95 million was a record for us, a near $19 million increase over the previous year. So it did not represent a poor performance. Given the circumstances it was a triumph," says McLoughlin.

For a year so well remembered for its angst, 1990 was one with a slew of awards. *Business Traveller* magazine named Dubai Duty Free the second best in the world, the readers of the *Middle East Economic Digest* voted Dubai Duty Free the best GCC duty free, while in the Pak-Emirates Forum Awards Dubai Duty Free scooped best duty free in January and then outstanding duty free in December 1990. To top that off, McLoughlin, Horan, and senior managers headed for Cannes and the Frontier Awards.

The previous year had been barren for Dubai Duty Free, something of a surprise perhaps, coming off the back of a quadruple stretch of successes that began with that famed success in 1985, when they nabbed airport duty free operator of the year. In 1986 Dubai Duty Free had scooped best Marketing Campaign and Duty Free Person of the Year (McLoughlin), in 1987 Airport Operator of the Year, and then in 1988 Retailer of the Year.

By contrast 1989 had been barren as far as the Frontier Awards were concerned. A question had hung over them in 1990. Was this an anomaly, or a slide?

"I went to Cannes full of confidence," says McLoughlin. "While things were not going swingingly in Dubai because of the crisis, I knew that in Finest Surprise we had launched a knock 'em dead campaign."

"I thought we were a shoo-in for the Oscar for best marketing campaign," says Bharat Godkhindi.

Cannes had less appeal that year for the Dubai Duty Free team there. They had left a crisis back home and there was not much appetite for the delights of the South of France. Even awards night, as ever a swanky black tie bash, lost its lustre in the circumstances. But the one reason for their interest, the Oscar in which Finest Surprise was entered, would hold no surprises. Dubai scooped Best Marketing Campaign for a Retailer.

"Don't forget," says McLoughlin, "this was ten months into what was, and probably still is, the most successful duty free marketing campaign in the history of the industry. I have no compunction in stating that. Our marketing team was at their brilliant best."

The Dubai Duty Free team returned home from France with their Oscar, and back to dealing with a running crisis.

"It was clear that the impact of the Gulf War would not be brief, and it would be hard," says Sheikh Ahmed. "There were two options facing Dubai Duty free: to throw up their hands in frustration and wait for the crisis to be over; or lay down the foundations of a post-war bounce."

Once again Sheikh Ahmed showed leadership. Elsewhere in the region it was a case of waiting. He pressed McLoughlin to be pro-active, readying Dubai Duty Free for the moment Kuwait was free and the Gulf began its slow return to normality.

"Sheikh Ahmed was there, in the office, excuding a business-as-usual confidence as much as was possible. His was a reassuring presence," says McLoughlin.

Looking beyond was an area that, in part, fell to Ramesh Cidambi, the company's IT man. He had first got involved with Dubai Duty Free when working for a sub-contractor, but had been 'borrowed' permanently by McLoughlin.

Based upon a realistic target of $150 million in the near future, and an average spend of, for example, $20 per passenger, the Dubai Duty Free shop floor was edging toward 7.5 million transactions a year, or over 20,000 transactions a day. Speed was of the essence.

"Our first cash registers, in 1983, had the memory of a modern calculator," says Cidambi. "But technology was moving on and it was recognised that we needed to do things at point of sale faster, simply to allow additional capacity."

Come Out Fighting

(top) Pictured with Salah Tahlak, despite being a multi-millionaire Sylvester Stallone could not resist purchasing a Finest Surprise ticket when he visited Dubai Duty Free.

(right) Stallone in more familiar guise, playing Rocky Balboa on the silver screen.

Fly *Buy* Dubai

Ramesh Cidambi is Dubai Duty Free's
Information Technology boffin.

With more megabytes available on a new generation of cash registers, it was time to look at the options available.

"With more memory capacity you have a much better user interface and (are able to) be very intuitive in terms of doing the transactions, you have a better quality of the receipts, you have the fastest printing of receipts and you have fastest scanning," he says. "But we even built upon that."

Working with the National Bank of Dubai, Dubai Duty Free's acquiring bank for all credit cards, American Express and Visa and MasterCard, Cidambi and his IT wizards put together a solution to take the whole credit card authorisation functionality and bring it on to the cash register itself. Nearly two decades on this seems slightly mundane, but in those days it was a step beyond in the Gulf.

Dubai Duty Free was the first company in the United Arab Emirates to do this as one transaction at the point of sale. The traditional method, as remains the case with a majority of retailers, was to register a sale and then go to a separate terminal for credit card transactions.

Two transactions took twice the time. Halving this would speed up the process dramatically. Throughout the second half of 1990 and into 1991 this project was underway. It was eventually rolled out onto the shop floor in 1991.

"It was a major achievement for the IT department. Some very bright people here, and in NBD, invested a huge amount of man hours to make this work," says Cidambi. "We had wed electronic fund transactions, had done the bank's own processes and authorisation, bringing in encrypting information into our own processes. But in the final analysis it was a coup for us."

While Dubai Duty Free had its boffins beavering away in the backroom, the company was again looking to its image and visibility.

As early as 1986, the first boat with the words 'Victory Team' emblazoned on its hull made its appearance on the scene, initially competing in events throughout the Middle East and the USA. In those days it was purely a sponsorship deal that tied Dubai into the sport. But gradually that changed. By 1990 'Victory Team', under Dubai-based management, competed in three US events, in Sarasota, Bay City, and Grand Haven, when they won two US National titles, finished runners-up twice, and established two world speed records. With some excellent media coverage worldwide, the sport began to prick interest in the emirate. Dubai was no longer wishing to be just another participant, albeit a successful one.

Offshore racing first came to the shores of the Arabian Gulf in 1989, when Dubai staged a powerboat race off the coast of Mina Seyahi. By this time the Victory Team had been formed, operating from a small workshop with a small crew. As part of its sporting strategy Dubai planned to promote the sport — and invest in the Victory Team, taking it into the UIM Class One World Championship by 1992.

"We signed on to support the Victory Team immediately," says Anita Mehra. "Not only was it a quickly growing sport, the speed and thrill was something that we were happy to be associated with.

"And then there was the potential for success. Dubai never did things by halves. If the Victory Team entered the world championship you could be pretty sure they would end up among the most successful teams in the world. That also appealed."

They soon became acquainted with Khalfan Harib. Today Harib is considered one of the most successful sportsmen in the history of the UAE.

Taking over as Managing Director of Victory Team in 1990, he would go on to shape seven Class One, four Class Two, and an astonishing five Pole Position World Championship titles, and personally be considered one of the

Dubai Duty Free's association with the multiple world championship winning Victory Team went beyond simple sponsorship and had a big impact on the sport.

greatest throttlemen to emerge in the history of offshore.

"Dubai Duty Free was one of our first sponsors, and remained loyal to Victory Team and the sport," says Harib. "But more than that, they helped create a template whereby this became a genuine spectator sport."

In 1991, the project would kick off when the emirate was scheduled to host a round of the UIM Class One World Championship. Offshore powerboat racing is typically point-to-point racing a kilometre or more off shore. Coupled with the astronomical cost of the boats and the fuel required to participate, it is an expensive and elite sport. Although there are team sponsors, it is still an amateur sport financed by a mix of private funding and commercial sponsors. Therefore it was not considered mainstream and lacked a support base among the general public, even where nations were successful or well represented.

This was a conundrum that Sheikh Ahmed offered to Dubai Duty Free. Dubai wanted to be at the vanguard of offshore racing, forging a sport that was popular and mainstream.

"We had the proven ability to create big, showpiece events," says McLoughlin. "We wanted a spectacle and to turn the UIM Class One World Powerboat Championship into the biggest powerboat racing event in the world," says Horan. "There was a vision of numerous noisy boats speeding in the azure waters of the Arabian Gulf, enjoyed by thousands of people."

The host venue of the event was to be the Dubai International Marine Club, established in 1988 and one of the most elegant yacht clubs in the region. Its importance in Dubai terms was only heightened in that the event was to be staged under the patronage of Sheikh Maktoum bin Rashid Al Maktoum, UAE Vice President and Prime Minister, Ruler of Dubai. Sheikh Maktoum rarely put his name to sporting events. On a domestic level, this made its success of strategic importance.

"We stepped forward and decided to put a very Dubai Duty Free stamp on proceedings. For Dubai and its prestige," says Salah Tahlak.

In April 1990 the emirate staged its first major event, followed by a second race in November 1991, the Dubai Duty Free Offshore Powerboat Race. The two races, UIM Class II and Class III events, were won by 'Victory One' and 'Victory Eight' respectively.

The second event was attended by an estimated 12,000 people. Dubai Duty Free had introduced a variety of beach-based entertainments for spectators. It was just the beginning.

"Our aim was nothing less than to take this established sport and, cooperating with the sport's administrators, make Dubai a hub of the sport and the world's most successful host in terms of spectators," says McLoughlin.

This required a shift in emphasis. Emirates, the airline, was co-opted as the title sponsor of the sporting event, while Dubai Duty Free was asked to handle the shore portion of events. The events of April 10, 1992 would prove a watershed for the sport of powerboat racing.

First came the race: Dubai International Marine Club announced that this would be the world's richest power boating race, with Dhs. 2 million in prize money for the 110 nautical mile Class M and 90 nautical mile Class S events. Then came the boats: Sponsored by Dubai Duty Free, Victory unveiled its new 35-foot inboard-engine catamaran, the 'M1'. This would compete against the very best in the world, some 60 entries in all.

Then came the spectators.

The Indianapolis 500 motor race at the Speedway in Indiana, USA is the largest single-day sporting event in the world, drawing 270,000 spectators annually. But the 'Indy 500' is an exception. During the 2006/07 campaign, England's FA Cup had an average gate of 13,960; in 2008, Rugby Union's Six

The Indianapolis 500 is considered the largest single-day sporting event in the world.

Fly *Buy* Dubai

*Many clubs in England's Premiership average lower gates than
Dubai Duty Free's powerboating days.*

Nations Championship had an average attendance of 70,893; 2004's
European football (soccer) championships enjoyed an average gate of 37,445;
the Cricket World Cup in 2007 attracted average attendances of 13,176; and
the Hockey World Cup 2,352 per match.

Where could Dubai go with a 'spectator' sport where the action takes
place 1 kilometre offshore, and one that had no history of crowds? That was
Dubai Duty Free's problem.

"We decided pretty quickly to make the event a day-long party," says
Anita Mehra. "It was an approach that we get people there, then we educate
them to the sport. That would set down the roots of the sport in the public's
consciousness, when they were introduced to the glamour and the speed of
the sport."

The party aspect started with music. And Dubai Duty Free was nothing if
not ambitious. First on board was Bananarama, the British girl group who
were still at the peak of their industry and had enjoyed ten Top 10 singles in
the UK and three in the USA, including 'Cruel Summer', 'Venus', 'Love in
the First Degree', and 'I Heard a Rumour'. Recognising that it would be a

mixed crowd, next on the line up was Amr Diab, an Egyptian singing superstar popular across the region, one of the highest-selling Middle Eastern artists of all time, and later a three-time winner of the World Music Award. Finally, Dubai Duty Free booked David 'Kid' Jensen as the event's DJ, one of the most familiar voices on Britain's Radio 1 and faces on Top of the Pops.

Today, we see the likes of Bon Jovi, Madonna, and Celine Dion, the biggest recording stars in the world, gigging in the UAE," says McLoughlin. "But a decade and more ago this was arguably the biggest line-up ever assembled for an event in the country."

Dubai Duty Free went on to add children's areas, fairground attractions, visual performance artists, huge BBQs, and booked a host of domestic bands for the musical line-up. With an eye on entrenchment of the sport itself, they produced a programme, erected giant screens on the beach on which the action would be relayed, and booked a commentator who could hold attention.

"We thought we had done a job, a good one. But when April 10 rolled around there were fraught nerves," says Mehra. "As much as we had laid on, and worked to publicise the event, because there was no real history of powerboat racing it was a matter of who would turn up on the day. That was the unknown."

Doors were due to open at 10.30am. McLoughlin and his staff were there not long after dawn putting the finishing touches. Nerves were high.

"We had said that we were expecting 15,000 people. If that many had come I would have said that we had done a good job," he says.

The first signs of what was to come became apparent at 8.30. Cars began arriving in the parking area. By 10 that morning parking was already becoming full and a queue was waiting impatiently. By 10.30 the doors opened and a flood of people turned into a surge.

The racing itself was not due to begin until early afternoon, yet by lunchtime police and civil defence forces were estimating 28,000-30,000 people on the beach.

"It was the biggest event ever staged in the UAE at that time, in terms of numbers," says Dubai-based sports journalist Cherian Thomas.

To give some perspective, the event had attracted more than the average attendance of British football (soccer) clubs Birmingham City (26,180), Blackburn Rovers (23,943), Bolton Wanderers (20,901), Fulham (23,774), Middlesbrough (26,709), Portsmouth (19,914), Reading (23,532), and Wigan Athletic (19,046) in last season's FA Premiership; and more than the average

Among the many acts Dubai Duty Free have brought to Dubai to entertain powerboating crowds have been Boney M, Lou Bega, Shaggy and Bananarama.

(top) Australian star Dannii Minogue was another act booked for Dubai Duty Free's powerboating days.

(left) Breeda McLoughlin with Minogue.

attendances of the most recent stagings of the Rugby League Tri-Nations, FIFA Women's World Cup finals, World Baseball Classic, World Cup of Hockey, and Cricket World Cup. There were people on the beach in Dubai than attended American Football's Million Dollar Game, more than the NBA Finals, significantly more than at ice hockey's Stanley Cup, and even beat Australian Rules football's AFL (Australian Football League) Grand Final crowd figures.

When the sporting action got underway, Dubai Duty Free achieved everything it set out to do. Live-action screens, powerful thunderous engines, close action, and a domestic team which claimed honours against entrants from Kuwait, Sudan, Italy, Bangladesh, the USA, Britain, Belgium, Norway, Lebanon, and Egypt, combined to make it a memorable sporting occasion. In Class M, the main event, Dubai also swept the boards when 'Victory 60' edged 'Victory 1' and 'Victory 7' into the minor placings.

"I knew we had got somewhere with the project when 50,000 people screamed, clapped and cheered their home team, Victory, across the finish line," says McLoughlin. "It was a great deal for Dubai and an excellent event for Dubai Duty Free."

Having nearly 50,000 people turn out for a powerboat race was a coup for the sport, and led to a revamped world series of the sport in 1992. Beginning with a series of races in Europe during the summer, starting in St. Tropez in May, by the winter action would turn to the Middle East where the world championship season would round off with two races, sponsored by Dubai Duty Free and Emirates. There was even acknowledgement, based upon Dubai's successes, that the sport needed to make itself more spectator-friendly. As well as similar, if less high-profile, PR and entertainment programmes adopted in other host cities, the sport introduced qualifying sessions, called Kilo Runs.

"I like to think that Dubai Duty Free played a role in transforming powerboat racing," says McLoughlin. "Today it is a big, glamorous sport that generates much media and attracts crowds. Dubai as a whole did so much to shape the sport."

Dubai was looking to establish itself further as a sporting capital.
Dubai Duty Free was set to bring world ranking tennis to the emirate.

Chapter Twenty

Major Walter Clopton Wingfield

I always turn to the sports section first.
The sports page records people's accomplishments.
The front page has nothing but man's failures.
— Earl Warren, American chief justice

On July 2, 1992, Colm McLoughlin arrived in his office, as usual. On his desk, as usual, were the previous day's sales figures. McLoughlin's daily programme varies, but generally comprised a briefing, a chat with Assistant Managing Director George Horan, and a daily management meeting. In the ante-room outside his office there are generally a few people waiting to be seen.

On this day, however, things were different.

With the Gulf War raging, the previous year had represented the only blip in an otherwise perfect record in increased turnover and profits year-on-year. Under the circumstances, 1991 had not been all that bad. There were stories of empty 'planes arriving in Dubai, and an arrivals terminal with a handful of passengers passing through at peak times. With Kuwait liberated, the second half of that year would see Dubai Duty Free flourishing. And Dubai Duty Free had not been content to tread water.

"Even in those circumstances, during the period of the Gulf War we had made considerable forward strides. When the conflict ended we were honed and hungry to carry on where we had left off," says Horan.

In 1991, World Snooker Champion John Parrott had claimed the first of two back-to-back successes in the Dubai Duty Free Snooker Classic, a year that had also seen Dubai Duty Free become established in powerboat racing. Outside the sporting arena Ramesh Cidambi and his IT team, had made a big difference to the shop floor with on-line credit card authorization. And then there was the impact of Tom Ellery.

McLoughlin had reportedly almost dropped his telephone when Ellery named his price in 1989, but the flamboyant Welshman went on to have a huge impact on the shop floor.

Ellery had cut his retail teeth in no less an establishment than Harrods in London. During his time there, in the late 1960s and 1970s, the famous Harrods motto 'Everything for Everybody Everywhere' had more than lived up to its meaning over the years. Noël Coward bought an alligator, while Ronald Reagan was on the receiving end of a baby elephant. Ellery was one of the architects of Way In, a hip, swinging, and ultra-trendy boutique that

Fly *Buy* Dubai

reinvigorated Harrods' image and brought Carnaby Street, one of London's coolest destinations during the Swinging Sixties, into the store. With these innovations on his *CV*, and a trendy persona that led him to move in the circles of bands such as The Beatles and Rolling Stones, and to be considered friends by hip British personalities including Mary Quant and singer Lulu, Ellery was at the top of his game in the most fashionable city in the world.

Ellery went on to revamp Thomas Goode, Asprey, and then Asprey Garrard, several of London's most upmarket shopping institutions. He was to retail what Muhammad Ali was to boxing, Pele to football, Borg to tennis, or Piggott to racing.

After 1989, Ellery had joined the Dubai Duty Free payroll on a freelance basis, visiting the emirate for 21 days twice a year, in the spring and autumn. His eye had helped transform the store.

On the shop floor, staff came to know the flamboyant character among them as 'Uncle Tom'. As well as enjoying the work, he had a profound impact on Dubai Duty Free. Ellery was a devotee of German firm Barthelmess, from where he would arrange purchase of the company's visual merchandising solutions… 'crafted using a holistic approach to

The Rolling Stones were close friends and contemporaries of Dubai Duty Free's visual merchandising guru.

conceptual design...' Ellery would order what he required for Dubai, and arrive in the emirate at the same time as his merchandise from Germany. There followed a three-week period when he would arrange, preen, spruce, and groom.

Dubai Duty Free looked great, and wherever he had worked there was a noticeable increase in revenue. Anything that Ellery did worked like a charm on consumers.

Throughout a difficult 1990 and 1991, a period when unnecessary expenditure was frozen and large projects were deferred, Ellery was an expense that was viewed as necessary. His impact was immediate and he gradually changed the entire face of the shop floor. By the time the Gulf War was over, the pre-eminent display consultant of his day had Dubai Duty Free ready for the inevitable post-Gulf War surge.

On July 2, 1992, McLoughlin arrived in the office and forewent the usual round of meetings. Something was on his mind. Two years earlier, before the invasion of Kuwait, Dubai Duty Free was hurtling toward a significant breakthrough. Some $100 million of sales may have been symbolic — but it was nevertheless a huge one. And if Saddam Hussein had not pursued his

At the beginning of July 1992, Dubai Duty Free was set to smash through the $100 million turnover barrier.

(top) A drawing of a Victorian-era tennis game.

(left) Major Walter Clopton Wingfield, considered by many the father of tennis.

mad plan, Dubai Duty Free would have ended that year well into nine figures.

In the latter weeks of June 1992 management had seen turnover edging upward. The post-liberation surge had continued. Dubai was back to its robust self. Dubai International Airport was enjoying a year that would go on to see traffic movements well up. All the work of the previous two years had seen a Dubai Duty Free that was lean, looking sharp, and ready for business.

"It was quite obvious that we would smash through the $100 million barrier that year, barring geo-political disaster or a world economic meltdown," says Mehra. "But nevertheless everyone working for Dubai Duty Free, from the shop floor to management, heard the rumours that it was about to happen."

In 1991, Sheikh Mohammed bin Rashid Al Maktoum had been behind the opening of the Dubai Aviation Club, a small social and sporting complex not far from Dubai International Airport. In 1992 it was quietly announced that management of this was to be handed over to Dubai Duty Free. Dubai Duty Free had a few ideas, and would over later years subsequentally roll out The Irish Village and The Century Village, which would go on to make this one of the entertainment hotspots of an emirate that is, today, alive with nightlife and social meeting places.

But as far as Dubai Duty Free was concerned, and within the framework of the Dubai brand, what was already afoot when Dubai Duty Free took over the Aviation Club was entirely significant for the emirate.

From 1859, and over a handful of subsequent years, Major Harry Gem and a Spanish friend, Augurio Perera, played and worked to develop a new sport. The Englishman and Spaniard developed a game which was rooted in two of their respective nations' most popular pastimes — the very British sport of rackets; and pelota, which was prevalent in Spain's Basque region.

Perera had a small estate near Birmingham, in central England, which possessed a flat and true croquet lawn. It was here that tennis was born.

Another name entered the scene of tennis' foundation when, in December 1873, a Major Walter Clopton Wingfield designed a similar game known simply as 'sticky', based upon real tennis. Wingfield left his mark on tennis, which continues today because of his use of the French vocabulary in his new game.

By the last quarter of the 1800s this new sport, with its French terminology, swept across the world. The first tournament at Wimbledon was in 1877, the first US Open four years later. The French Open dates from

Andre Agassi was at the pinnacle of the sport in 1992. Within a few years he would be plying his trade in Dubai.

Major Walter Clopton Wingfield

1891 and the Australian Open since 1905.

These Grand Slam events would come to underpin the sport, as did the International Lawn Tennis Federation's rules, forged in 1924. Two years later the first professional tennis tour was formed, mostly with American and French players. Only in 1968, however, with the abandoning of the amateur era, did tennis become a recognised, global professional sport. The advent of what is deemed to be the open era saw top players able to turn professional, make a living, and become genuine stars. A world dominated by footballers, F1 drivers, and golfers, suddenly got used to names such as Bjorn Borg, Billie Jean King, Jimmy Connors, Margaret Smith-Court, Chris Evert, and John McEnroe.

In 1992, Dubai Duty Free organised the 'Aviation Club Tennis Cup'. That year's Grand Slam winners were Stefan Edberg, Andre Agassi, and Jim Courier, while Pete Sampras was also starting to come into his own on the circuit.

The Dubai Duty Free Classic snooker was probably at its height around this time, but McLoughlin and his team were looking higher. The World Professional Billiards and Snooker Association had done an admirable job with the sport, but even the greats of the 1980s and 1990s, like Steve Davis, Stephen Hendry, John Parrott, and Jimmy White, were big names only in a handful of countries. Snooker had not set down its roots as a major sport around the world.

"We loved the snooker, the players and the sport, and our tournament got bigger and bigger," says Bharat Godkhindi. "But Dubai Duty Free was about promoting itself, and promoting Dubai. Although we would continue to support and manage the Dubai Duty Free Classic for several more years, we had, in fact, outgrown snooker."

"You have to be different, you have to be outrageous, if you like," explained Colm McLoughlin. "Our marketing effort is unrivalled in the duty free industry and we are considered to be the example of how to do things."

Even before the Aviation Club Tennis Cup began, Dubai Duty Free had signed papers with the ATP. Indeed, the ATP agreement was a result of two years of hard lobbying on the part of Dubai Duty Free.

McLoughlin says: "When I look back now I am amazed at how much it has all grown. Each idea was a small one and it all just snowballed and became what we see today. We have always received lots of support and have a great team at Dubai Duty Free."

The Dubai Tennis Championships grew out of the Aviation Club Tennis Cup. Many commentators have recorded that Dubai Duty Free's affiliation with the sport grew from an idea when "Colm, over coffee with friends, dreamed that a tennis tournament would be a great sponsorship opportunity for a company such as Dubai Duty Free."

But McLoughlin is reluctant to take credit for the popular event.

"I don't remember who first mentioned tennis, but I took it to Mr Binhendi and he won the backing of Sheikh Ahmed. When the idea was introduced to Sheikh Mohammed, he immediately offered this his full support and was very keen," says McLoughlin. "I never understand why everyone is so keen to trumpet their influence on such things. It think it is clear that the concept was championed by Sheikh Mohammed and Sheikh Ahmed. Without that support it would never have happened, no matter whose idea it was."

On November 16, 1992, Dubai Duty Free and chief supporter BMW announced officially that in Dubai in ten weeks' time they would host the first-ever world-ranking tennis tournament in the Middle East. Boasting a prize fund of $1 million, Dubai had set out its stall to create a major event.

Building work was already underway at the Aviation Club, creating five new championship courts and providing seating for 3,000 spectators.

"Sheikh Mohammed believed in this and gave it all his support. He is himself a keen tennis player," says Sheikh Ahmed. "So as an enthusiast, and someone aware of the size and scope of the professional circuit, he could see the benefits for Dubai in hosting a top class event."

Sheikh Ahmed adds that Sheikh Mohammed's only stipulation was that "…our event should be one of the best in the world…"

With the full backing of Dubai's Ruling Family, the work began in earnest. The work, of course, had gone on long before November 16.

"You don't put on an ATP event in ten weeks," says Godkhindi, "let alone a first of its kind in the region. It was a big, big undertaking.

"The key to the success of the event then, and until today, is that Dubai Duty Free is the owner, the organiser and the sponsor of the event. It creats a cohesion that breeds success," adds Godkhindi, whose huge influence over the tournament is widely recognised.

The Dubai Desert Classic golf tournament remained the only world event staged in the emirate. The snooker was far smaller and, relatively parochial, in terms of its mass appeal, as was powerboat racing. Horse racing under Rules just got underway in 1992, and the Dubai World Cup was still four years away.

"Unlike the days when the snooker began, there was now a core of competencies and experience in staging big events. But it was still hard to bring a new event to the emirate," says Salah Tahlak, who would later go on to be Tournament Manager for the event.

Tahlak joined Dubai Duty Free just weeks before the first tournament.

"Yet organising a snooker tournament is vastly different from a tennis tournament. A thousand things can go wrong. If one does indeed go wrong, it can have a domino effect and impact on everything. Military-style precision is required."

Throughout the second half of 1992, a committee comprising Dubai Duty Free members, the management of The Aviation Club, Dubai and UAE tennis authorities, the police, civil defence, Dubai Airport immigration, and others huddled regularly in order to plan the event meticulously.

Dubai Duty Free had been warned not to expect draws such as Edberg, Agassi, Courier, and Sampras to enter the first staging of a tournament, especially one slotted into the calendar so soon after the Australian Open. That rarely happened unless huge appearance fees were involved. But when the ATP announced its entry list there were a few surprises. The top seed was Alexander Volkov, runner-up in three ranking tournaments the previous year and most famous for his shock straight sets defeat of Stefan Edberg —

Karel Novacek entered the first tournament in Dubai and became a crowd favourite over future years.

The temporary stands which hosted Dubai's first international tournaments.

(inset) Thomas Muster, who would go on to be a World Number One, competed in Dubai's first event.

Fly *Buy* Dubai

Dubai's tennis tournament would grow quickly and become one of the biggest non-Grand Slam events on the international calendar.

then ranked the World Number One — in the first round of the US Open. Also there was Thomas Muster, an Austrian who was heading up the world rankings and would eventually be World Number One, winning 44 career titles including the French Open. The third seed was Karel Novacek of The Czech Republic, who was at his peak, with wins in Auckland, Hamburg, Kitzbühel, and Prague in 1991, and Hilversum, San Marino, and Prague in 1992. Like Muster, Novacek was a clay court specialist, but 1993 would mark the   beginning of a love affair with Dubai and its hard courts for the Czech.

The event began at the end of January and there was luck for Dubai Duty Free in the qualifiers. Moroccan 22-year-old Youness El Aynaoui became the only Arab player in the 32-strong singles line-up for the Dubai Duty Free/BMW Tennis Open when he was one of the four qualifiers who swept past his opponents and made it through to the tournament proper. The charismatic young El Aynaoui was another player who would become a fan favourite over successive years, returning to Dubai as often as his injury-troubled career would allow.

The tournament proper got underway on February 1. Unlike the first year of the snooker, where there was a late rush for tickets, resulting in some sleepless nights for organisers, the tennis was an immediate attraction.

The likes of Volkov, Muster, and Novacek put 'bums on seats', as did El Aynaoui, and the parochial nature of the Dubai public also showed.

Briton Jeremy Bates reached a career-best fourth round of Wimbledon in 1992, only won one singles tournament in his pro career, was the British national champion six times, and enjoyed career-high rankings of World Number 54 in singles, in 1995, and Number 25 in doubles, in 1991, winning two Grand Slam mixed doubles tournaments. But although he was not a star as such, organisers found that Bates was a crowd-puller. Later, the multi-national nature of Dubai's population would ensure that any matches with players drawn from big domestic populations, such as Britons or Russians, would be popular.

The tournament as a whole would prove a success — although this would be one of those rare times when wet weather and gales show themselves in the UAE. Dubai, with its year round sunshine, had its ATP debut to a backdrop of play lost to rain and the venue pounded by destructive winds. That week, a Royal death also meant that Dubai and the UAE went into an official mouring period, ensuring a domestic television blackout. The weather conspired to force the tournament into a Monday final.

"We were surprised — surprised at the strength of ticket sales — and very pleased at the media coverage. It was global," says Bharat Godkhindi.

The week-long event was reported on CNN each day, and broadcast live in a handful of channels across the world. Fifth seed Emilio Sanchez gave an inkling as to what was to come over future seasons when he told a press conference: "This is a great place and the arrangements are super."

On semi-finals day wild card and subsequent eighth seed Frenchman Fabrice Santoro first eliminated top seed Volkov in the quarterfinals, and then outmaneuvered Bates in the semifinals. Novacek also made it to the final.

Finals day was a sellout, and the crowd, including Sheikh Mohammed and Sheikh Ahmed, was treated to an excellent doubles final, with John Fitzgerald and Swedish legend Anders Järryd defeating Grant Connell and Patrick Galbraith. In the singles, Santoro played with his usual guile and two-hands on forehand and backhand, and would prove a tough opponent for Novacek, although the Czech went on to capture the first Dubai Tennis Open 6-4, 7-5. Santoro would have his day — he won the singles title in Dubai in 2002, and the doubles twice in 2004 and 2007, the latter 14 years after his first appearance in the emirate.

Fly *Buy* Dubai

Sheikh Mohammed presents trophies on court to the finalists of the singles and doubles. He would champion the growth of the event.

Although Dubai had signed contracts with the ATP that represented a long-term commitment to stage a tournament, in the wake of the events of 1993 it was clear that the sport was going to be big business for Dubai. Domestically it was well received, but internationally the event was an outstanding success. In terms of media, the exposure was worth millions to Dubai and Dubai Duty Free. It was a good sign of a job well done on this score that, in November 1993, at the ATP Tour Awards in London, Dubai scooped the category for Outstanding Media Relations.

"The Dubai Men's Open is a success each year because of the fantastic team we have working with us," says Godkhindi. "The event is run in-house and all our staff pull together to make the event a reality. Almost everyone employed by Dubai Duty Free has a job either pre-, during, or post- the championships."

The year 1993 was a year in which Dubai Duty Free's sponsorship budget also extended further to golf. Dubai Duty Free had been a key supporter of the Desert Classic since the first tournament. In 1993 Dubai Duty Free operated and hosted the annual industry-linked Dubai Golf World

Cup for the first time, attracting international duty free and aviation industry representatives. Their portfolio would extend to a UAE Junior Development Programme, the Dubai Duty Free UAE Nationals Cup, Dubai Duty Free Golf Cup, and the Dubai Duty Free Seniors Cup.

But the tennis swamped everything else.

"The success of that first tournament convinced us that we should really build this into a major international event," says Sheikh Ahmed. "Dubai of course would come to be seen as the very best host of top sporting events. While we could not hope to host a Grand Slam, we could nonetheless aim to be the best of the rest."

The life of a tennis tournament lasts one week as far as the public are concerned. But behind the scenes it is a 52-week process. It took a team and plenty of commitment. And there were, in the wake of 1993, big plans being forged.

"Within weeks we were discussing a tennis stadium," says Tahlak. "In Dubai, we do nothing by halves, and with the government supporting us there were big plans being hatched."

A 1952 advertisement for Courvoisier cognac that highlights the link with Napoleon Bonaparte.

Chapter Twenty-One

Colm's Tuxedo

The word impossible is not in my dictionary.
— *Napoleon Bonaparte, French statesman*

Courvoisier is a brand of cognac produced by a company that is now based in the town of Jarnac in France. Legend has it that Courvoisier cognac was the favourite drink of Napoleon Bonaparte. According to the company's website:

> *'The origin of our history goes back to the beginning of the 19th century with Emmanuel Courvoisier and his associate, Louis Gallois, running a wine and spirit merchant company, in the Parisian suburb of Bercy. In 1811 Napoleon visited their warehouses in Bercy and he was hosted by Louis Gallois, the Mayor, and Emmanuel Courvoisier. Legend has it that Napoleon I later took several barrels of cognac with him to St Helena, a treat much appreciated by the English officers on the ship who named it 'The Cognac of Napoleon'.'*

Legend also has it that when Bonaparte was faced with disgrace after his defeat by the British, he attempted to escape to America with a ship stocked with '*le Cognac de Napoleon*'. In the 1800s, Napoleon III was also a big fan. A clever deal was forged by Courvoisier, and from this association it was agreed that a bust of Napoleon would appear on every bottle of Courvoisier.

A silhouette of the little emperor can still be found today on the distinctive bottles.

"Courvoisier is one of the most distinctive and popular brands of cognac we stock," says George Horan.

In the 1990s, Courvoisier was an established luxury brand, a term that indicated a high-income elasticity of demand: as people become wealthier, they will buy more and more. It also held that Courvoisier was part of that socio-economic phenomenon called conspicuous consumption. Some 190 years on from Napoleon's visit to Bercy, such was the brand's cachet that the company had launched its own guide to elite lifestyles. Perhaps it was more of a guide for the *nouveau riche* — French for 'new rich' — a person who has acquired considerable wealth within his or her generation, but the Courvoisier did ensure that people sat up and noticed. This guide pre-dated many of the other luxury guides that would follow, and therefore became something of a definitive.

Fly *Buy* Dubai

In 1994, Dubai Duty Free quite unexpectedly found itself named within the pages of the 'Courvoisier Book of the Best' as the Best of the Best when it came to world duty free.

"I already thought that," jokes McLoughlin. "But it was nice to have some reaffirmation!"

Essentially, some said, this was a book for snobs and those who attached importance to what the rich and upper class did. As one reviewer noted: '…if you have the money you couldn't go too far wrong in following the guide's recommendations… I recommend the Courvoisier guide if you want to be familiar with where the rich are seen, or not seen. Or if you wish to err on the safe side in traveling throughout the world.'

Courvoisier's reach may not have been mass market, but nevertheless the kudos was well received in Dubai, coming on the back of a slew of awards. A year earlier *Executive Travel* had presented Dubai Duty Free with an award as 'Best Duty Free in the World'. *Business Traveller* magazine had chipped in with an award of the same name some months later. A *Business Traveller* readers poll had been somewhat out of step in October when naming Dubai Duty Free second in its 'Best Duty Free in the World' category, while 1993 had gotten back on track when, at the Arab Travel Awards, Dubai Duty Free had been named 'Best Duty Free in the World'.

"After 1993, we decided that Colm should have two tuxedos," says Breeda McLoughlin. "It proved a smart move."

By 1994 the awards were coming thick and fast. Perhaps the most deserved came in June at the ATP Tour Awards. Even allowing for the hard work of the previous, inaugural, year the 1994 Dubai Tennis Championships were a stretch better.

"After 1993 we spent one month looking at the whole thing, from every conceivable angle, in minute detail,' says Salah Tahlak. "It was an exhaustive process, but from it so many lessons were learned. We also spent a lot of time visiting other tournaments around the world, watching and learning what others did.

"The lessons learned elsewhere were brought back and built upon," says Tahlak. "We were conscious not just to copy, but to do things better."

A look at the top eight seeds for the second championship shows growth: Sergi Bruguera, Thomas Muster, Petr Korda, Magnus Gustafsson, Ivan Lendl, Wayne Ferreira, Karel Novacek, and Alexander Volkov. Bruguera was the French Open holder, Gustafsson had just reached the quarter finals of the Australian Open, and Novacek was Dubai's defending champion. Lendl was in the twilight of his career, a career that had seen eight grand slams wins.

Colm's Tuxedo

Indeed, Lendl announced his retirement from professional tennis on December 21, 1994, due to chronic back pain, something that was in evidence during his visit to the UAE.

"It was a magnificent field," says Mehra. "Other tournament organisers were commenting that it was unheard of to get such a quality field in just the second year of an event."

Lendl lasted until the quarters, when he was ousted by the eventual winner, Sweden's Gustafsson, who claimed his second title of the year. In the doubles event 'The Woodies' — Australia's famed pairing of Todd Woodbridge and Mark Woodforde — claimed the honours.

Four months later McLoughlin's tuxedo was dusted off for the ATP Tour Awards in London. Indianapolis won its fifth consecutive gong as best International Series Gold venue, while South Africa's Sun City claimed the International Series best host title, but in its second year Dubai was voted, by players, one of the top tournaments of the year. McLoughlin was on his feet for a second time when Dubai scooped 'Most Improved Facilities'.

"As I was receiving the award for our facilities I reflected on what was coming," says McLoughlin. "A few weeks earlier we had presented to Sheikh

As the awards nights came thick and fast, Colm McLoughlin invested in a new tuxedo.

Fly *Buy* Dubai

(top) Dubai Duty Free had seen turnover jump from $20 million to $120 million in eight years.

(left) Dubai International Airport was doing so well that there was a need for expansion.

Colm's Tuxedo

Mohammed plans and a model that would see the creation of a full-blown tennis stadium. As is his way, when Sheikh Mohammed is convinced of the merits of a project he gives the green light immediately.

"Here we were in London receiving an award for our facilities in 1994, and I knew that by 1996 Dubai was set to boast something comparable to many of the best tennis stadiums in the world. It was tremendously exciting for the emirate."

In 1992, Dubai Duty Free crossed the $100 turnover mark *en route* to a mammoth $132 million. Both marks were a source of jubilation. More than awards and kudos, the bottom line is what fed success. It had taken eight full trading years to leap from $20 million to $132 million.

"Only then had we reached a point of critical mass," says Horan. "The Dubai Duty Free brand was growing, Dubai had emerged from the Iran-Iraq War and the Gulf conflict — in top shape."

The shop floor, with 'Uncle Tom' Ellery weaving his magic, was trading at its very best. Globally, the industry was thought to register between $5 to $10 in revenue per passenger. Dubai Duty Free had smashed through that figure and more than doubled it.

In 1994, Dubai International Airport recorded an above ten per cent increase in movements. This was mirrored on the shop floor when Dubai Duty Free saw its turnover grown again, by another whopping $11 million, to $145 million, representing just a fraction under $400,000 a day. On a more domestic note this created an avenue for public relations as this drew Dubai Duty Free across the Dhs. 500 million mark.

The 'Bottom Line', in airport terms, is about carriers, flights, passengers, and cargo. And, in 1995, Dubai International Airport reached a series of milestones. Perhaps the most symbolic was flights. In 1984, 51,350 aircraft landed in Dubai, a shade over 140 per day. Topping 100,000 movements in 12 months may have been more symbolic than anything else, but it was nevertheless a milestone.

"At Dubai International Airport the event was received with a great deal of delight and satisfaction," says Mohammed Al Khaja. "In both 1994 and 1995 traffic had leapt by over ten per cent. It was a ringing endorsement for the government's belief in aviation and the investment that it had made in the airport. The airport was staffed by a lot of amazing, dedicated professionals.

"In the final analysis it was also a testimonial to the vision of the late Sheikh Rashid. In the late 1950s the Gulf was a very different place. We had

Sheikh Ahmed was set to lead Dubai International Airport into a period of almost constant expansion and development that would bring it to the present day.

been isolated for generations, the modernity of the 20th century had all but passed us by. Yet Sheikh Rashid knew and understood the opportunities presented by aviation. He was years ahead of his time, and his vision, and his Open Skies policy, set in motion the construction of an airport, and led us to 1995 when over 50,000 aircraft called at Dubai International Airport. It is beyond belief what had been achieved."

Al Khaja's sentiments were captured in a 1996 aviation supplement produced by the US-based *Arab Times*.

> '...*Opened in 1960, years ahead of most airports in the Gulf, yet well after many of its present-day competitors in Asia and the West, Dubai developed its airport against the wishes of the Imperialist government and amid a wave of disquiet over the cost...three and a half decades on Dubai International Airport has grown up to be the Gulf's major aviation artery...*

> '...*from the point of view of Dubai International Airport, the emirate...weathered the tough market conditions of the 1980s with limited, yet positive growth, and began the 1990s with a plethora of new airlines from around the world initiating services...this year it is expected that nearly four million... passengers will use the airport...*

> '...*Dubai began its aviation years with an Open Skies policy and resisted the obvious temptation to become protectionist when it began its own carrier, Emirates, a decade ago...If the industry needed a lesson as to the benefits of Open Skies, then Dubai is an excellent case study.*'

In 1995, Dubai Duty Free was ahead of the curve. As the airport added 13 per cent on its movements over the previous year, Dubai Duty Free saw its turnover rocket, announcing annual turnover of $173 million. Anoth slew of awards followed.

"It's not just about business. It's important to reflect on the other thing we do, the promotions, the awards. It's easy to become blasé when we win so many," says McLoughlin, who donned his tuxedo several times that year. "But I see the awards we win as an endorsement of the quality that Dubai Duty Free strives for. They are also an endorsement of our staff.

The bottom line, however, is that trophies don't equate directly to profits. McLoughlin had claimed a hatful of gongs, but he had also turned around Dubai Duty Free from a floor of concession shops to a slick operation that was showing a double-digit annual increase in turnover.

Fly *Buy* Dubai

"I was aware we were reaching saturation point, where our operation simply had no capacity to increase and grow," says McLoughlin.

It was a view shared by Sheikh Ahmed and the government of Dubai. The old airport, despite the investment in it, was simply reaching its logical point of capacity.

In early 1994 Costain International, architects of a Dubai Airport Master Plan, were ordered to prepare studies on a logical next step. The solution was an entirely new terminal building.

"The way things were going, you could see the need," says McLoughlin. "From Dubai Duty Free's perspective, around half of all passengers were shopping with us, and on average they were spending $24 each. This was well in excess of the international average, and possibly the highest in the world. We were delighted.

"But could we do better than a turnover of $140 million? I was in no doubt. No doubt at all that we could achieve far more if given the space."

There were those around McLoughlin who whispered of $500 million turnover — and more. And envisioned a larger Dubai Duty Free competing with the likes of Heathrow, Incheon, Singapore, Amsterdam, and Frankfurt. It was a vision that would have seemed fanciful just a couple of years earlier.

A new terminal was always included in the Dubai Airport Master Plan but, given Dubai's explosive results, the government was forced to look at the issue far earlier.

In the late summer of 1994 Sheikh Ahmed presented Sheikh Mohammed with a detailed plan for a $200 million development. With subsequent phases of work included, the medium-term bill for development work at Dubai International Airport was estimated to be $500 million.

"Sheikh Mohammed wants what is best for Dubai. That is his primary requirement on any given project," says Sheikh Ahmed. "On the fate of the airport, we went to Sheikh Mohammed only when there was a thorough case to be made, backed up by the solid figures."

No-one needed to convince Dubai's Crown Prince, Sheikh Mohammed, as to the merits of civil aviation. Once the case for a new terminal was made he needed no further persuasion.

Toward the end of 1994 and into 1995, planning work continued in earnest. DCA had stated their belief that Dubai would be receiving nearly 12 million passengers a year by 2000, and therefore required the initial phase of the Dubai Airport Master Plan to be completed by 1999. Achieving these aims would be an inclusive process. In the planning stages Sheikh Ahmed drew in the managements of Emirates and Dubai Duty Free, along with those at DCA.

"Planning the new terminal was a very exciting period," said Mohammed Al Khaja, Emirates Senior Vice President, Safety & Standards, and one of the most longstanding emirati aviators. "There was a real belief that we had embarked upon a programme that would create a wondrous, 21st century airport. All the input from the various stakeholders meant that it was a very practical design, but from the outset the look of the terminal was one that sent shivers down your spine."

"We were consulted, and we were pleased to have input," says McLoughlin. "It was clear that duty free had a big future in Dubai. The more that planners could do to accommodate the needs of Dubai Duty Free, in order to help us grow stronger, the more we could prosper for Dubai."

That prosperity was not just financial in terms of profits, but equated to what Dubai Duty Free could do to promote the Dubai brand and to help make Dubai International Airport one of the most attractive in the world.

After months of work, Costain unveiled a proposal that would establish Dubai International Airport at the forefront of the industry. It encompassed

The expansion programme being discussed would allow Dubai International Airport to handle some 12 million passengers a year by 2000.

Fly *Buy* Dubai

Sheikh Maktoum, Sheikh Mohammed and Sheikh Hamdan during an inspection of the shop floor, with Sheikh Ahmed and Colm McLoughlin.

a new stand-alone terminal building, linked to the present one by two tunnels for the incoming and outgoing passengers and cargo. The existing building would be designated for verification and finalising departure procedures. Twenty-four departure gates would be constructed, boasting modern mobile aerobridges, the number of gates later to increase to 32. The new terminal would include a 100-room hotel for transit passengers, a health centre and business centre, elite first class lounges, and spacious departure and arrival terminals. A smaller building would also be constructed for the departure and arrival of pilgrims. Plans also called for a new control tower and 182 high-speed check-in and ticketing counters. Downstream projects on the drawing board included a multi-storey concourse, and a free trade zone business park.

Dubai Duty Free was to move. Its area would be doubled. Its position, instead of being down an escalator, away from the life of the airport, would be at the very heart of it.

"We were thrilled," says Horan. "It was a breathtaking plan that would transform Dubai Duty Free. They were talking about creating one of the busiest airports in the world. Life at the airport would ebb and flow through the duty free. We were at its heart."

Commenting on the plan, which became public knowledge on April 29, 1995, when Dubai Ruler Sheikh Maktoum visited DCA in order to review the project, India's *The Statesman*, one of India's oldest English newspapers, stated:

> '*From the point of view of Dubai and its continued development, the plans unveiled this week are a firm statement of intent. The Dubai government has never shied away from being ambitious... yet one cannot help but wonder if the emirate has not extended itself on this occasion, especially given the scope of airport developments already underway in the United Arab Emirates, around the Gulf and indeed there is also the Chek Lap Kok factor to consider...*'

Ambitious? Yes. Over-extended? In Dubai no-one believed that, least of all the management of Dubai Duty Free.

"During the mid-1980s the airport was seeking a near ten per cent increase, year on year, in traffic movements," says Al Khaja. "The growth was extraordinary and showed no signs that it would abate."

Gerard Kearney (left) on the steps of Dubai's iconic Irish Village, with food and beverage manager Dave Cattanach (right) and two patrons.

Chapter Twenty-Two

The Sporting Life

Sports is human life in microcosm.
— *Howard Cosell, American sports journalist*

Irish pubs are renowned throughout the world for their vibrant and friendly atmosphere, full of character and characters. They define public meeting places as a place in which you feel immediately at home. It was a mood that was integral to the continued development of the Dubai Duty Free-managed Aviation Club. In 1996 'The Irish Village' opened, going on to become one of the most popular venues in the emirate, as well as receiving an honourable mention in *Time* magazine as one of the world's top meeting places, steeped in character and traditional ethnicity.

"The Irish Village was at the heart of everything we were trying to do with the Aviation Club complex," says Gerard Kearney. "All in all, 1996 was a big year."

Days after the 1995 Dubai Duty Free Men's Open, the developers moved in. They were armed with plans that would transform the Aviation Club into a major international tennis venue.

The world's largest tennis-specific venue, the Arthur Ashe Stadium in New York, holds 22,547 spectators. This dwarfed anything Dubai would require. In conjunction with designers, tournament managers looked at a prospective capacity and had settled on a capacity of 5,000 for centre court, identical to that of Kungliga Tennishallen, home of the Stockholm Open, and Sportlokaal Bokkeduinen, home of the Dutch Open Amersfoort. This was bigger than MTTC Iphitos in Munich, Germany, venue of the BMW Open and even Barcelona Tennis Olímpic, where the tennis tournament for the 1992 Olympics was staged. A 5,000 capacity was also 1,500 more than the number required by the ATP at the time.

Hindsight, perhaps, dictates that 5,000 was too low. But in the mid-1990s Dubai's population was less than 500,000, one million less than it is today. In February 1996, Sheikh Mohammed inaugurated the Dubai Tennis Stadium, a magnet for people seeking entertainment in Dubai, and a swish self-contained stadium. It boasted a 5,000-seat centre court, VIP stand and Royal enclosure, press office, press interview rooms, media complex, tour offices, television commentary boxes and camera positions, state-of-the-art changing rooms, and administration block.

"The players were thrilled, the media were thrilled, the spectators were thrilled. Dubai Tennis Stadium was, and is, one of the best in the world,"

The Irish Village, part of the Dubai Tennis Stadium,
is one of Dubai's great social hotspots.

says McLoughlin, who had seen most of the world's top tennis venues. "1996 was the year when the tennis world suddenly sat up and took notice."

One of the key parts of the Dubai Tennis Stadium business plan was that it would not just be a sporting venue a few weeks each year, but would provide the emirate with a fresh music and sporting outlet too. This would be the case, having played to acts such as Sting, Gerri Haliwell, Bryan Adams, Venga Boys, Asha Bhosle, Coolio, Shaggy, Sash, Maxi Priest, Big Mountain, and Bally Sagoo, while former world boxing champion, Chris Eubank, staged his first Middle East bout on centre court in 1997.

Most of the world's tennis legends would also have the opportunity to show their skills there. Croatian giant Goran Ivanisevic, who would become the only person to win the men's singles title at Wimbledon as a wildcard, dominated the tournament, trounced Spaniard Albert Costa in the 1996 final. But, with all due respect to Ivanisevic, a former world number two, the star of the third Dubai Tennis Championships was the new stadium.

"During and after the tournament many tennis people — officials, players, managers, agents and media — reckoned this to be one of the finest facilities in the world after the four Grand Slam venues of London, Paris, New York and Sydney," says Tahlak. "Dubai was the talk of the circuit.

"That year, in the international media there were almost as many profiles on the tournament venue as the tournament itself!"

The February launch of the Dubai Tennis Stadium would prove a high point in what would become a watershed year for Dubai Duty Free. Since the beginning, Managing Director Colm McLoughlin had set out to create a brand. Duty free industry norms dictate that two per cent of turnover is invested back into advertising and promotions. Dubai Duty Free had set out its stall to do more — with a five per cent budget mark.

"It was deliberate," says McLoughlin. "Sheikh Ahmed wanted Dubai Duty Free to become a brand, and to play a role within the evolution of Dubai as a brand itself."

With revenues crossing $170 million in 1996, Dubai Duty Free's marketing team were now — to use horse racing vernacular — given their head. That is to say they now had at their disposal a budget that would stretch further and do more.

By 1996, tennis, golf, and snooker were the main elements of Dubai Duty Free's sports portfolio. Supported by an award-winning advertising campaign — 'Fly Buy Dubai' — Dubai Duty Free had done well.

Although there were many examples prior to the 1980s, it is generally agreed that the explosive growth of sports marketing began in 1984, when

The Sporting Life

(clockwise from top left) Maxi Priest, Bryan Adams, Sting and Cheb Mami have all performed at Dubai Tennis Stadium, while master puglist Chris Eubank fought there.

The Sporting Life

*The 5,000-seat Dubai Tennis Stadium remains one of
world tennis' most renowned stadiums.*

Fly *Buy* Dubai

(top) Colm and Breeda McLoughlin.

(left) Chinese star Yi Jian Lian. Sports marketing is a global $250 billion industry.

the Summer Olympics in Los Angeles took sporting commercialism to a new level. A plethora of corporates used the Games as a platform to market their brands. Foremost among these was Coca-Cola, which spent nearly $30 million in support of its official sponsorship of the Games.

As CEO and chief organiser of the 1984 Olympics, Peter Ueberroth is credited with demonstrating the power of sports marketing, heralding in an era when sport came to be seen as just as, or more, effective than more traditional print and television. According to the *Sports Business Journal*, today sport is a $250 billion industry. This figure includes sports-related advertising and venue signage, athlete endorsements, stadium naming rights, sporting goods and licensed merchandise, event management and marketing services, sponsorship and ticket sales, media broadcast rights, and multimedia — including sports-related websites, magazines, books, and video games.

"In the early 1990s, we took the view that if sport was going to be our emphasis, then we needed to get it right," says McLoughlin. "We had done well with tennis, golf and snooker. It was right to widen that base and look at additional options."

Dubai Duty Free did not have to look far.

Over millions of years primitive breeds of horse migrated from their North American homeland to the Old World, across the Bering land-bridge which used to connect Alaska and Siberia where the Bering Sea is now. Among the wild Equidae, horses had probably the largest area of distribution. During the Ice Age they were able to survive under diverse living conditions on moor and tundra, in forests, mountains, steppes and desert-like regions. One of these was a small graceful finely-boned almost gazelle-like horse evolved on the bleak expanses of the deserts of southwest Asia. With a fiery temperament which guaranteed a lightning reaction to danger, and a broad thorax allowing plenty of room for efficient lungs and a strong heart.

This horse emerged as an integral part of life on the unknown and largely uncharted Arabian Peninsula. The Bedouins of the wild barren deserts bred sheep and goats, and used camels as riding and draught animals. In the southwestern region of Asir and Nejran, archeologists have repeatedly found equine remains within the settlements and townships of the region.

"A Bedouin needed three things: his horse, his camel and his rifle," stated former Godolphin trainer Hilal Ibrahim, whose family ancestry is filled with noted horsemen. "The horse was entirely significant to the area."

Fly *Buy* Dubai

Sheikh Hamdan bin Rashid Al Maktoum (centre) — one of the world's foremost owner-breeders — receives a trophy from Colm McLoughlin (right) and Salah Tahlak (left).

Arabians, along with closely related breeds such as the Barb, are believed to have raced on a rough track laid out in Yorkshire, England. In 208 AD, the Roman Emperor Lucius Septimius Severus led a campaign to Britain. There he settled and lived out the rest of his life in Yorkshire, where he is reported to have laid out that first track and organised horse races.

In the late 1920s and early 1930s English racing was being dominated by the likes of Derby winners Gainsborough, his son Hyperion, and Mahmoud. In America the likes of Gallant Fox and Omaha were achieving their own immortality by winning the Triple Crown. Half a world away, a young Crown Prince of Dubai, Sheikh Rashid bin Saeed Al Maktoum was developing into a horseman of some repute locally. He loved riding and was seen in the saddle nearly every day, taking his beloved Arabian, named Al Sqalawi, on a punctual mid-afternoon tour of public work. Even after buying his first car, in 1934, Sheikh Rashid still preferred to ride Al Sqalawi. No surprise then that the keen rider found time away from his relentless task of building Dubai to tutor his sons, Sheikh Maktoum, Sheikh Hamdan, Sheikh Mohammed, and Sheikh Ahmed, in this noblest of Arab pursuits.

The Sporting Life

In 1969 Sheikh Maktoum was the first to open what could be called a Western-style racecourse, when he developed a small training yard, a grandstand, and tight oval racecourse, complete with wooden running rail, at a site in Al Ghusais, now overrun by Dubai International Airport.

During the early years of the 1970s, the four brothers—Sheikh Maktoum, Sheikh Hamdan, Sheikh Mohammed, and Sheikh Ahmed—were playing an increasingly important role in the fortunes of Dubai and the fledgling United Arab Emirates. It was in his capacity as head of the Dubai Police Force that Sheikh Mohammed came into contact with the man who is identified as having laid the foundations of the Maktoums' entry into the sport in Britain.

"I've met this charming Arab who would like to buy a few horses. I think that one day he could be a very big owner." That was how the late Colonel Dick Warden recounted to colleagues a meeting with Sheikh Mohammed. Warden had just completed a commission on behalf of the Curragh Bloodstock Agency to supply horses for the Dubai Police force. His trip was subsequently to change the course of racing history.

While the four brothers had made their mark in the West, Sheikh Mohammed also believed that it was time to bring the sport home, back to its roots. He had re-developed a track in the Nad Al Sheba area of Dubai and, after establishing racing under Rulers in 1993, had resolved that Dubai would stage the world's richest race.

The final two decades of the 20th century will be remembered within racing as the years the sport went global. Cross-border competition became inter-continental, encouraged by the huge purses which followed the 1981 staging of the inaugural Arlington Million. America's Breeders' Cup, the Japan Cup, Melbourne Cup, and Hong Kong Invitational Races followed.

When Sheikh Mohammed decided to bring international racing to the UAE his team set out to ensure the participation of the best thoroughbreds on earth, an event which would finally be capable of claiming such a mantle.

Carrying $4 million of prize money, the inaugural staging of the Dubai World Cup in 1996 fulfilled the wildest dreams of racing lovers everywhere, bringing together champions from Europe, Oceania, Asia, the Americas, and the UAE at Nad Al Sheba, for an event which was officially recognised as the strongest race ever run. While Emirates would be title sponsor of this new 2,000 metre classic, Dubai Duty Free was approached to back the day's main support race, which would be titled the Dubai Duty Free.

"This was another example of Sheikh Mohammed's long-term thinking. When you heard what the Dubai Racing Club were going to do with the World Cup meeting, you could not help but be impressed," says

Fly *Buy* Dubai

Sheikh Hamdan bin Mohammed Al Maktoum presents a trophy to Sinead El Sibai in appreciation of Dubai Duty Free's sponsorship of the Dubai World Cup.

McLoughlin. "We have never looked back."

That 1996 meeting was an amazing year. Alanudd, the greatest Arabian racehorse of all time, won the Arabian race that opened the meeting, watched by 30,000 spectators. Top class mile and sprint races followed. By the time night had fallen and Nad Al Sheba was illuminated, both the Dubai Duty Free and the Dubai World Cup were broadcast live on the BBC and on satellite channels around the globe.

In the Dubai Duty Free American superstar Gary Stevens won on Key of Luck, in the colours of Sheikh Saeed bin Maktoum Al Maktoum, while the main event Jerry Bailey and wonder-horse Cigar claimed the $2.4 million winner's purse. Dubai Duty Free won global exposure from the race, enjoyed one of the year's premium days for corporate hospitality, and just as importantly contributed to an event that again helped place Dubai on the international map.

Horse racing abroad was also set to become a fixture on Dubai Duty Free's marketing planner, courtesy of Dubai Ruler Sheikh Maktoum bin Rashid Al Maktoum.

The first recorded racing at Newbury took place in 1805, but Newbury Racecourse didn't come into existence for another century. With the backing of King Edward VII, in April 1904 the Newbury Racecourse Company was formed.

Newbury came to be seen as one of the fairest tracks in Britain, with good racing ground and a shape that is very well suited to a horse that likes to gallop. From the classic trials in the spring, the Greenham Stakes and Fred Darling Stakes, to the Mill Reef Stakes for two-year-olds in September and the Horris Hill Stakes in October, the course boasts a top class flat, and jumps, programme.

One of those who enjoyed Newbury was Sheikh Maktoum, a skilful and adroit horseman. In 1986 he suggested that Dubai Duty Free may like to look at the Fred Darling Stakes, named after Fred Darling, an English trainer who trained a joint-record seven English Derby winners, as an ideal sponsorship opportunity.

"Such was the respect that people had for the late Sheikh Maktoum that we took up that suggestion straight away," says McLoughlin. "And it is a sign of the success that that race has been for us that we support the Fred Darling until the present day."

The Fred Darling Stakes is a Group 3 race for three-year-old fillies over seven furlongs (1,400 metres) in mid April. The length of the race, one furlong (200 metres) short of the 1,000 Guineas trip, and the timing of the

Fly *Buy* Dubai

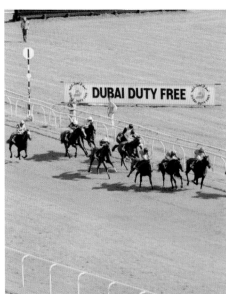

(top) Newbury
Racecourse is one of the
premier tracks in Britain.

(left) Dubai Duty Free
sponsored races now take
place all over the world.

race, made it one of the best trials for the 1,000 Guineas.

Since the race has been run as the Dubai Duty Free Stakes, four winners of the race have gone on to win the 1,000 Guineas — Salsabil, Shadayid, Bosra Sham, and Wince. The first pair was owned by Sheikh Hamdan bin Rashid Al Maktoum, as was Lahan, who finished fourth in the Fred Darling Stakes and went on to win at Newmarket.

"For Newbury, Dubai Duty Free has been one of our most successful associations, and the stability of that relationship has meant that we got to know each other very well," says Mark Kershaw, former managing director of Newbury Racecourse. "It went from a simple sponsorship to a friendship, a very strong relationship which has allowed Newbury Racecourse to understand everything that Dubai Duty Free wants from its association with us and with the sport."

That relationship seemed to be mutual, as Dubai Duty Free's interest in Newbury quickly burgeoned to include a high-summer race, the Group Three Arc Trial, with a purse of £47,000, which sits at the heart of what is now branded the Dubai Duty Free Race Day. The day includes The World Trophy, a Group 3 sprint branded under the name of Dubai International Airport.

"Certainly this is one of the longest continuous relationships between any sponsor and any racecourse," adds Kershaw. "Building that relationship is a hands-on job, but it has paid off for Newbury Racecourse and paid off for Dubai Duty Free as April and September have grown into institutions on the British racing calendar."

Kershaw adds that in a commercial climate where many sponsors come and go, the consistency of knowing Dubai Duty Free will be there means that Newbury, for example, will defend television coverage of these events harder, and can build print media attention. In 2005, Dubai Duty Free added Newbury's Group 3 John Porter Stakes to its portfolio, a race named after yet another English trainer who trained seven English Derby winners.

Sheikh Mohammed bin Rashid Al Maktoum brought a unique driving force and energy to directing the development of Dubai.

Chapter Twenty-Three

Quality

Quality is not an act. It is a habit.
– *Aristotle, Ancient Greek philosopher*

On January 3, 1995, Dubai Ruler Sheikh Maktoum bin Rashid Al Maktoum signed two decrees that appointed his younger brother, Sheikh Mohammed, as Crown Prince of Dubai. It was a move that would harness for the emirate what was acknowledged to be a driving force and energy. Sheikh Mohammed would serve as Crown Prince for nine years, a period when he set out to modernise the very functioning of Dubai, preparing the emirate for a new era of growth. If any project came to symbolise his progressive intent it was Burj Al Arab; but the new Crown Prince also had an eye on the nuts and bolts.

Sheikh Mohammed had launched e-Dubai, an e-government initiative. He had overseen improvements in the education and health systems, championed the Dubai World Trade Centre Exhibition Centre as it grew to become the Middle East's leader, added Emirates Golf Club and Dubai Creek Golf and Yacht Club to the emirate's portfolio, while Jumeirah Beach Hotel and the iconic Burj Al Arab had opened their doors in 1997 and 1999.

He conceptualised and drove forward Dubai Shopping Festival and Dubai Summer Surprises and, while supporting Dubai Duty Free's Dubai Tennis Championships and Dubai Desert Classic, had added the Emirates-sponsored Dubai World Cup, the world's richest horse race, to the global sporting diary.

Dubai Media City and Dubai Internet City were typical of his thinking.

The city was changing and evolving, later to be named by London's *Financial Times* as the 'Middle Eastern City of the Future'.

The Dubai Quality Award (DQA) would become a driving force behind the quality and continuous improvement movement in Dubai, a model considered as a quality roadmap for all organisations operating in the emirate, driving forward contemporary practices in quality management. Built upon an international framework of business excellence, awards were designed to help organisations in Dubai to position all their quality activities and, most importantly, provide them with the mechanism to measure their performance.

"Although we had already paid attention to a methodology that would create a quality and excellence, we were interested in the Dubai Quality Awards for two reasons," says McLoughlin. "Firstly it was important for

Fly *Buy* Dubai

Dubai Duty Free to blaze a trail. We were among the best duty frees in the world, if not the best. Secondly, and most importantly, as one of Dubai's best known companies it was incumbent upon us not just to support Sheikh Mohammed's initiative, but to embrace it.

"The Quality Awards represented the new direction in which Sheikh Mohammed was taking Dubai. We wished to be a part of that."

Dubai, it was said, was set to become a world class quality centre — one organisation at a time. Success would ensure that Dubai could maintain its competitive edge, meet the challenges of an increasingly crowded market place and realise the vision of becoming the world's leading centre for trade and commerce.

The DQA presents a model framework based on nine main criteria, comprising five 'Enablers' and four 'Results', each criteria differently weighted and each with a number of sub-criteria.

Enablers cover what the organisation does, while Results cover what the organisation achieves, all achieved through 'Leadership driving Policy and Strategy, People, Partnerships, Resources and Processes'.

"It was a big thing for us," says Ramesh Cidambi. "Sheikh Mohammed had instilled a pride in Dubai, the staff and management wanted to be a part of it, and for Dubai Duty Free to be at the vanguard of those receiving awards."

Over an extended period, led by a committee appointed by McLoughlin, Dubai Duty Free pulled together a top class entry, to be submitted to the DQA Secretariat.

In November 1996, Dubai Duty Free was named the Dubai Quality Awards' Company of the Year — Trade. This was the final chapter of an awards season that had seen Dubai Duty Free named 'World's Best Airport Duty Free' at *Business Traveller*'s Asia Pacific Awards, 'Best Duty Free in the World' at the *Arab Traveller* Awards, 'Gulf Retailer of the Year' from the Institute for International Research, 'World's Best Airport Duty Free' at *Business Traveller*'s Europe Awards, and named 'Best Duty Free in the World' by *Executive Travel*.

It was a year when McLoughlin's tuxedos were again in evidence, but it was November's Dubai Quality Award that stole the year.

"So many people within Dubai Duty Free worked on the Dubai Quality Award programme," says McLoughlin. "But every employee, every single one, laid the foundations for it through their excellence in general. We deserved it — no question about it — but that reaffirmation was important.

"Of course, in the first place Dubai Duty Free was a product of Sheikh

Quality

Mohammed's vision, and we felt it enormously important that we contribute in whatever way we could to his wider vision of Dubai and the UAE as a whole."

Dubai Quality Awards night, in November 1996, came weeks before Dubai Duty Free would round off its most successful ever trading year. In early January the company announced turnover of $184 million.

"We were squeezing every ounce of turnover we could out of our existing set-up," says Cidambi. "There had been plenty of improvements on the shop floor, and indeed in our systems, but the fact is Dubai Duty Free already boasted what was probably the highest spend per passenger of any duty free in the world."

Over preceding years, in order to maximize potential, Dubai Duty Free had opened a Luxury Watch Shop, launched its own fashion merchandising brand, AKARU, and Tom Ellery was still weaving his magic on the shop floor. Yet the fact remained that the existing floor space was as maxed out as many of the credit cards making their way up the escalator and out of Dubai Duty Free.

Ramesh Cidambi led Dubai Duty Free's efforts within Sheikh Mohammed's Dubai Quality Award initiative.

Fly *Buy* Dubai

Terminal 2 would alleviate some passenger congestion at the airport, and provide Dubai Duty Free with new shop floor capacity.

Away from the shop floor, the biggest relief for this pressure was being forged on the drawing board of Bechtel International. While today there are comments from several stakeholders that they were not involved in development of the $450 million new terminal, Dubai Duty Free was satisfied.

"From the earliest stages I found we were listened to," says McLoughlin. "From our point of view, this was the most important development in our history since 1983. It would transform Dubai Duty Free. We worked hard to ensure that we maximised our own benefits within the project."

While the architects were beavering away during the mid-to-late-1990s, elsewhere on the airport site there were practical developments taking place that would help relieve some of the pressure.

Situated directly across the runways to the north of Terminal 1, on the other side of airport grounds, Terminal 2 was under construction. Although this would be smaller and far less prominent, it would help alleviate congestion from Terminal 1 and allow into Dubai International Airport many smaller and newer airlines who were simply unable to get a foothold because of the dearth of space.

"Terminal 2 was a good opportunity. We had maximised our location in Terminal 1, this offered at least some outlet for expansion," says Horan.

Set over 12,000 square metres, Terminal 2 had the capacity to process 500 arriving and 1,000 departing passengers per hour through 22 check-in counters, equating to some 2.5 million passengers per year. The terminal also included 1,300 square metres of duty free shopping. In addition to some scheduled flights, Terminal 2 also catered for charter, executive and special flights, such as those of *Haj* pilgrims.

So confident were Dubai Duty Free that they introduced a special bulk purchasing desk at the duty free, in order to aid those who wished to buy a great deal of merchandise.

Bringing in British-based CIL International, Dubai Duty Free pushed the boat out.

"After opening an Arrivals Duty Free in 1987 and the main shop floor expansion in 1989, Terminal 2 was the first major increase in floor space we had enjoyed in nearly a decade," says Horan.

Based in Harlow, near London, CIL International's manufacturing plant had, over two decades, built a reputation for manufacturing, supplying, and installing retail stores, high street banking, and leisure environments. On the company's *CV* were major multi-site projects with Lloyds TSB, Panasonic, Fred Perry, Samsung, and Dunhill, among other.

"CIL came recommended for delivering innovation, but also for delivering projects on time and within budget," says McLoughlin.

For six months Dubai Duty Free plotted and schemed with CIL International, working up designs that would maximise and tease every ounce of benefit from that limited 1,300 square metre space in Terminal 2.

In the end it proved to be a success. Dubai Duty Free's twice yearly contract with the shop floor guru was still going on, and Ellery was heard to voice his approval.

On May 1, 1998, Sheikh Ahmed inaugurated Terminal 2. Today, the terminal handles around 35 scheduled carriers, along with a plethora of charter, executive aircraft, and specials. Peak season is usually around the time of *Haj*, when dozens of special flights may be programmed. Among them a plethora of carriers from the subcontinent, such as Pakistan's Airblue and India's Air-India Express, along with small Gulf-based airlines such as Falcon Express, many based in Iran, the likes of Caspian Airlines and Iran Aseman Airlines, along with a surprising number from Iraq.

Fly *Buy* Dubai

"Terminal 2 has been invaluable to the growth of Dubai International Airport," says Sheikh Ahmed.

The terminal was also a hit with Dubai Duty Free, as soon as it grew fully operational, providing an initial few per cent of additional turnover. After just several years this grew to around seven per cent.

Also growing was an awareness within Dubai Duty Free of the leadership role it could play in one of the most pressing issues of modern times. The Islamic Golden Age ranged from a period between the Eighth and Thirteenth centuries. It was a golden era for the Middle East, a time when the region's engineers, scholars, and traders made significant contributions to the sum of human knowledge and achievement in the arts, agriculture, economics, industry, law, literature, navigation, philosophy, sciences, and technology. Part of this renaissance saw a fundamental period of development in the way man approached agriculture.

This is known as the Arab Agricultural Revolution, and coincided with what can be described as humanity's first burst of 'environmentalism'. Many of the region's historians and authors commented on what they viewed as air pollution, water contamination, soil contamination, and other problems, all of which have only become all too apparent in more recent centuries. Books produced by Alkindus, Costa ben Luca, Rhazes, Ibn Al-Jazzar, al-Tamimi, al-Masihi, Avicenna, Ali ibn Ridwan, Isaac Israeli ben Solomon, Abd-el-latif, and Ibn al-Nafis all discuss these pressing issues, but are dated, in some cases, over a millennium ago.

It was the Industrial Revolution that set in motion modern environmental issues over the burning of immeasurable quantities of coal and other fossil fuels. Global warming became a household word, as evidence began to mount that something untoward was going on. Swedish chemist Svante Arrhenius had speculated about the problem in 1897, but it was not until 90 years later that serious evidence emerged. Increased amounts of carbon dioxide and other greenhouse gases were being proven to be a primary manmade component of warming, caused by burning of fossil fuels, land clearing and agriculture, among others, and led to an increase in the greenhouse effect. In 1987 the world population reached five billion, in 1999, just 12 years later, it reached six billion.

"The world was only just waking up to the damage done," says McLoughlin.

In the 1970s the Chipko movement was formed in India, influenced by Mahatma Gandhi. Their peaceful resistance to deforestation by literally hugging trees, which led to the coining of the term 'tree huggers', was

Quality

(top) The planet's environment was in crisis and corporate responsibility was a buzzword within Dubai Duty Free.

(right) Ibn al-Nafis was one of the writers from the Islamic Golden Age who wrote about the environment.

Fly *Buy* Dubai

another step on a long road that would culminate in the Earth Summit in Rio in 1992 and the Kyoto Protocol of 1997.

Post-Rio, Dubai Duty Free had begun to look at itself. Hard. The retail industry was at the cusp of a sea change. From being regarded as a sector where environmental impacts were of little concern, the general public were beginning to hold their retailers to account.

"Not only in response to public pressure, but for ourselves and a corporate responsibility, we decided to have a look at our operations and see what could, within reason, be done," says McLoughlin.

The retail industry had, in general terms, sought to maintain the view that as the industry did not manufacture anything, it had limited impact.

"It was clear to all of us in the company that Dubai Duty Free, along with the rest of retail, would see its stance shaped by consumer awareness, pressure from NGOs, increased media attention, new laws and regulations. We were going to have to be pro-active," says Horan. "Not just because we had to be, but we ourselves wanted to be."

Environmental integrity would be an increasing part of Dubai Duty Free's set-up. This started with identifying internal environmental and social impacts, which would become an integral part of business practices.

"From top to bottom, we looked at everything," says McLoughlin. "It was an enormous challenge."

This included addressing transportation and distribution issues, supply chain management, introduction of environmentally friendly products and recycling, as well as balancing the availability of locally produced products, which had always been a concern anyway.

"It was something that the government of Dubai endorsed whole heartedly," says Sheikh Ahmed. "Sheikh Mohammed recognises that, in this part of the world, for thousands of years life was only sustainable through man living in balance with the desert and its surrounds."

With the blessing and support of Sheikh Ahmed, during the mid-1990s, Dubai Duty Free's management pushed ahead with a review of its green credentials and acted where it was possible. Areas such as distribution and transport, energy use and carbon dioxide production, use of refrigeration, waste management and recycling, were all studied and amendments to Dubai Duty Free practices made.

In the Developed World, it is believed that two thirds of firms belonging to the retail industry have developed an environmental policy. The quality of the policies varies, but the most frequently covered issues are energy use, compliance with applicable laws, packaging and waste management,

Sheikh Ahmed had actively attempted to participate in, and promote,
Dubai Duty Free's environmental policy.

recycling, resource efficiency, and a reduction of the impact of operations. Most of these companies have implemented programmes to improve their environmental performance, though the extent of this work varies greatly.

During the Uruguay Round of trade negotiations of the General Agreement on Tariffs and Trade (GATT), the ISO 14000 series emerged, enhanced by the Earth Summit in Rio in 1992.

The International Organisation for Standardisation — ISO — is a Geneva-based international standard-setting body. The organisation benchmarks proprietary, industrial, and commercial standards around the world and has, for the most part, become the defining body in this area.

Its ISO 14000 environmental management standards have led the way for corporate environmentalism. While ISO 14000 was being snapped up by companies in the west, it was still all but absent in the Middle East.

"When you look at the ISO and see that a vast majority of the world nations are member bodies, correspondent members, or subscriber members, it shows the importance of its work," says McLoughlin.

Indeed, the nations without ISO Status today are mostly drawn from those countries mired in broken economies or considered, new or recently, failed states, including Haiti, Liberia, and Somalia.

"We weren't ready for ISO 14000, but that was no excuse for not striving toward many of its basic tenets," says McLoughlin.

Carbon footprint was still not a trendy jargon when Dubai Duty Free began identifying hot spots of energy consumption and optimising energy efficiency.

Next Dubai Duty Free also began a dialogue with its suppliers.

"Much of Dubai Duty Free product range is luxury, which means in most cases a great deal of high-quality packaging. No retailer would be prepared to cut its own throat and issue edicts that affected its bottom-line, but over time discussions with suppliers on product-specific issues such as PVC, and encouraging sustainably-managed forests in products that involved paper and packaging, would pay dividends.

"Just as we took the issue seriously, increased global awareness saw significant changes in the products and packaging of some of the world's biggest and most luxurious brands," says McLoughlin.

In Dubai, his team looked at recycling, labeling, stocking more energy efficient products, and others.

"During the 1990s Dubai Duty Free did a lot to reduce its carbon footprint," says Sheikh Ahmed. "It is all about corporate responsibility, something demanded of us by both the government and the general public."

Around 12,000 years on from the extinction of the Dire Wolf, Smilodon, Giant beaver and Mammoth, the world was only now beginning to wake up to the chilling fact that humanity itself might join that unhappy list. And of its own accord.

In December 1997, the Kyoto conference called on countries to ratify its protocol and commit to reducing their emissions of carbon dioxide and five other greenhouse gases.

More than ever, environmentalism was hip — and being legislated.

Within Dubai Duty Free this process was already underway, using ISO 14000 as a template, an international standard allowing organisations to focus environmental efforts against internationally accepted criteria.

"At present many countries and regional groupings are generating their own requirements for environmental issues, and these vary between the groups," says ISO President Mr Håkan Murby. "A single standard ensures that there are no conflicts between regional interpretations of good environmental practice."

Quality

While, in general, environmental policy in the GCC and Middle East was behind on the international curve, ISO 14000 had presented Dubai Duty Free with an internationally recognised set of standards that would draw the organisation ahead of the region at large.

"By the early 1990s, we were among the most environmentally aware companies in the UAE and arguably the region," says McLoughlin. "In all areas we were sharpening our approach."

It was an effort that was adopted by Dubai Duty Free staff. At their various housing complexes in Dubai, in an initiative from within their own ranks, they requested recycling bins and worked to reduce their carbon footprint.

"It is surprising how much an individual can contribute," says Anne Smith. "For example, a study in Britain showed that the UK generates 12 tonnes per capita per year of carbon dioxide emissions. It is about lifestyle and awareness."

"Our staff have helped us lead the way," says Smith. "It is humbling to see such effort. Over the years, through their own personal efforts in

Long before Al Gore had helped to drive the environment onto the global agenda, Dubai Duty Free was firming up its green credentials.

recycling and other areas, they have cumulatively saved thousands of tonnes of emissions."

In 1996, ISO 14001 was first published. This specified actual requirements for a comprehensive environmental management system. It applied to all the environmental aspects which an organisation has control over, and which can have a powerful environmental impact, both in terms of its locality and in the overall picture of global environmental degradation.

Dubai Duty Free, it was recognised, needed to provide a template for the UAE and Gulf, especially as a government-owned entity. To lead the project, McLoughlin turned to his Executive Office Manager and personal enforcer, Anne Smith.

"Anne was perfect to lead this initiative. No-one messes with her," says McLoughlin.

ISO 14001 sets organisations the task of implementing, maintaining, and improving an environmental management system, demands continual and demonstrative conformance, and seeks compliance with environmental laws and regulations. Certification is undertaken by an external third party organisation.

"ISO 140001 specifies requirements for establishing an environmental policy, determining environmental aspects and impacts of products, activities and services, planning environmental objectives and measurable targets, implementation and operation of programs to meet objectives and targets, checking and corrective action, and management review," says Smith. "It was a formidable task."

Organising a system that would systematically reduce the impact of Dubai Duty Free's activities on the environment required a root and branch assessment of Dubai Duty Free, with an even tighter eye than during the initial assessment several years earlier. The International Organisation for Standardisation is not without its critics. Computer security entrepreneur and Ubuntu investor, Mark Shuttleworth, stated: "...ISO is an engineering old boys club and these things are boring so you have to have a lot of passion..."

While the ISO and its vast compliance documents did not in themselves inspire passion, the cause itself was something else.

"The management of Dubai Duty Free — and indeed the staff, who invested themselves heavily in the project — showed a dedication to this project which was commendable," says Sheikh Ahmed. "It was gratifying to see such effort — and the resultant impact has ensured that Dubai Duty Free reduced our Carbon Footprint."

Quality

One of the most visible aspects of 'green thinking' is on the shop floor. Product stewardship initiatives such as packaging minimisation and refill solutions are to a certain extent consumer-driven, but their introduction and widespread use also depends on a commitment to environmental thinking, on the part of producers and the outlets in which they sell. It is a question of what comes first, the chicken or the egg, or in this case — consumer demands or consumer awareness.

"We have worked with Dubai Duty Free and indeed it is Nestlé company policy to ensure that our products are environmentally sound," says Alan Brennan, Regional Business Manager of Nestlé International Travel Retail. "Colm and his team are the most environmentally aware customers we have."

In an industry highly sensitive to consumer trends, greater focus on enlightening end-users to recycling, refill solutions, and environmentally sound packaging is sensible business practice. Brennan adds that Dubai Duty Free, while conscious not to compromise quality, is highly encouraging of its suppliers' initiatives in this area.

In addition to the aforementioned root and branch analysis of company operations, Smith led a drive to formulate and (later declare) its primary environmental objectives, those that would have most environmental impact. In order to gain most benefit for the environment, these would become primary areas of consideration within the process. Care had to be taken as Dubai Duty Free would be required to set specific goals and targets. An Environmental Management System established procedures, work instructions, and controls, all of which would target these achievable aims.

In 1999, Dubai Duty Free won its coveted ISO 140001.

"It was a drive in which every employee of Dubai Duty Free would have a responsibility," observes Smith. "Gaining ISO 140001 was a powerful message of our intention toward the environment. Losing it would be another message altogether."

Dubai Duty Free's Environmental Management System undertakes a comprehensive periodic audit to ensure effective operation, while a commitment to undertake four 'eco events' in the UAE each year takes the fight beyond being an internal effort. Over the years this has included a Kids Eco Garden at Dubai's Tennis Championships ('… a very subtle way of teaching kids about the environment…'), a Kids Club at the airport, and a high-profile event each November, where Dubai Duty Free teams up with the Emirates Diving Association to undertake a major, well-publicised beach cleaning operation on the beaches of Fujairah.

Fly *Buy* Dubai

ISO 140001 was the culmination of a vast amount of work, not least by Smith, who proved her mettle by pushing through a huge array of initiatives during the process that would claim certification. As the designated 'Tree Hugger' in Dubai Duty Free, Smith would also be the point-person when it came to one of the most contentious issues in retail today — plastic bags.

Plastic shopping bags are the world's most common type of shopping carrier, for the most part intended for a single use to carry items from a store to a home. The disadvantages are clear in that they are made of petrochemicals, a nonrenewable resource; when disposed of improperly they represent a hazard to wildlife; and as litter they clog drains. It was a growing and international problem. In Turkey, for example, where plastic shopping bags are a major environmental problem, Turkish people use on average 1.2 bags per day each.

Around the world there is a growing backlash against plastic bags.

The Australian federal government has considered action that would result in plastic bags being phased out. Charging is the most commonly used method of control. Generally, most German supermarkets charge between 5 and 25 cents per single-use bag, while Ireland introduced a €0.15 levy on every bag. This led to a 90 per cent reduction in use.

Other nations have taken a more radical approach. In the mountain kingdom of Bhutan, plastic shopping bags — along with tobacco and MTV — have been banned on the grounds that they make the country less happy, while in Bangladesh they are forbidden, thought to cause flooding during monsoons by clogging drains. San Francisco has become the first US city to ban plastic shopping bags, while the island of Zanzibar prohibited their import and use.

The conundrum for the duty free industry as a whole is what it can do.

"It's a compromise in environmental terms, and not really a contradiction," says Smith. "We have to operate, we have to give people something to carry their purchases in…what are the options?

"As well as being unsuitable for duty free, paper bags are far more than an issue for environment — cutting down trees, from bleaching, the chemical processes."

According to the *Worldwatch Institute*, plastic bag production requires 40 per cent less energy, results in 80 per cent less solid and 94 per cent less waterborne wastes, and generates 70 percent less air pollution than the manufacture of paper bags.

Plastic bags also take up less room in landfills. Reuseable canvas shopping bags continue to be touted as the natural alternative to plastic. In some ways this is true, but for airports canvas is unlikely to be viable.

"We have looked at jute," says Smith. "But you don't keep a jute bag at the back of your car when you are going to the airport, it's totally different. But we tried and ordered a large consignment, selling them at the checkouts for just a couple of dollars each. Only a few ever sold. When you purchase through a duty free you need something reliable to carry them in that will get your purchases all the way to your destination…and a businessman traveling is not going roll up a big reusable bag and carry it with him, is he? No, we must be realistic…"

"In the beginning, we used only the very thick, very good quality plastic bags. And that was a luxury rather than necessity," says Smith. "What we've done now is isolate the differing needs of the shop floor. Some areas require heavy bags, such as the liquor shop, or the food shop where people buy huge tins of Nido or Tang. They need very thick and very good quality bags. In the areas where light bags are suitable, such as for soft toys or small items, we reduced the thickness of the bag."

High quality bags are 120 microns and lesser quality 45 microns.

Silver screen star Julia Roberts pictured shopping with organic canvas shopping bags — a practical step in some retail environments.

Fly *Buy* Dubai

Ordering the latter equates to far more bags per ton — making environmental sense overall, and economic sense for Dubai Duty Free itself. Dubai Duty Free's turnover has increased by 20 per cent a year for the last 10 years, while the consumption of plastic bags has increased only by about 20 per cent overall during the same period.

According to *Worldwatch Institute*, factories around the world manufactured four to five trillion plastic bags in 2007. The same year Dubai Duty Free still used 550 tonnes of plastic shopping bags. In general the recycling rate for plastic bags is very low. According to the United States Environmental Protection Agency, only one per cent of plastic bags were recycled in 2000. Nearly 80 per cent of litter in the ocean comes from land-based sources.

Most aquatic life is threatened through entanglement, suffocation, and ingestion. One animal dissected by Dutch researchers contained 1,603 pieces of plastic. All sea creatures are threatened by floating plastic, from whales down to zooplankton; for example, sea turtles die as they mistake plastic bags for jellyfish. Dolphins are routinely found dead with plastic bags in their stomachs or windpipes.

"....Animals die because the plastic eventually fills their stomachs," Ocean Conservancy vice president Warner Chabot said. "It doesn't pass, and they literally starve to death."

"Our society, for thousands of years, lived by being in harmony with nature," says Sheikh Ahmed. "The seas represented a huge bounty. This is why we take such initiatives seriously."

Smith had led as Dubai Duty Free has reduced its usage of bags and struggled to use bags with a lower micron count. Yet she acknowledges that heavier 120 micron variety are probably better environmentally.

Heavy-duty multiple-use shopping bags are often considered environmentally better than single-use paper or plastic shopping bags, suitable for multiple uses as shopping or storage bags.

"Our bags must be the most reused plastic bags that ever existed!" observes Smith.

Quality

(top) A sea turtle with a strip of plastic bag in its mouth. Sea life is particularly affected by man's pollution.

(right) Anne Smith has driven the company's green efforts.

Quality

Sheikh Ahmed receives an OHSAS 18001 certificate from Colm McLoughlin, Anne Smith and Osama Al Gergawi.

The next phase of Dubai International Airport expansion would be defined by an iconic new control tower.

Chapter Twenty-Four

Five Thousand, Four Hundred

The great thing in the world is not so much where we stand,
as in what direction we are moving.
– Oliver Wendell Holmes, American author

"The Master Plan was, for the most part, ahead of schedule," says Sheikh Ahmed, referring to Dubai International Airport. "Through constant review Dubai International Airport coped well, but we were looking to 2020 and this was a challenge."

At the foundation of the airport, in the late 1950s, the then Ruler Sheikh Rashid bin Saeed Al Maktoum had backed his personal judgment that Dubai could become something in aviation. With little money at his disposal, it had been a leap of faith. By the late years of the century the emirate was now the region's aviation hub — but the next step, becoming an international hub, would require a leap of faith every bit as pronounced as that of Sheikh Rashid decades earlier.

Re-developing Dubai International Airport was an ambitious process that would take many years. The first phase — development, design, and building of a huge new terminal — would cost $450 million. This development began in earnest in 1998, when construction commenced on one of the biggest civil projects ever undertaken in the Gulf. But the actual process, from a Dubai Duty Free perspective, went well beyond the prolonged period of construction.

As they embarked upon the design process, Costain International was instructed by the Dubai Department of Civil Aviation to meet with stakeholders. Dubai Duty Free and Emirates were foremost among these.

"This was the starting point of a long relationship between ourselves and planners," says McLoughlin. "Between the start date and the opening of the new terminal, there would be literally hundreds of meetings and thousands of man hours invested in discussions between ourselves and project managers."

These would take the new terminal from concept to design board and then into reality. This was undoubtedly the biggest thing that had happened to Dubai Duty Free since its inception. The operation had grown far too big for its base, in a disused former kitchen in what was effectively a basement. Any amount of expansion, on the shop floor, through an arrivals shop, landside outlets, and with Terminal 2, were effectively stopgap measures as Dubai Duty Free sought to expand it sales. Through the likes of Tom Ellery, shop space on the main floor had been maximised and utilised to its fullest potential. There was little room for improvement.

"With the expansion, we were effectively morphing from our launch operation and being given the opportunity to forge exactly what we would become during the years of the new millennium. This was a key event that would define this company for years to come," says Horan.

Therefore the pressure was on to get it right. Over the months Dubai Duty Free defined what it would become and how the public would perceive both it and the shop floor. Failure to correctly transmit to Costain the essence of the company, and its operational requirements from a new concourse, would wreck everything that had been achieved. There was no room for mistakes.

Given that, Dubai Duty Free spent months on an internal project to assess the logistics of growing its business based upon a shop floor of around 5,000 square metres. As the company's management understood, the growth that Dubai International Airport's Open Skies policy allowed, in terms of passenger arrivals, meant a great deal of anticipation was required. DCA estimates were for a passenger throughput of 30 million by 2010, a huge increase.

In 1998, the Dubai Department of Civil Aviation unveiled plans for the spectacular new Sheikh Rashid Terminal, boasting a futuristic 118,000 square metre concourse, 800 metres in length and comprising five levels, designed to meet the expanding needs of travellers and airlines well into the new millennium. In addition to 27 fixed aerobridges and 47 movable passenger loading bridges, the plans called for 28 boarding lounges, 45 escalators, 17 moving walkways, a 7.5 kilometre baggage handling system, a new runway, and a 84 metre-high control tower equipped with state-of-the-art landing systems. The new facility, it was said, blended technology with the requirements of a burgeoning airport. A vast underground tunnel connecting Concourse and Terminal Buildings was 340 metres long, 33 metres wide, and over five metres in clear height. The terminal also boasted a 100-room hotel, cafés, bars, snack bars, and restaurants throughout the length of the new concourse. This development, claimed Costain, would push Dubai into a ranking as one of the top 20 airports in the world.

At the heart of this $450 million facility, its living, beating heart was a duty free complex spanning some 5,400 square metres of real estate.

"We felt we had got it right," says McLoughlin. "But having achieved that, the transition would in itself be a task."

Work began on the structure in 1998, a vast enterprise that would throw up its own demands on Dubai Duty Free, as thousands of labourers

Five Thousand, Four Hundred

Dubai Duty Free had gone as far as it could within its old environs. The huge airport development project represented a seismic opportunity.

Fly *Buy* Dubai

descended on the site and hundreds of construction vehicles arrived. The disruption that this giant project would create would go on for two years.

In 1999 Dubai International Airport recorded growth of 10.5 per cent. Some 10.7 million passengers passed through the airport, one million up on the previous year's 9.7 million. Total aircraft movements reached 132,708, an increase of 7.6 per cent. Some 90 airlines were operating out of Dubai International Airport, serving 130 destinations.

While the airport was achieving record results, Dubai Duty Free was mirroring this record-breaking achievement — posting a 4.4 per cent increase in sales for 1999, with turnover of $188 million.

It was a year characterised by well-managed turmoil, given the construction. In addition to preparing for a transition to the new terminal, the existing shop floor was in a state of flux as development work, specifically the connecting tunnel, meant huge interruptions in normal service. It was a very demanding period because contractors were being required to work in areas that were shop floor, and immediate stock holding areas. At some points in 1999, as much as a quarter of the shop floor was blocked off.

"It was a vast project," says McLoughlin. "There were upwards of 5,000 labourers on site, and, in addition to that small army, hundreds of construction vehicles and huge earthworks to contend with."

It was not just the impact on shop floor space. The airport site was dominated by cranes, trucks, tankers, and the like. The usual dozens of Dubai Duty Free transporters, feeding the shop floor with merchandise, often had restricted access issues and faced many hold-ups. The logistics of running a duty free became a complication, which several management members recall being a constant battle as they worked to maintain supply chains and keep the vast operation afloat.

Dubai Duty Free's record of year-on-year growth, announced at the end of 1999, would be maintained with significantly reduced floor space and a marked reduction in the number and variety of products available.

"Considering the interruptions and logistical problems, a 4.4 per cent increase in turnover, in fact, represented a remarkable achievement," says Sheikh Ahmed.

In view of an estimated average of a 15 per cent loss in floor space over the year and a 10 per cent loss in product lines and product variety due to the same reason, an increase in turnover of nearly one twentieth can be viewed as somewhat remarkable. The one advantage that Dubai Duty Free had during this difficult year was increased turnover from the Terminal 2

Five Thousand, Four Hundred

The vast building programme at the airport mean that shop floor operations were often in flux and the company fought to keep working smoothly.

shop floor, reflecting Dubai International Airport's need to increase passenger traffic there. But this was marginal.

"As management, we can plan things out to an enormous degree, overcoming major obstacles and achieving great things on paper," says McLoughlin. "But the success of this period sat squarely with our staff, who responded to the demands upon Dubai Duty Free stoically and rose to a grand challenge."

From the outset of the year there had been an expectation that Dubai Duty Free would see reduced revenues. Overcoming the odds and boosting revenue was a success that each of Dubai Duty Free's staff — by now over 600 — took a role in.

"We had launched with 100 employees and this had grown to over 600 at this point, in 1999," says McLoughlin.

A duty free operation is only as good as the team that works within it and certainly at Dubai Duty Free its teamship had been at the heart of growth. From the original 100 members of staff there are 59 who remain today. And that says a lot for any organisation, particularly after 25 years. It's not just

How the new Sheikh Rashid Terminal looked during its construction. (inset) The designer's model looked futuristic and unique, but creating it would prove a logistical challeinge.

Fly *Buy* Dubai

The company's success is recognised to be built upon its team, among them Lilian Vargas, Saba Tahir, Mohamed Nagutha, Mathew George, Antony Joseph, Richie Burley, Pascal Fernandes, Fiona Nagi and C.P. Joseph.

Five Thousand, Four Hundred

loyalty which has made people stay on — particularly when one considers that the majority of staff are expatriates longing to eventually get back to their homelands — it's the fact that they feel a total sense of belonging and being part of a 'family'.

There are so many different nationalities represented at Dubai Duty Free that it would be, for any human resources manager, a perfect nightmare to integrate everyone under one umbrella cohesively. But that has been the incredible situation at Dubai Duty Free. Today, there are more than 33 nationalities. They have been recruited not only from Dubai and other GCC countries but from such a diverse range of nations as the Philippines, the CSA countries, China, Pakistan, Lebanon, Morocco, Myanmar, Tunisia, India, Sri Lanka, Europe, and even from the Antipodes…and, of course, Ireland. In other words, from all corners of the globe.

They have been united in friendship, share the common language of Dubai Duty Free, and ardently adhere to the vision that began 25 years ago with the pioneering Irishmen.

Together they cover every aspect of a successful duty free operation, from management to office boy. And while new staff are constantly being taken on and trained, they have a very firm foundation of mentors to look up to — the many personnel who have been part of the Dubai Duty Free team since day one. Several arrived in the weeks before the operation opened in 1983 while others had merely days to adjust to new surrounds and the frenzy of activity which was going on as the last nail was being hammered into place and the final lick of paint was transforming the former kitchen into a shop floor.

McLoughlin — the 'father' of them all — has his own memories of the family he has created and shaped. He recalls the first people he recruited; the excitement everyone shared when the first inter-staff marriage was celebrated; and when people had their first babies.

"Over the years we have had fathers and sons working for us — and I think that says a lot for family loyalty," he remarks. He has been proud to watch those early pioneers move up the career ladder with Dubai Duty Free, and has felt a personal satisfaction with each long-service award he has presented and each promotion letter he has personally signed.

"I think the important thing is that people should work hard," said McLoughlin. "I think they should work honestly. I don't expect people to do anything I wouldn't do myself." And it is this philosophy that drives everyone forward at Dubai Duty Free.

From the day when the first training manuals were written in 1983 and

Fly *Buy* Dubai

the training sessions were held in whatever free space was available at the time, Dubai Duty Free has placed great emphasis on quality teaching. There is now a fully equipped training facility within the operation — a far cry from those early days when new recruits huddled in corners to learn the rudiments of the operation from experienced members of staff.

Each new recruit today enjoys at least a week of intensive training in the operation's classroom learning about Dubai Duty Free, its aspirations and its machinations, before each is moved to his or her respective area of work. The programme for new employees who will be interfacing with customers is more intense. This includes sales techniques, product knowledge, and the art of customer relations. Following the initial induction new recruits move into their respective areas of responsibility to learn alongside more experienced colleagues. But every so often they return to the classroom for anything from refresher courses and new product seminars conducted by suppliers' representatives to programmes which will help elevate them to higher positions within the company. Training is an ongoing process but it all helps employees to have sufficient knowledge of the products they are selling and of their industry. Training is not only for those on the shop floor — it covers every single department within the organisation and even management have to go back to the classroom from time to time.

Today, there are over 200 training courses conducted throughout the year.

"We had always kept pace with the need for training, as Dubai Duty Free has morphed from a new enterprise into a world class company, but the impending move to the Sheikh Rashid Terminal meant a great deal of change," says Nic Bruwer, head of Human Resources.

In 1997, slightly over 600 people were on the Dubai Duty Free payroll. By 2000, the year that the new Sheikh Rashid Terminal was scheduled to open, this would grow to well over 900. This represented a growth of 50 per cent.

"Achieving this, and getting the right people in all areas, was yet another challenge on the road to expansion," adds Bruwer.

While the internationalist nature of the operation meant that Dubai Duty Free was now recruiting from more nationalities than ever before, again emphasis swung to the Philippines.

Since day one, the archipelago had provided the biggest segment of staff for Dubai Duty Free. The company, by now, had a reputation.

By the 1960s, the Philippine economy was regarded as the second-largest in Asia, next only to Japan. However, the presidency of Ferdinand Marcos would prove disastrous to the local economy, sliding the country into severe economic decline. It was during this decline that the Philippines began to

Five Thousand, Four Hundred

export in bulk its most important natural asset — an educated and skilled workforce. The Philippine economy has grown heavily reliant on remittances as a source of foreign currency, surpassing even foreign direct investment. By 2007 there were over one million Overseas Filipino Workers (OFW), and just under 3,000 workers leaving the country for overseas jobs each day. Remittances from OFWs in 2007 was $14.4 billion, the fourth highest in the world behind India, China, and Mexico. According to some published estimates, workers in the six Gulf Cooperation Council states, whose number is estimated to be 10 million, transfer $30 billion annually to their countries. Based on Philippine Overseas Employment Administration data, the six GCC member-states employed 435,190 Filipinos as of December 2006, just under 100,000 were in the UAE.

"Colm visited Manila before Dubai Duty Free opened and the group of staff that eventually went to Dubai had begun to spread the word about the sort of employer that Dubai Duty Free is," says Angelito Hernandez, President of one of the Philippines' leading foreign recruitment specialists. "Inside a decade, whenever we were asked to seek a new batch of recruits for

Nic Bruwer,
Dubai Duty Free's
Human Resources
Manager.

Fly *Buy* Dubai

Among those influencing the fortunes of the company today are June Reid, Mohammad Tayyeb, Sayed Saifoddin, Vinayak V. Sirat, Magdy Al Sheikh, Christine Feliciano, Shirrin Sarkaree, Krishnan Valeri and Jasmin Micoyco.

Five Thousand, Four Hundred

Dubai Duty Free, the places were massively over subscribed."

Nearly half the extra 300 places made available during this pre-Sheikh Rashid Terminal period would be filled via the Philippines.

Dubai Duty Free's policy in the Philippines is one of inclusion. Most industries are concentrated in the urban areas around metropolitan Manila, while metropolitan Cebu is also becoming an attraction for foreign and local investors in recent times. Therefore other regions tend to be ignored by foreign employers — meaning there is a great deal of employee potential.

"Dubai Duty Free insists that jobs are advertised in provincial newspapers throughout the country," says Bruwer. "In many areas, otherwise ignored by many recruiters, Dubai Duty Free gets to cherry-pick some very talented young people."

Dubai Duty Free's reputation now precedes it.

"People get to know, through family members, friends, an informal network, about employers and what they are like," says Bruwer. "In the Gulf people were wary, because there were horror stories.

"The excellent way Dubai Duty Free looks after and treats its staff quickly became well known, with the result that when positions in Dubai Duty Free are advertised there is an overwhelming response."

At times, by the late 1990s, such was Dubai Duty Free's reputation that positions advertised in the Philippines are oversubscribed by as many as 200 applications for every position that became available.

"This means that Dubai Duty Free applicants include a great many high-quality people. Many graduates, top class personalities, committed workers," says Bruwer. "There is no doubt that Dubai Duty Free has benefited from the way it is set up, the way it works with its employees, as this has attracted the cream of the employment market in the Philippines and elsewhere."

With 300 new employees coming in during 1998 and 1999, representing a 50 per cent increase in Dubai Duty Free's employee base, it was a quality on which the company would come to rely. During this period the company's training programmes grew in size and scope.

"We were being provided with the real estate, a vast new shop floor inside a superb terminal, Dubai's Open Skies policy was working, and we were bringing in and developing a strong employee base," says Horan. "Although there was a great deal going on, coping with ongoing construction work and preparing for the new terminal, we had a sense that things were going in the right direction.

"It was a time of tremendous optimism."

Five Thousand, Four Hundred

As Dubai International Airport expanded, so did the Dubai Duty Free family.
Thousands of new positions were being created.

Deputy Managing Director George Horan on the shop floor of the new Sheikh Rashid Terminal.

Chapter Twenty-Five

A New Beginning

A journey of a thousand miles must begin with a single step.
— Lao Tzu, Chinese philosopher

On April 15, 2000 the new terminal at Dubai International Airport opened. Four decades had passed since the inauguration of Dubai International Airport itself. But the genius behind the airport was not forgotten.

"It was named the Sheikh Rashid Terminal in honour of the success of his vision," says Sheikh Mohammed. "Around a half a century earlier, Sheikh Rashid had saved Dubai with his Creek Development Scheme. It is remarkable to think that his determination, leadership, and courage set in motion the development of Dubai from its very humble beginnings until the present day. The new terminal was a 21st century artery into the emirate, the airport an example of his vision, and I believe quite appropriately named in his honour—the Sheikh Rashid Terminal."

The late Dubai Ruler's legacy has never been forgotten. Aviation had been one of Sheikh Rashid's tools for progress. DCA's $540 million expansion programme was led by this spectacular new terminal, a futuristic 118,000 square metre concourse, 800 metres in length, and comprising five levels, designed to allow capacity. The terminal blended the latest in passenger-interfacing and airline technology with a very human understanding of passenger and airline needs, drawn from the expertise of many.

"The human element was drawn from hundreds of meetings, DCA officials concerned with the terminal, and the architects and planners, all interfacing with carriers and other stakeholders," says Jamal Al Hai, Director Strategy and Management Excellence, Dubai Department of Civil Aviation. "This allowed Dubai's terminal to be as advanced as any in the world."

April 2000 had been the focus of Dubai Duty Free operations for some time. From hundreds of man hours with Costain International, when the die was cast and designs for the new terminal were completed, a new phase began.

"The building in itself was 21st century. It was incumbent upon Dubai Duty Free to look the part," says McLoughlin.

During 1999, Dubai Duty Free's management team and designers worked on the look that, it was hoped, would propel Dubai Duty Free not only into the new millennium, but also drive the company into the world's top five duty frees worldwide in terms of turnover.

"We had the space, plus also the customer base, as the airport itself was doing better each year. The expansion, we believed, would allow us to shoot for one billion dirhams in turnover, around $272 million, and then on to $500 million within a few years," says Horan. "The figures were mind-boggling, but that was the stated objective and we believed within the realms of possibility."

During the early part of 1999, the 5,400 square metres of space allocated to Dubai Duty Free shopping in the new terminal were shaped and finalised through an elongated design and consultation process.

"From the beginning, Dubai Duty Free had forged a relationship with us, and other suppliers, which was well beyond simply a business transaction," says Ramesh Prabhakar, CEO and Director of Rivoli, one of the UAE's most important watch retailers and brand representatives. "Colm and his team worked with us. This allowed our expertise of our products to have an effect on the shop floor. When it came to the Sheikh Rashid Terminal, ourselves and others were allowed an input which impacted upon the design process, which ultimately helped both ourselves and Dubai Duty Free through better sales."

Prabhakar's view is mirrored by others. Gangu Batra, the venerable and widely respected boss of newspaper and book giant Jashanmal, adds: "Since 1983 Colm, George and their team set out to work with us, as a partnership, and the loyalty they projected has been repaid by their suppliers over the years. Dubai Duty Free is one of the best clients you can have in Dubai, a fact borne out by the number of commercial relationships that remain in place since 1983."

In the late spring of 1999, after nearly a year of development work, a reasonably final working design had been reached. It had encompassed thousands of man hours, and including dozens of meetings with suppliers, and a huge internal Dubai Duty Free process.

During this period Sheikh Ahmed was presented with some drawings that represented the direction that Dubai Duty Free intended to go — if they could secure his blessing.

"The work that had been done was outstanding," recalls Sheikh Ahmed.

Sheikh Ahmed's green light was the starting point for a 1999 dominated by a development programme far bigger and more complex than anything the company had previously entered into, even considering the difficult days of late 1983. The shop floor was huge. But so were the logistics of managing it on a day-to-day basis. Dubai Duty Free would require a bigger logistics network, including a vast new warehouse and more supply trucks. A 50 per cent increase in staffing levels also meant more housing, transport, catering, and support services. Dubai Duty Free's suppliers also needed to be on board. A larger, busier shop floor equated to higher volumes and therefore a larger product base. They too had to tool themselves for the anticipated leap in trade.

"We were used to a growth in business with Dubai Duty Free. Such was their

A New Beginning

The new shop floor was a result of thousands of man hours of design and consultations with suppliers.

success that this was normal," says Tawhid Abdullah, chairman of Damas. "But what we were gearing up for was now, instead of a large, yet steady annual increase in supply demand, something of a surge. No supplier was unhappy at this, of course, but it did mean that we had to increase stock levels and be far more deft in assessing the needs of the shop floor and staying on top of them."

At the end of 1999, some four months before the new terminal was due to be inaugurated, Dubai Duty Free announced annual turnover of $188 million. This represented well over half a million dollars a day and well over $20,000 per hour.

Given preparations for the Sheikh Rashid Terminal, and the interruptions on the shop floor that this caused, it was a satisfactory year. Dubai Duty Free had scooped its usual slew of awards, including from the Raven Fox Awards, *Business Traveller*, and *First Class* magazine.

Frenchman Jérôme Golmard had won the Dubai Tennis Championships in February, defeating Nicolas Kiefer in the final. He reached a career-high ranking of 22 in 1999. The 6ft 2in left-handed Frenchman was arguably the least renowned of all Dubai winners in the history of the tournament, before or since, but was enjoying his best ever year and would reach a career-high ranking of 22 that year. Yet Golmard's unexpected success came in a year when Dubai won two ATP Tour Awards: as World Series tournament of the year for the 1998 rendition of the tournament; and later in 1999 an award for excellence. Dubai's rising stocks in the tennis world came at a time when Dubai Duty Free was already working to increase its interest within the sport.

There were also pre-Sheikh Rashid Terminal preparations in cyberspace. The USSR's launch of *Sputnik* in 1957 spurred the USA to create the Advanced Research Projects Agency, known as ARPA, in February 1958, which led to the foundations of cyberspace, but the Web as we know it today is recognised as being invented by English scientist Tim Berners-Lee in 1989. By 1992, the Internet had one million hosts. By 2008, there were an estimated 1,407,724,920 users, or 21.1 per cent of the world population, according to Nielsen/NetRatings. In 1993 the White House opened its first home page, a year later it was joined by the Vatican. In April 1994, two students at Stanford University started a guide to keep track of their personal interests on the web. They named this guide 'Yet Another Hierarchical Officious Oracle' — Yahoo!.

Just as Dubai Duty Free was entering a new phase in the physical world , it was time to update a company website that was looking decidedly 1990s, in a project led by in-house IT expert Ramesh Cidambi.

In 1999 www.dubaidutyfree.com went live. After an initial surge resulting from launch publicity, traffic leveled off at around 400,000 hits per month. In addition to the latest company press releases, the site offered details of Dubai Duty Free's

A New Beginning

products and features, competition winners, news, calendar of Dubai Duty Free events, and details of the company's environment policy.

Before the end of the year another feature was to be added.

"We were brainstorming for a long time, wanting to do a special one-off, both to mark the passing of the Millennium, and to recognise the inauguration of the Sheikh Rashid Terminal," says McLoughlin. "I recall one idea being that we should sell x amount of tickets and draw, at the same time, a whole bunch of $25,000 winners. For a while this was considered."

Eventually this idea lost ground and Mohi-Din Binhendi, Bharat Godkhindi, and McLoughlin kicked around several concepts for a time.

"I forget who came up with a million dollars," says Godkhindi. "But as soon as this idea was raised there was no other concept discussed."

A millionaire is measured as an individual whose net worth exceeds one million units of currency. For the most part the threshold is nominally measured in dollars, both because this is a global currency and because the unit value of the dollar gives possessing one million dollars a certain level of prestige.

Currently, depending on which publication is read, there are around 10 million millionaires around the globe. The 11th annual World Wealth Report from Merrill Lynch/Cap Gemini found that there are 9.5 million individuals of High Net Worth (HNW), this being the 'measurement' of a millionaire, with total assets of $37.2 trillion. Of these, three million are in North America, 2,900,000 in Europe, 2,600,000 from Asia-Pacific, 400,000 are Latin American, 300,000 Middle Eastern, and 100,000 African.

"At first, we believed that we would create one, maybe two if the promotion had legs," says Binhendi. "But I always suspected that the idea would catch fire."

In late summer, Dubai Duty Free went public with its latest ground-breaking promotion. Every passenger arriving, departing, or transiting through Dubai International Airport is welcome to enter the draw. The draw is limited to only 5,000 tickets, so there is a great chance to be a Dubai Duty Free Millennium Millionaire. The 5,000 tickets were to go on sale at Dhs. 1,000 each, or $278, and there was no restriction on the number of tickets that each passenger could purchase.

"I thought, 'we are on to something here'. We really believed that people would respond, and that there would be mileage for Dubai Duty Free and Dubai International Airport," says Binhendi. "I was not ready for what happened after the announcement."

Dubai Duty Free believed that it would take the autumn, and perhaps toward the time of the opening of the new terminal, in April 2000, to shift 5,000 tickets. Only if sales went well, along these lines, would the Millennium Millionaire be extended to a second draw.

Fly *Buy* Dubai

Dubai Duty Free's innovative Millennium Millionaire promotion has created millionaires all over the world.

Fly *Buy* Dubai

"The tickets, let's face it, are not cheap when you compare them to draws elsewhere in the world, so we thought that while there would be demand, it would probably be steady. But then again the prize was far grander than most," says McLoughlin.

Draws originated in southern Italy, the word 'tombola' is in fact Italian. The concept was by now well established around the world. But very few had ever had a prize of such value, less still one million dollars cash. The annual Christmas lottery in Spain, the Sorteo Extraordinario de Navidad, is believed to be the largest in the world and in 2003 its prize fund reached $2.2 billion, with a first prize of $470 million. Yet every number entered in this lottery is on 170 tickets, which are often sold in fractions, and therefore the *El Gordo* prize is usually split by many winners. *El Gordo* ('the big one') therefore creates many millionaires.

Yet with a one in 13,000 chance of winning any prize at all, even *El Gordo* paled into insignificance against a guaranteed one in 5,000 chance of winning $1 million.

The media lapped it up. Working this out for themselves, the international media responded with a flourish of interest. Dubai Duty Free received millions of dollars of free publicity on television, radio, in newspapers, and on the Internet, across the world.

For several news cycles, Dubai Duty Free won a great deal of praise, and in some places a little derision. Some commentators believed that the public would not respond. It was a view that was not without merit, and there were a few within and around Dubai who had quiet doubts.

"Although we had sold thousand upon thousand of tickets for Finest Surprise — at Dhs. 500, or $139 — we thought that there would be some reticence, as $278 is, of course, a lot of money," says McLoughlin.

Few people will forget the ecstatic images of Dubai Duty Free's first Millennium Millionaire, with Taiwan-based Ashok Nankani being presented with his $1,000,000 cheque by Sheikh Ahmed. Tickets for this first draw had sold out weeks before, and well over 2,000 of the 5,000 tickets for the second draw had been sold. It was clear that Dubai Duty Free had another extraordinary success on its hands.

As often would be the case, every winning ticket had its own story. After purchasing the ticket during a business trip to Dubai in October 1999, Nankani returned home to his office in Taiwan at a consumer electronics company he runs. He mentioned the promotion to his employees and gave them an opportunity to share the purchase price of the ticket with them — if, of course, they were interested in taking a chance. Three employees took him up on the offer. And when, a few weeks later, the phone call came through to tell Nankani that he'd won, each became a quarter of a million dollars richer just through that visit to Dubai Duty Free — and his good luck! Nankani, like many winners after him, donated some of his money to

A New Beginning

Sheikh Ahmed, Colm McLoughlin (left) and Abdulla Ansari (right) officiate over a draw that would create yet another Millennium Millionaire.

charity and enjoyed a luxury family holiday. He also bought himself a prestige luxury car. This was his way of compensating for never having won with his Finest Surprise tickets that he'd bought during previous visits to Dubai.

His three members of staff had other ideas for their win from ticket number 1237. They variously invested their shares, spending the money made from the investment; built homes, or ensured their children enjoyed a good education.

It's the sort of thing that dreams are made of, and in ensuing years Dubai Duty Free would go on to make dollar millionaires out of travellers representing nearly 25 nationalities.

The tickets — which take the form of stylish credit cards — can be bought by departing, arriving, transiting, or online buyers, and details required at purchase include passport number and flight number. Online buyers have to provide further details including credit card particulars and nationality.

In most cases, and when he is able to, Sheikh Ahmed is the person presenting the million dollar cheque to winners. He acknowledges that while other duty free outlets around the world have 'borrowed' the concepts of Finest Surprise and Millennium

Fly *Buy* Dubai

DUBAI DUTY FREE
MILLENNIUM
MILLIONAIRE
WIN $1,000,000

Date: 5th April 2005

y ~Mr. Giuseppe Depetro .... against this cheque

DOLLARS One ~Million Only .... US$1,000,000

5·3698·000·000   Sheikh Ahmed Bin Saeed Al Maktoum

Australian Millennium Millionaire winner Joe Depetro.

A New Beginning

Millionaire from Dubai Duty Free to their own benefit, 'imitation is the sincerest form of flattery'!

Over the years since the first Millennium Millionaire draw, the ecstatic winners have all expressed incredulity when they have been notified of their win. A great many have reported feeling they were the butt of a hoax or even a joke when they were telephoned by Dubai Duty Free to be told of their win. But when reality kicks in nothing can beat the astonishment and the utter glee. A Bahraini who won the draw in 2003 said: "Winning one million dollars is the biggest surprise of my life." Another recipient, a Syrian who won in 2003, was so delighted he said his heart began to beat really fast. "I want to thank Dubai Duty Free for the opportunities they are giving to people. It's a fair and square deal and everybody gets a chance to win a million dollars. This win has really made my day."

And so the thank you messages roll in and Dubai Duty Free management could be forgiven for feeling like benevolent benefactors when they see the happiness etched across the many faces of the people who have taken a chance and become millionaires!

As the region's duty free industry began to grow and take prominence on the world stage, the Middle East Duty Free Association (MEDFA) was formed in 2000 as an officially recognised entity within the global duty free and travel retail business. Among the founding members was Dubai Duty Free — and it has remained a strong player in the Association since the beginning. MEDFA is set up as an establishment within the Dubai Airport Free Zone.

McLoughlin, a past President of MEDFA who remains a board member, explained that the *raison d'être* behind MEDFA was to create a body which would bring official recognition to the region's duty free industry, raise awareness of the industry's contribution to the greater travel and tourism industry infrastructure, and provide representation for its member companies.

Its main objectives are to encourage closer links between retailers and brand suppliers in the Middle East to facilitate the growth of the industry in the region; to group together all people who are active or who show an interest in these fields; and to organise seminars, conferences and training programmes related to the region's duty free retail industry. Moreover, its aim is to represent the region's duty free industry *vis-à-vis* government agencies and the travel industry.

*A stylistic view of the shop floor. In 2000 Dubai Duty Free
reached turnover of $222.3 million.*

Chapter Twenty-Six

2001

If you mean to profit, learn to please.
— *Winston Churchill, British statesman*

From the second quarter of 2000, Dubai Duty Free traded from its new 5,400 square metre shop floor. The Sheikh Rashid Terminal was an instant success, both from the perspective of the company and the airport itself. The Sheikh Rashid Terminal was a fundamental part of a $450 million expansion plan for Dubai International Airport. Along with Terminal 2, this gave the airport capacity to handle up to 22 million passengers a year. In 2000, 10.7 million passengers passed through Dubai International Airport. Toward the end of 2000 Dubai International Airport was serving 100 airlines, nine new carriers scheduling flights that year — Finnair, Angel Air, Ugandan Airlines, Condor, Mozambique Airlines, Tchad Airlines, Martinair, CSA Czech Airlines, and APA International Airlines. The same year scheduled arrivals rose by over eight per cent, to 57,632.

In January 2001, McLoughlin signed off on a press release that announced that the company had reached annual turnover of $222 million on the year, an increase of $46 million, or just under 20 per cent, over 1999.

"2000 was a memorable, memorable year," says McLoughlin. "The Sheikh Rashid Terminal gave us a huge lift. The brilliant staff at Dubai Duty Free had done the rest."

In addition to operations in the new concourse, Dubai Duty Free had opened 'The Irish Village', a pub in the terminal styled after the successful outlet with the same name based in The Aviation Club complex. There was an announcement with Tejarji, the UAE's leading Business-to-Business online marketplace, MEDFA, a new vendor support programme launched, and a Dubai Duty Free Service Desk opened at the 598-room Jumeirah Beach Hotel.

"What was more exciting," says McLoughlin, "was the knowledge that 2001 was going to be the first full year that we traded from the Sheikh Rashid Terminal. That meant we would surely build on our 2000 results markedly. Aside from this, there were so many great things happening away from the shop floor, a plethora of fresh initiatives."

For a year that will be remembered in the annals of modern history as one of darkness, there were several positives in 2001 that, with a distant view several years on, make up what was a seminal year in the short history of

Fly *Buy* Dubai

Dubai Duty Free. There was the inauguration of the Shergar Cup, the launch of Cultural Voyages *(see Chapter 27)*, the first Dubai WTA Tennis Tournament, and a co-branded card with American Express (Amex). But arguably the biggest, as far as the shop floor was concerned, was an extraordinary milestone.

The now-famous Dubai Duty Free Finest Surprise promotion had been launched in December 1989 to coincide with an extension of the shop floor. It had been viewed as a short-term thing, even a one-off, but bloomed into a concept that was not only intrinsic to Dubai Duty Free, but by now the longest-running promotion in duty free history.

Not only that, but in 2001, tickets went on sale on the shop floor for the 1,000th luxury car offered by Dubai Duty Free.

"One thousand luxury cars of this calibre represented some $100 million of vehicles," says Salah Tahlak. "That makes Dubai Duty Free Finest Surprise one of the biggest promotional events ever staged worldwide."

The Finest Surprise concept had been so successful that dozens of airports around the world had adopted the concept and run their own promotions. If copying was the sincerest form of flattery, Dubai Duty Free was flattered.

"When I travel somewhere and, passing through an airport, see a car, or a yacht, or a motorcycle, or some other luxury prize being raffled, it is with a sense of pride that this idea has had such an impact not only on Dubai, but on the industry in many countries," says McLoughlin.

On from 1989 and some 999 vehicles later, Dubai Duty Free was aware of the additional publicity that would come with the milestone.

"We looked for a special car for number 1,000, something that would attract attention," says Tahlak.

The signature vehicle that would be offered as Finest Surprises car #1,000 was unique. The Ferrari 550 Maranello was a two-seat Gran Turismo sports car produced by the Italian auto giant. First built in 1996, the 550 was a powerful front-engined V12 coupé. Car lovers acclaimed what was the first of its kind not seen since the Daytona. The Ferrari 550 Maranello was positioned as the company's highest-end model, from a stable of vehicles that were all top class. The model number is derived from total engine displacement — 5.5 litres — and Maranello referred to the town where Ferrari's headquarters are located.

Initially intended as a one-off promotion, 12 years later Finest Surprise was now offering to its customers a prize that was the marquee car produced by the world's top marque car producer. How far they had come?

Dubai Duty Free also branched into fresh pastures. As early as 1999,

*The elite Ferrari 550 Maranello was the 1000th Finest Surprise
car offered by Dubai Duty Free.*

discussions had begun with New York City-headquartered American Express, that would lead to Dubai Duty Free's first venture into the fast-expanding co-branded credit card market. It was an area that the duty free industry as a whole had mostly skirted at that point.

Co-branding is when two major brands join hands to enhance the usefulness and image of their product. In the case of a credit card, it is a partnership between the issuer and, in most cases, a retail service-provider. Many co-branded cards, the model on which a Dubai Duty Free card was proposed, are also rebate cards that provide the consumer with benefits such as extra services, cash or merchandise. The aim of both associated brands is to gain market share, promote loyalty, and propagate use. By the turn of the millennium, in the USA this category of credit card was the fastest-growing segment of the credit card industry. Therefore the concept was steadily gaining ground around the world.

"By 2000, our turnover had topped $220 million, and our growth had attracted several credit card firms, who made overtures to us.

"Around this time we gave the idea some consideration," says

(top) Krishnamurthy Kumar.

(left) The American Express brand is estimated to be the 14th most valuable in the world.

Krishnamurthy Kumar, Finance Manager.

Many retailers continued to push their own in-house proprietary cards that could mostly only be used in-store. Yet while major names, such as Harrods, and chains, such as Marks and Spencers, for example, due to their notoriety or size, could press home a viable case for their in-house efforts, most others were opting for wider use credit-cards. Certainly, given inherent access restrictions in the case of a duty free operation, however large, an in-house card would be largely impractical. It was not a direction that Dubai Duty Free could take with any degree of success.

With co-branded cards, both parties reach a wider customer base. The credit card issuer is responsible for distribution, while the partner offers the benefits that differentiate between the cards and target customers. The benefit to card holders comes in the form of reward schemes and discounts offered by the credit card company.

There were definite plus and minus factors that demanded Dubai Duty Free's consideration. The main downside was that Dubai Duty Free did not wish to peddle credit card debt to anyone. The global credit crunch was still maybe a decade away, but even then newspapers were full of comment about a black hole of debt in which a growing number of households worldwide had anchored themselves.

"We didn't do that," says McLoughlin. "It wasn't our business. So as the idea was mooted within our management team we looked hard at the firms that had approached us."

American Express is best known for its credit card, charge card, and travellers cheque businesses, and is one of the 30 stocks that comprise the Dow Jones Industrial Average. *BusinessWeek* would go on to rank American Express as the 14 most valuable brand in the world. As Dubai Duty Free looked at its credit card operations, it was also clear that Amex was noted as being careful as to whom it offered credit cards to. There were no unwieldy credit limits. Their business practices toward consumers were sound. Because of this, Amex also had a certain cachet.

American Express had been founded in 1850 with the merger of the express mail companies owned by Henry Wells (Wells & Company), William Fargo (Livingston, Fargo & Company), and John Butterfield (Butterfield, Wasson & Company), as an express business. In 1882, American Express expanded into financial services. The first cards were paper, with the account number and holder's name typed. It was 1959 before the plastic cards with which we are familiar today were used. In 1966, American Express introduced the Gold Card, and in 1984 the Platinum Card.

Fly *Buy* Dubai

"The more we looked at Amex and several others, the more Amex stood out as an ideal brand to be associated with," says Kumar. "By 2000 we were locked in negotiations."

BusinessWeek had put the worth of the American Express brand at $14 billion. While Dubai Duty Free's own brand was growing, the link required that both brands should benefit.

"It was also incumbent upon us to ensure that our cardholders enjoyed benefits beyond those enjoyed by holders of the bog standard Amex card," says Kumar. "From the outset there was a decision made that card holders would receive ten per cent discount within Dubai Duty Free, yet we hoped to build more."

As co-branded credit cards proliferated, many examples were criticised for failing to negotiate good terms for their members, and comment that the organisation fronting the card often looked at immediate benefits and did not care how badly these cards reflect on their brand.

"From the outset we looked at the co-branded market carefully. One of the prime complaints was that many tended to set punitive interest rates on late payments or defaulters," says financial analyst Malcolm Corrigan.

The average default rate set by the major cards was 25 per cent, while co-branded cards were, in some cases, set a default rate at over 30 per cent. With such issues dealt with between both, over a period of months Amex and Dubai Duty Free put together a portfolio of restaurants and shops around Dubai that would offer discounts to customers utilising the Dubai Duty Free/Amex co-branded card.

"The response was amazing. Even Amex was surprised," says Kumar. "Within weeks, hundreds of hotels, restaurants malls, shops and retail organizations had committed themselves to the programme."

From a few per cent off a final bill, to a basket of free items from some, and discounts from others, the list grew into a compelling programme. It was the first time that Amex was called upon to produce a full booklet, detailing card members' benefits.

"It was an eye opener, for sure," says Kumar. "The card was due to launch with spectacular support form merchants around Dubai."

Of course, the Dubai Duty Free link also had enormous benefits for American Express, in that a secure foothold in Dubai encouraged more merchants to accept Amex in preference to, or alongside, Visa and MasterCard, the industry leaders in terms of volume, if not brand.

In 2001, the co-branded card was launched officially. Within a year thousands of cards were in circulation. But this was far from the end of work

The Dubai Duty Free/Amex credit card would go on to boast one of the broadest packages of benefits of any co-branded card in the world.

Fly *Buy* Dubai

on the Amex deal.

"It is easy to launch a card and sit back. They quickly lose relevance," says Kumar. "Colm dictated that we should ensure that our card remains fresh and attractive, in a market place that would increasingly become crowded as other card companies and other Dubai and international brands joined hands."

The UAE federation turned 30 years old in 2001, the nation's constitution having been signed on December 2, 1971. The seven emirates — Abu Dhabi, Dubai, Ras Al Khaimah, Sharjah, Ajman, Fujairah and Umm Al Quwain — had long since combined into a cohesive state where citizens thought of themselves as Emiratis. But Dubai Duty Free's co-branded card would go on to have a strong pull for 'Dubaians', be they Emiratis or expatriates.

"Irrespective of nationality Dubaians were defined as those living in Dubai and across the UAE, who value the cosmopolitan and spirited lifestyle of Dubai and seek to experience the best of the city," says Kumar. "Since 2001 we have constantly built upward."

In 2007 the co-branded card was revamped with a fresh, sleek,

Shergar was one of the greatest thoroughbred racehorses of all time.

modernistic design and an embedded smart chip to enhance security. At the same time, Dubai Duty Free announced a fresh slew of participating outlets that ensured that the card 'provides greater rewards and the best of everyday shopping, entertainment, sporting, dining and travel experiences to Cardmembers.

Over half a decade, the card programme had grown to encompass a vast array of outlets in the emirate.

"This gave our card one of the biggest footprints of any co-branded card in the world," says McLoughlin. "It grew beyond any expectations we had at the beginning."

The card now entitled holders to special rates at the First Class, Business, and Marhaba lounges, and Marhaba Services at the Dubai International Airport, offered entries into Millennium Millionaire and Finest Surprise, and tickets for the Dubai Tennis Championships and other Dubai sporting events.

"We have witnessed remarkable success in the use of the co-branded Dubai Duty Free American Express Card and worked to take it several notches higher to enhance card holders' everyday lifestyle needs. Dubai is growing as a consumers' paradise, which makes it important for us to align the offerings of the card and to ensure that the benefits are in line with consumers' expectations," adds Kumar.

From a thoroughbred credit card, to actual thoroughbreds, Dubai Duty Free's stable was expanding. In 1981, a horse owned by the Aga Khan achieved that rare feat of transcending the sport of thoroughbred racing and becoming a sporting icon. In winning the Epsom Derby by a record ten lengths, the longest winning margin in the race's 226-year history, the son of Great Nephew earned a spot in *The Observer*'s 100 Most Memorable Sporting Moments of the Twentieth Century. Shergar went on to be named European Horse of the Year in 1981 and was retired from racing that September.

His place in history was assured, but the story of the bay colt with a distinctive white blaze would become infamous. On February 8, 1983, he was kidnapped by masked gunmen from the Ballymany Stud in County Kildare, Ireland. Shergar's body was never found.

In 2001, 20 years on from his record-breaking summer, the champion's name was adopted as the title of something new in racing. The element of team competition was traditionally confined to well-meaning but uncompelling international jockeys' challenges. The Dubai International Jockeys' Challenge had been one of the most successful of these. Dubai Duty Free had been one of the principal sponsors. For four years this event had brought together pairs of top jockeys representing Asia, Europe, North America, Australia, and the UAE.

The movement behind the Shergar Cup was bold, unusual and — for a sport bound to its traditions — most non-traditional. Taking its inspiration from golf's Ryder Cup, the concept was of a team event, comprising two teams of five jockeys, competing on a six-race card at Britain's Goodwood racecourse, later moving to Ascot.

The venture was the brainchild of then British Horseracing Board chairman Peter Savill. Leading a progressive new administration, Savill was looking to introduce something new to the sport in many areas. While a team event would take some time to take root, Savill believed that, in time, racing could replicate golf. A sport based on individualism, golf occasionally eased itself into team competition and, over the years its Ryder Cup burst into life and by the millennium competed with the four Majors as the sport's premium event.

"Racing has always allowed us to spectate, participate and socialise," said Savill. "But it has lacked team competition. This exciting new event will help bring to racing the dynamism and interest of international team competition. It has the potential to establish itself in equivalent terms with golf's Ryder Cup."

The Shergar Cup was to have a similar international theme to golf's bi-annual classic, but where Europe's finest took on America, Europe's opponents would be the Middle East. In later years, as the event evolved, the Middle East would become the Rest of the World.

Internet betting firm Blue Square would be title sponsors of the Shergar Cup in 2001, but Dubai Duty Free also moved to add the event to their growing sports portfolio.

"By this time we were sponsoring top class races in several countries, perhaps most notably at home where the Dubai World Cup meeting had grown into the world's most important meeting and the Dubai Duty Free was second only to the big race itself," says McLoughlin. "But there was also a growing commitment to Newbury and other European tracks."

The Shergar Cup had clear appeal. The vision of forging something of the scale of the Ryder Cup had appeal. It was something that Dubai Duty Free was happy to get involved with from the beginning, during early years as a support sponsor.

That year's team captains were arguably the two most influential men on turf racing: Robert Sangster for Europe and Sheikh Mohammed for the Middle East. And over ensuing years, as the event grew and matured, other

The ebullient John McCririck with Breeda McLoughlin (right),
Carmel Horan (left) and Sinead El Sibai.

famous names took charge of the teams, and the Middle East team became Rest of the World. Then England manager Kevin Keegan, a keen racegoer and golfer, was one team captain.

Keegan's Europe recorded a convincing 157-83 victory over the Rest of the World, after which he said: "I've not lifted too many trophies recently so it makes a pleasant change. The lessons from last year have been taken on board and in ten to fifteen years this could be one of the big events in the calendar.

The inaugural Shergar Cup set down the roots of a competition that continues to grow and, soon afterward Dubai Duty Free became the event's title sponsor. But while the 2001 event was a milestone for the sport, it, like everything else during that difficult summer, would become secondary to one of the most infamous events in modern history.

The winning European team following their success in the 2008 Shergar Cup.

*A unique and appalling photograph of the World Trade Centre site in the
days after the September 11 atrocity.*

Chapter Twenty-Seven

September 11

Islam is a civilising religion that gives mankind dignity. A Muslim is he who does not inflict evil upon others. Islam is a religion of tolerance and forgiveness and not of war, of dialogue and understanding.
— Sheikh Zayed bin Sultan Al Nahyan, father of the UAE

Summer is traditionally a busy time at Dubai International Airport. The summer of 2001 was no exception. Ensconced in the Sheikh Rashid Terminal, the main Dubai Duty Free shop floor was humming.

The company had anticipated a rise in sales, not only due to the extra floor space but also thanks to a vastly expanded product range and a swathe of new innovations — coupled with a sharp increase of passengers.

In 1959, Dubai's tiny airport had opened with its then ruler, Sheikh Rashid, dictating an 'Open Skies' policy. Over four decades later this had established Dubai as a genuine international hub. The new terminal, named in his honour, gave the emirate a renewed sense of direction and purpose. International airlines across the world were responding. 2001 was shaping like a record year.

"It was an exciting time," says Sheikh Ahmed. "The Dubai government's investment had captured attention in the industry. We were seeing strong growth."

September 10, 2001, had been a typical day. Tens of thousands of passengers passed through the airport. On their way, they purchased their KitKats, bottles of whiskey, newspapers and chocolate. Dubai Duty Free's employees were, it seemed, helping to drive the company to yet another record year.

"For many members of management, plus our pioneers, the staff who had joined us at the beginning, this was our eighteenth year in Dubai," says George Horan. "The Rashid Terminal had injected a fresh sense of purpose and excitement. The company had such an amazing sense of direction."

The morning of September 11 went more or less the same as its predecessor. The tills on the shop floor hummed with activity.

"It was a nondescript day," says Mathew George, a pioneer. "One which had come and, seemingly, was set to go without anything out of the ordinary to make it stand out."

In Dubai Duty Free's management offices all had gone as normal on the morning of September 11, 2001. Perhaps the most notable element of a mostly ordinary day was when the tennis committee had met, a regular feature on the 12-month programme between tournaments in Dubai.

"Even in those dark early moments of the attack, it was clear to me that this would have huge repercussions for aviation, and the Middle East," says McLoughlin. "While our hearts were with those whose lives were being taken in the United States, my mind was already working out the immediate impact upon Dubai Duty Free."

The situation in America grew worse with channels reporting that other aircraft were under the control of terrorists. Then came the Pentagon and Pennsylvania incidents. All air traffic in North America was grounded. Like hundreds of millions of others, the routine of McLoughlin's life was lost as the unthinkable events of that day unfolded on his TV screen.

International reaction to the disaster was unanimous. Shocked governments around the world offered condolences. UN Secretary-General Kofi Annan called the attacks "deliberate acts of terrorism, carefully planned and coordinated".

A sombre and visibly shaken British Prime Minister Tony Blair said the world's democracies must "fight this evil", adding that this sort of attack was "perpetrated by fanatics, utterly indifferent to the sanctity of human life".

The Muslim world expressed similar sentiments. Turkish Prime Minister Bulent Ecevit was reported by Reuters as saying: "The United States of America is face to face with one of the greatest tragedies in its history, something that could affect the entire world."

Palestinian President Yasser Arafat said: "We are completely shocked. It's unbelievable. We completely condemn this very dangerous attack, and I convey my condolences to the American people, to the American President and to the American administration, not only in my name but on behalf of the Palestinian people."

From the United Arab Emirates, President Sheikh Zayed and Vice-President and Prime Minister Sheikh Maktoum both sent private cables of condolence to George W. Bush, while the Minister of Information and Culture, Sheikh Abdullah bin Zayed Al Nahyan, stated: "The government of the United Arab Emirates condemns these terrorist attacks. These criminal and horrifying attacks necessitate a strong and comprehensive international campaign to eradicate terrorism in all forms and manifestations.

On September 13, UAE Foreign Minister Rashid Abdullah Al Nuaimi spoke with US Secretary of State Colin Powell, and conveyed the condolences of the UAE leadership, government and people. President Sheikh Zayed bin Sultan Al Nahyan was not a leader given to public admonishments, but the hour required leaders across the Muslim world to issue a clarion call and offer a true view of their religion. He stated:

> *'Islam is a civilising religion that gives mankind dignity. A Muslim is he who does not inflict evil upon others. Islam is a religion of tolerance and forgiveness and not of war, of dialogue and understanding. It is Islamic social justice which has asked of every Muslim to respect the others. To treat every person, no matter his creed or race, as a special soul is a mark of Islam, that makes us so proud.*

> *'In these times we see around us violent men who claim to talk on behalf of Islam. Islam is far removed from their talk. If such people really wish for recognition from Muslims of the world, they should themselves first heed the words of God and His Prophet. Regrettably, however, these people have nothing whatsoever that connects them to Islam. They are apostates and criminals. We see slaughtering children and the innocent. They kill people, spill their blood and destroy their property, and then claim to be Muslims.'*

The venerable UAE President Sheikh Zayed bin Sultan Al Nahyan was outspoken in his condemnation.

Fly *Buy* Dubai

The shop floor was subdued in the wake of September 11 as the public deferred travel amid a world crisis.

September 11

There was a markedly subdued atmosphere on the shop floor of Dubai Duty Free that afternoon and evening. The world was experiencing a 'JFK' moment. It was a defining moment. Few adults would not remember where they were when they heard, and experienced vicariously, the horrors that day.

The aviation world reeled. All North American air traffic was grounded. Elsewhere in the world, amid the uncertainty, passenger cancellations spiked. Those who arrived at Dubai International Airport were full of apprehension.

"I had never felt such a strange atmosphere in the airport," says Khalifa Al Zaffin, Director of Engineering and Projects, Department of Civil Aviation. "It is normally a place of anticipation and excitement."

Author Douglas Adams had written in his *The Long Dark Tea-Time of the Soul:* "…It can hardly be a coincidence that no language on Earth has ever produced the phrase, 'as pretty as an airport'. Airports are ugly. Some are very ugly. Some attain a degree of ugliness that can only be the result of a special effort…"

Yet Dubai International Airport had been at the vanguard of a global transition from sterile, grey buildings that sought to simply shift passengers around, to 21st century buildings, living communities that many would dub Airport Cities. The Rashid Terminal had a soul, and a personality. Its visitors did not simply pass through. In ordinary times they browsed and shopped, chilled out in its many breezy cafés and bars, tucked into meals, and passed their time a world away from the draughty halls of airports past.

On September 11, however, the convivial atmosphere was gone. A pall of apprehension hung over those who chose to travel. Elsewhere in the world aircraft had been hijacked. People had died. No-one wanted to be in an airport under such circumstances. Those that were looked uncomfortable. Their mind was certainly not on shopping.

"Although September 11 was an anomaly, in that the public were simply not buying at all, this was the beginning of a dip in revenue as international confidence in aviation stuttered," says Ramesh Cidambi.

The US authorities quickly pinpointed Osama bin Laden and his Al Qaeda organisation as chief suspects behind the events of September 11. Bin Laden was in Afghanistan. A brief stand-off would lead to an invasion of the country that would oust the Taliban.

Operation Enduring Freedom, a military campaign to destroy Al Qaeda camps inside Afghanistan, began in late 2001 when British and American Special Forces infiltrated Afghanistan while aiding anti-Taliban militias, backed by air strikes against Taliban and Al Qaeda targets.

In December 2001 leaders of the former Afghan mujahideen and diaspora met in Germany to agree a plan for the formulation of a new democratic government. Hamid Karzai was appointed Chairman of the Afghan Interim Authority and would go on to become President.

Once again the Middle East was in the international news for all the wrong reasons. Some 49 countries were recognised as being a part of the international coalition taking on the Taliban, including Australia, Bahrain, Canada, Egypt, France, Germany, India, Jordan, Kuwait, Pakistan, Russia, South Korea, Turkey, the United Kingdom, and the USA. There were newsmen embedded with troops on aircraft carriers, based in neighbouring countries, reporting from throughout the region. Just as the world had been there for that 'JFK' moment on September 11, during the last weeks of the Taliban régime the news media fed the world a constant stream of coverage.

The terrible acts of September 11, resulting in in-depth coverage of the Taliban and their extreme ideals, along with the instability of the war, created another set of conditions to be overcome. The Middle East was in the midst of a series of public relations body blows that served to cast a shadow on the region and to allow those armed only with ignorance to influence global perception of Islam.

Particularly in the USA, but also across the western world, there were numerous reports of incidents of harassment and hate crimes against Muslims, Middle Easterners, and 'Middle Eastern-looking' people. There were reports of verbal abuse, attacks on mosques and other religious buildings, and assaults. On television screens across the world so-called experts, some with a paucity of fact to support their statements, were given free reign to opine.

You won't find anyone in Dubai Duty Free who links their campaign of late 2001 with these circumstances. But you will find many outside of the company who give them credit for what became one of the most noted campaigns ever to feature on CNN.

"We have always been aware of our responsibilities in promoting Dubai and the UAE," says McLoughlin. "The timing of the campaign was coincidental. If there was a residual impact then we were happy for that."

At the same time that an international Coalition was executing a war in Afghanistan, in the autumn Dubai International Airport and Dubai Duty Free had commissioned and were at the latter stages of working on one of the biggest cultural promotion exercises ever undertaken on international television.

September 11

The TV campaign, which took the viewer on a 'Cultural Voyage' of Dubai, would commence broadcasting on CNN on November 4. The campaign had a reach to 241 million viewers in Europe, Africa, Asia, the Middle East, and Latin America, and would run for nearly two years.

As a whole, 'Cultural Voyage' consisted of 24 different vignettes, or mini-documentaries, conceived, produced, and filmed in Dubai. Each would provide a global audience with insight into a separate aspect of Dubai, UAE, and Arab-Islamic culture. The themes included falconry, henna, pearling, perfumery, Arabian horses, architecture, dhow-building, and Arabian music and dance.

"Although Dubai is already established as a top business and leisure destination, there is a need to go beyond the commercial success story and focus on aspects of Dubai's heritage that are still relevant to modern day life in Dubai," said Sheikh Mohammed bin Rashid Al Maktoum at the time. "This CNN campaign is a great initiative by Dubai International Airport and Dubai Duty Free. It perfectly captures our rich and diverse culture and sheds light on the people and traditions of Dubai."

While Dubai spoke for itself, the campaign came to be seen as speaking for the Middle East as a whole and, in pursuing its goals, promoted regional culture. Over two years, a total of 24 vignettes were created, filmed and produced by CNN. An initial schedule of eight vignettes were produced and a further 16 mini-documentaries produced over the ensuing 12 months, the filming schedule tapered to ensure that subject matter remained relevant.

"This campaign has provided CNN International with a unique opportunity to visually capture the essence of Arabia and broadcast that to millions of people, many of whom are unaware of the rich diversity of life in Dubai," said Kevin Razvi, Executive Vice President of TBS International's Advertising Sales for News, who worked on the project. "In each vignette the people we feature are real-life characters who talk about their own particular job or hobby with a genuine passion, whether they are a pearl diver, a boat builder or a henna artist. The end result is a visually compelling mini-documentary that we believe will appeal to a global audience."

Each spot was introduced by a co-branded Dubai International Airport and Dubai Duty Free billboard, and was followed by a 45-second TV commercial featuring either the airport or the duty free. An average of four ran each day over the two-year period.

"It was an enormously successful campaign," says Sheikh Ahmed, "both in terms of promoting Dubai and in terms of the exposure generated for Dubai International Airport and Dubai Duty Free."

(top) The Dubai International Airport and Dubai Duty Free campaign was hugely successful and had wide ramifications.

(left) CNN anchor Wolf Blitzer. CNN International's reach is more than 200 million households and hotel rooms in over 200 countries.

September 11

"For the investment, which was not insubstantial, Dubai Duty Free received massive exposure and the vignettes were themselves very well received," adds McLoughlin.

A caveat to the Dubai-specific benefit of the 'Cultural Voyages' campaign still remains unspoken. The late 2001/early 2002 period was a key time in world affairs. The post-September 11 period unleashed tensions and saw the Middle East fixed in an uncomfortable spotlight. For a time, no-one could predict what would come next.

'Cultural Voyages' provided global insight into the region, its heritage and what the Middle East stands for," says Sinead El Sibai. "The campaign could not have come at a better time. Hundreds of millions of people were offered a window into the region, precisely at a time when such a thing was needed."

A difficult year ended, despite the unforeseen events of September 11, with Dubai International Airport and Dubai Duty Free having fought their way through the tight spot. Despite some difficult weeks during the summer, a total of 13.5 million passengers passed through the airport, registering a growth of 10 per cent over 2000. Some 14 million passengers had been projected; however the international crisis, coupled with airlines utilising larger aircraft, meant that aircraft movements were in negative territory for the first time, registering a five per cent drop. The number of airlines operating out of Dubai International Airport stood at 96, serving 137 destinations.

For Dubai Duty Free, that post-September 11 wobble did just enough to prevent the company crashing through the quarter billion dollar mark. But nonetheless, record annual sales of $245 million represented an 11 per cent increase over sales in 2000. The previous year's $222.3 million had driven Dubai into the world duty free top ten. An increase of over $23 million placed Dubai as the seventh biggest in the world.

The Cannes Film Festival is one of the biggest cultural events in the world today —
a focal point of The Belle Époque.

Chapter Twenty-Eight

The Belle Époque

So, where is the Cannes Film Festival being held this year?
- *Christina Aguilera, American singer*

Dubai Duty Free ended the year seventh biggest in the world in terms of turnover, but resoundingly the best in terms of status. In October, McLoughlin and his team returned to Cannes, as they did every year.

Years earlier, Dubai Duty Free's management had attended the Tax Free World Association Exhibition in Nice. No-one had heard of Dubai and they were very much the outsiders. However this did not last. Some 18 months after Dubai Duty Free opened, in 1985, they had secured the industry's highest accolade: a Frontier Award. Considered the Oscars of the duty free industry, not only did the small team from Dubai leave with an Oscar, but they bagged the biggest award, Airport Retailer of the Year.

By 2001, McLoughlin and his team were no longer the new kids of the block. If anything they were old pros. By now there were six Frontier Awards at home in Dubai.

Nice had by now been discarded by TFWA for the glamour of Cannes in southeastern France, one of the best-known cities of the French Riviera and, of course, host of the annual Cannes Film Festival. A city famed for its various luxury stores, fancy restaurants, and prestigious hotels, Cannes' American sister city is Beverly Hills.

Archeological evidence suggests that there were civilisations in the area around Cannes by the 2nd century BC, a fishing village, which over subsequent centuries grew to be a small Ligurian port and later a Roman outpost. By the 10th century the town was known as Canua, a name that seems to have been derived from 'canna', meaning a reed. In the 18th century, both the Spanish and English attempted to capture the nearby Lérins Islands, but were defeated by the French; but it was the early 1800s before Cannes itself grew in importance. June 1838 is viewed as the beginning of the Belle Époque, the Beautiful Era, when construction of a harbour began. This brought new life to Cannes and the population rose. The 20th century marked the height of Belle Époque, marked by new luxury hotels such as the Miramar and the Martinez, while the city was itself modernised.

The summer casino at the Palm Beach and the Cannes Film Festival are probably the best facets that Cannes is known for today, but it is a striking and beautiful city that has much more to offer than gambling and film stars.

Fly *Buy* Dubai

These include La Croisette, the Musée d'Art et d'Histoire de Provence, the Quartier des Anglais, and the 21 days Carnival on the Riviera.

In May 2001 the Cannes Film Festival was 55 years old, by now by far the most influential and prestigious film festival alongside Venice and Berlin. That May 20 films had competed for the prestigious Palme d'Or. Italian director Nanni Moretti's La stanza del figlio ('The Son's Room'), the tale of how a psychoanalyst and his family go through profound emotional trauma when their son dies in a scuba diving accident, claimed the Palme d'Or.

But while the Cannes Film Festival was undoubtedly the focal point of Cannes' calendar, the attractions and glamour of the modern Belle Époque era attracted a weight of conferences. The economic environment is based on tourism, a majority of which is drawn from business fairs. Among those are the Cannes Lions International Advertising Festival, the International Festival of Games, and Festival de la Plaisance. And one that remained the fastest-growing during this era, in terms of stands sold, delegates attracted, and companies represented, was the Tax Free World Association Exhibition.

In 1990, organisers had been forced to make a public statement on Frontier Awards night, defending moans within the industry that Dubai was dominating the industry's Oscars.

A decade on from that statement, and 15 years on from Dubai Duty Free's arrival at the Tax Free World Association Exhibition for the first time, McLoughlin and his team flew to Southern France, landing at the Côte d'Azur International Airport. A decade and a half earlier, the team had been outsiders.

"No-one wanted to know," says Breeda McLoughlin, who was seconded to the task of leaflet distribution. "They did not know where we were from, nor did they care too much."

"In those early days, we were out of a limb," says George Horan. "By now we were under siege from suppliers and by those wanting to be suppliers."

Horan was not kidding. In 1985 some of those gathered for this annual industry fest thought Dubai was either in Saudi Arabia, or perhaps rural America. But now McLoughlin, Horan, and others lived much of their time in Cannes, not browsing the Musée d'Art et d'Histoire de Provence and wandering the Quartier des Anglais but trapped in a diary of meetings spaced 30 minutes apart.

As industry leader, Dubai Duty Free's shelves at the Sheikh Rashid Terminal now had cachet - as well as millions of potential customers flowing through Dubai International Airport each year. At an event which brought together the world's duty free industry, and a vast majority of international suppliers, the emphasis was on persuading Dubai Duty Free to give more space to existing products, or persuading them of the merits of new ones.

"A lot of friendly persuasion goes on," says Horan.

Toward the end of these long Cannes days comes the industry's black-tie dinner - the Frontier Awards. In 1985 Dubai Duty Free was, to borrow racing terminology, the rag of the field, a complete outsider. By 2001 it was odds-on that McLoughlin would be called to the stage to claim the company's seventh Frontier Award and its third as Airport Retailer of the Year.

"We would take nothing for granted," says McLoughlin, "but I would have been disappointed if we had not been in the running given Dubai's record over the previous year."

It was a period in which the Sheikh Rashid Terminal had boosted Dubai Duty Free turnover and standing, and concepts based upon the Millennium Millionaire and Finest Surprises had continued to sweep across the industry. Post-September 11, Dubai Duty Free had come out fighting with its CNN 'Cultural Voyage' campaign, while there had also been the tennis.

The early years of the Dubai Tennis Championships had been won by a roll call of some of the best tennis players of the 1990s, the likes of Karel Novacek, Magnus Gustafsson, Wayne Ferreira, Goran Ivanisevic, Thomas Muster, and Àlex Corretja. The latter was a lively Spaniard who reached a career-high singles ranking of World No 2 in 1999, a year after winning in Dubai.

For a week each year, Dubai Tennis Stadium thronged to the rhythmic sounds of top class tennis and staccato volume of 5,000 people a day. Adding to an impressive tally of industry awards, the Dubai Tennis Championships had been awarded the ATP Tour Award for services to players in 1998, in 1999 the International Group of ATP Award for Excellence, along with World Series Tournament of the Year.

"The players looked forward to visiting Dubai," says Salah Tahlak. "The time that had been invested in building relationships with managers, trainers, players, and the tennis world had seen the Dubai Tennis Championship grow. Within five years Dubai had risen from its inaugural event to become a recognised stop on the tour calendar. Each year, the field grew in quality."

The ATP Tour comprises of tennis tournaments including the ATP Masters Series, ATP International Series Gold, ATP International Series, ATP Challenger Series, and Futures tournaments. It is a crowded calendar, in which the ATP Entry Ranking, a 52-week rolling ranking and ATP Race, a year-to-date ranking, decides the best players in the world.

(top) Martina Hingis brought glamour and plenty of attention to the women's game.

(left) Salah Tahlak with Swiss star Roger Federer.

The Belle Époque

Away from the glamour of the court, it is one that demands a great deal from players. Mark Philippoussis observes that most people "don't realise that I live out of a suitcase". It is a widely repeated complaint.

"From the outset, Dubai has set out to define itself from other tournaments by being clearly the best when it came to looking after players," says Tahlak.

Dubai began looking at the Womens' Tennis Association (WTA) Tour in 1999.

"No-one ever told us, 'You cannot have the WTA Tour here', it was never indicated," says Tahlak. "So before the idea went anywhere we defined the clothing parameters that would be adopted."

The WTA Tour is the elite tour for professional women's tennis, including the four Grand Slam tournaments, tracing its origins back to the inaugural Virginia Slims event of 1970. If the Seventies had been the years of Margaret Court-Smith, Billie Jean King, and Chris Evert, the 1980s had belonged to Martina Navratilova. The 1990s, however, had been kind to the WTA Tour with household names like Steffi Graf and Monica Seles vying for attention, and the glamour of Gabriela Sabatini and Martina Hingis ratcheting up the glamour associated with the sport.

And 1998 had been the breakthrough year for a young Russian player named Anna Kournikova, when she burst into the WTA's top 20 rankings for the first time and scored impressive victories over Hingis, Lindsay Davenport, and Graf. Most of Kournikova's fame has come from the publicity surrounding her personal life, as well as numerous modelling shoots. During Kournikova's debut at the 1996 US Open, the media began to take notice of her beauty and soon pictures of her appeared in numerous magazines worldwide.

"Anna Kournikova was also a good player, people tend to forget or discount that," observes Tahlak. "She reached the semis at Wimbledon and the quarters in Australia."

Some thought Kournikova's non-tennis activities a distraction from the sport itself, but the WTA's profile grew immeasurably.

"There were no real doubts from our side," says McLoughlin. "When a ladies tournament was suggested, we agreed that this should be looked at closely."

The WTA was very keen. Dubai had been a big success story on the men's circuit and its stadium was considered one of the very best outside of the Slams. What was more, Dubai Duty Free was looking to offer a $600,000 prize fund for its event.

411

Fly *Buy* Dubai

"Negotiations were relatively simple with the WTA. Dubai had everything in place and a top notch record," says Tahlak. "The only concern was scheduling. We went into this hoping to create a fortnight of tennis, running the men's and women's events back-to-back."

The WTA comes out of the negotiating process with praise from Tahlak, who led Dubai's negotiating team. In 2000, when the WTA announced its tour calendar for 2001, there, in February, was the Dubai Women's Tennis Open.

"We did a lot of work to introduce ourselves to the players," says Tahlak. "Just as between our tournaments we spend time talking to players and their agents, we presented ourselves to the WTA Tour and looked to introduce Dubai to that new audience."

Founded as a Tier II event, with a view to quickly becoming bigger. There was an explosion of interest in the hard courts of the Dubai Tennis Championships. The men's week, in 2001, ended when Spaniard Juan Carlos Ferrero won an abridged final after Russian star Marat Safin retired through injury in the second set.

But the stars of Dubai's fortnight of tennis that year were the ladies.

"There was tangible excitement," says McLoughlin. "All the hard work in telling people who we are, and the reputation we had built as one of the very best hosts in terms of looking after players, paid off when we attracted some of the best women players in the business. This included the then current World Number One Martina Hingis and French Australian Open and French Open winner Mary Pierce.

Hingis arrived in Dubai at, arguably, the very peak of her career. Weeks earlier, in the Australian Open she had defeated Serena Williams 6-2, 3-6, 8-6, and gone in to pummel Venus Williams in a semifinal, handing Venus her career-worst defeat, 6-1, 6-1. The Swiss starlet was in a 209-week run as World No 1 and had won five Grand Slam singles titles - three Australian Opens, one Wimbledon, and one US Open.

"Martina was one of the world's top sporting names," says Tahlak. "It was important for the growth of Dubai to get someone of her class here, especially for the inaugural tournament."

The buzz surrounding Hingis' appearance added something special to Dubai's tennis that year, and despite her stardom Tahlak reports that she was one of the easiest players with which he has had to deal.

"She was completely unaffected and a pleasure to work with, always ready to do anything within reason to help promote the tournament and the sport," says Tahlak. "Sometime later the WTA would name this the Best

The arrival of the WTA tour in Dubai was a source of much excitement and created a tennis fortnight for the Dubai Tennis Championships.

Tennis starlet Anna Kournikova competed several times in Dubai and brought with her a great deal of publicity for the Dubai Tennis Championships.

Fly *Buy* Dubai

Tournament of the Year. This was a big, big honour for us."

It was then, perhaps, poetic justice when Hingis made smooth progress into the final, where she dispatched French Wimbledon finalist Nathalie Tauziat 6-4, 6-4.

The 2001 Dubai Tennis Championships had generated millions of dollars worth of media and television coverage for Dubai. Hingis, her colleagues in the WTA Tour, and the men's event, had been filmed and photographed for two weeks with an ever-attendant Dubai Duty Free logo somewhere in the background. The fortnight was a resounding success for Dubai Duty Free itself.

Seven months after Hingis' presentation with the Dubai Women's Open trophy on centre court closed the two-week Dubai Tennis Championships, another sort of trophy was in focus. McLoughlin and his team had put on their tuxedos and evening gowns and were seated prominently at the Frontier Awards dinner. Fifteen years earlier there had been no expectation, now the group from Dubai had the burden of expectation on their shoulders that rests with a favourite.

"In a way, we were enjoying our own Belle Époque," he observes.

After the year they had - and returning to Cannes having won Airport Retailer of the Year the previous year - the weight of expectation was heavy. But worth it. Dubai Duty Free became the first duty free operation at that time to win two consecutive Airport Retailer of the Year Awards.

The Belle Époque

Colm McLoughlin with a Frontier Award statuette, won at the end of a year that Dubai Duty Free could well consider their own Belle Époque.

A stylised satellite image of the coast of Guinea-Bissau on the west coast of Africa.
The country has the world's 175th largest economy in terms of GDP.

Chapter Twenty-Nine

Matching Guinea-Bissau

Unidade, Luta, Progresso.
— 'Unity, Struggle, Progress' the national motto of Guinea-Bissau

President Kumba Ialá's tenure as President of Guinea-Bissau was not viewed as a success, characterised as it was by sackings of ministers and other officials. Poor financial management led the World Bank/IMF to suspend aid. A former Portuguese colony, the Republic of Guinea-Bissau in western Africa is one of the smallest nations in continental Africa, bordered by Senegal, Guinea, and the Atlantic Ocean. Yet if President Ialá (a.k.a. Yala) is not recalled as the most successful head of state since the nation's hard-fought independence in 1974, at least his tenure marked a period of calm. In January 2000, he won a Presidential election with 72 per cent of the vote, the final chapter of a disruptive civil war that took place between 1998 and 1999.

President Ialá's job was to build upwards in a country attempting to recover from a long period of instability, within a fragile political situation. This meant building upon the nation's valuable agricultural base and developing its fishing, palm kernels, timber, cashew nut, and ground nut exports.

In 2002, exports would total $54 million, Guinea-Bissau's main trading partners being India, the USA, Nigeria, and Italy. That same year the International Monetary Fund (IMF) rated the Guinea-Bissau economy as the world's 175th biggest, sorted by gross domestic product (GDP), the value of all final goods and services from a nation in a given year. Calculated at government official exchange rates, the nation's GDP was around $296 million.

While the around 1.3 million Guinea-Bissauians lived in hope of a brighter future, some 7,564 kilometres away from the capital, Bissau, Dubai Duty Free was enjoying the fruits of the sort of steady leadership that was being hoped for from President Ialá. At the end of 2002, the company issued a press release that announced that Dubai Duty Free had smashed through the one billion dirhams barrier. At the close of business on December 31, turnover for 2002 stood at $306 million, equating to around $840,000 a day and nearly $35,000 an hour.

"It was an extraordinary effort, more than $50 million up on 2001. And, this propelled us into the world's top five duty frees in terms of turnover," says Colm McLoughlin. "Dubai International Airport was growing at such a rate that this reinforced the belief that we would, in time, reach half a billion dollars."

According to figures released on 2002 by the International Monetary Fund, World Bank, and CIA World Factbook relating to GDP, Dubai Duty Free's turnover also exceeded that of the likes of Dominica, Tonga, São Tomé and Príncipe, Kiribati, Micronesia, Palau, the Marshall Islands, American Samoa, the Cook Islands, Anguilla, and Tuvalu, these 11 having a total of nearly one million citizens. Dubai Duty Free's turnover was more than the combined GDPs of the world's ten smallest economies in 2002, as published in the CIA World Factbook, including the Falkland Islands and its half million sheep.

Recognising social responsibility has never been a problem for Dubai Duty Free. The company was green (ISO 140001 had been certified in 1999) and socially aware, having launched an educational support programme for needy children. But, considering the company's turnover, management began to look at what could be done to develop a charitable arm.

Dubai Duty Free's turnover is in excess of the Falkland Islands with its half million sheep and many penguins.

420

Matching Guinea-Bissau

While many businesses make regular charitable donations as part of their corporate social responsibility programmes, a special few are prepared to go that extra mile to give something meaningful back to the wider community.

"We were determined to be one of those," says Horan. "At the beginning it was done on a piecemeal basis, when the need arose or a good cause was brought to our attention."

This effort grew into an education programme launched for needy children whereby for a number of years grants were made to pay for school teachers in developing nations such as Mongolia and Vietnam, and several Dubai-based charities received regular donations.

In addition, the Dubai Duty Free Staff Benevolent Fund chips in with a donation each year.

"Informally, at least, there was a committee of management. But as the company grew, and could do more, we did," says Horan. "But as requests and demand grew, we decided to make it more formal."

Considering that Dubai Duty Free had a higher turnover than many poor countries' GDP, it was a natural progression. Says Sheikh Ahmed, under

The 750 square kilometre Caribbean island of Dominica depends on tourism and agriculture for its economy.

Fly *Buy* Dubai

(top) In the wake of the Asian Tsunami, the Foundation participated in several support efforts, including the rebuilding of a village in Sri Lanka.

(left) A rehoused family in Sri Lanka.

whose patronage these efforts occurred: "It is a responsibility that Dubai International Airport, Emirates, and Dubai Duty Free have never shirked. Every year hundreds of thousands of dollars are channelled to good causes and into excellent, well-managed projects abroad. I like to think that Dubai International Airport is a global hub, so we are behaving responsibly as a corporate citizen of the world."

The increasing demands on Dubai Duty Free as a 'corporate citizen of the world', would lead to ever more formal recognition of that responsibility. Hundreds of thousands of dollars were channelled into good causes in 2002 and 2003, which led to the formation of the Dubai Duty Free Foundation in October 2004.

Driven by Sheikh Ahmed, the Foundation aims to raise funds for needy causes around the world with a particular emphasis on causes that directly benefit children. It is the first large-scale initiative of its kind in the duty free industry. The original concept was to help to make an impact on the lives of many people around the world, particilarly with emphasis on children.

The Foundation grew out of the operation's 20th anniversary charity drive which raised $1.9 million for a number of institutions. Initially it was suggested that Dubai Duty Free would donate 20 per cent of its revenues that day to charity. Instead it was decided to donate all revenues, but to offer a 20 per cent discount to customers in order to boost sales.

While it was a very successful one-day event to mark the operation's milestone, the wheels had been set in motion. Management looked at the wider picture and knew that a properly established Foundation would be able to do greater long-term good. In addition to start-up funds donated by Dubai Duty Free, collection boxes for the Foundation were set up throughout the operation at Dubai International Airport. Funds are also gleaned from events which tie in with the operation's many local and international promotional activities.

"The idea really moved forward as we made preparations for our twentieth anniversary," says McLoughlin. "Rather than throwing a party for ourselves we decided to give away all our birthday sales revenues. Those sales totaled $1.9 million, and the money went to five local charities. The reception to donations made us think that we'd like to do something more permanent, and so through the Dubai Duty Free Foundation we'll now give a percentage of our revenue every year to worthy causes."

As it is not dedicated to any single cause, the Foundation will have the ability to respond to urgent requests for assistance such as disaster relief funds in the wake of the Asian tsunami.

Fly *Buy* Dubai

Funds had also been flowing to Orbis, a non-profit organisation famed for its DC-10 'flying eye' hospital airplane and ophthalmology training centre. With the $25,000 received from Dubai Duty Free Foundation in 2003, Orbis was able to save the sight of 1,600 people who otherwise could not gain access to expert medical care. Shocked by the shootings at the Beslan school in southern Russia in September 2004, the company's management also ordered that funds be made available to support local families in the aftermath of that atrocity.

Other major partnerships were forged with the likes of Seeing is Believing, a partnership of Standard Chartered Bank and International Agency for Prevention of Blindness working to help tackle avoidable blindness. Also supported is Sightsavers, which works to combat blindness in developing countries, restoring sight through specialist treatment.

Also benefiting from the Foundation is Right To Play an international humanitarian organisation that uses sport and play programs to improve health, develop life skills, and foster peace for children and communities in some of the most disadvantaged areas of the world.

"It just seems appropriate for a company whose business is to serve people from all over the world to give aid where we can across the world," says McLoughlin. "We'll never forget our causes in Dubai, but like the city of Dubai we will always be looking outwards."

Superbrands was founded by Marcel Knobil in 1995, beginning as a radio show on GLR (now BBC Radio London) aimed at giving ordinary customers an insight into the significant brands that touched their lives. Today, the enterprise aims to identify brands that perform above and beyond others within their respective markets.

Superbrands is a worldwide arbiter of branding excellence, and the official Superbrands book is published in 47 countries and has launched its programmes in many key global markets and has publications in close to 90 countries.

The UAE's Superbrands Council consists of some of the nation's most eminent media and communications personalities, such as Gangu Batra, CEO, Jashanmal; Bhawani Singh Shekhawant, Managing Director, AC Nielsen Amer; Joseph Ghossoub, Managing Partner, TEAM Young & Rubicam; Robert Mitchell, Managing Director, Saatchi & Saatchi; and Sheikha Lubna Al Qasimi, CEO, Tejari.com, later the UAE's Minister of Economy, and the country's first female cabinet member.

"Brands are invited to participate in the Superbrands project based on criteria such as market dominance, longevity, goodwill, customer loyalty,

Matching Guinea-Bissau

(top) Foundation head Anne Smith (second from right), with First Lady Nasreena Gayoom (extreme right), hands over a cheque that will help children in the Maldives with thalassaemia.

(right) The Foundation supported the community in the wake of the grim Beslan School siege.

Fly *Buy* Dubai

*Colm McLoughlin and Sinead El Sibai receive an acknowledgement of
Dubai Duty Free's Superbrand status.*

and market acceptance," says McLoughlin. "When one considers the
international names connected with UAE Superbrands, it is obvious that it
was something we wished to be aligned with."

The list of UAE Superbrands includes the likes of American Express,
Aramex, Burger King, Canon, Castrol, Colgate, Gillette, Hertz, Jaguar, JVC,
Land Rover, MasterCard, Nokia, Philips, and Shell. In 2002, the same year
that Dubai Duty Free smashed through the one billion dirham turnover
barrier, the company was named a Superbrand.

"It means a lot to me personally," says McLoughlin. "The staff of Dubai
Duty Free worked very hard to establish and have done well to build it with
the management, being considered alongside such long-established
international names is a ringing endorsement for what had been achieved, in
addition to our bottom line, which continued to grow."

Other out-of-the-ordinary and notable endorsements flowed in that year.
In February each year, the Dubai Quality Awards presentation evening had
become established as one of the business community's focal points. In 1997,
DDF had claimed a Quality Award in the Trade Category.

Matching Guinea-Bissau

Sheikh Mohammed presents Colm McLoughlin with the prestigious
Dubai Quality Award — Gold.

"From then we were shooting for the highest level award — gold," says McLoughlin. "This was an enormous effort, as the concept was to drive forward quality in Dubai and there were stringent guidelines on how to reach the level required."

The Dubai Quality Award Gold Category is presented to organisations from all sectors of the economy that have been previous winners of the Dubai Quality Award, but only after demonstrating tangible sustained improvement over past performance.

The Gold Award set standards in such diverse areas as Leadership and Constancy of Purpose, Customer Focus, Results Orientation, Management by Process and Facts, People Development and Involvement, Continuous Learning Innovation and Improvement, Partnership Development, and Corporate Social Responsibility.

"The Gold Category required much, much effort in almost every area of the business," says Ramesh Cidambi. "But there was a determination that we should be Gold, and indeed we were one of the first companies to step up to the Dubai Quality Award Gold Category."

*Philippines President Gloria Macapagal-Arroyo presents Colm McLoughlin
with a Presidential Award of Distinction.*

Matching Guinea-Bissau

In February 2002, Sheikh Mohammed presented McLoughlin with a trophy marking Dubai Duty Free's Dubai Quality Award — Gold.

"It was another important step for us," says McLoughlin. "We were a top Dubai brand, Sheikh Mohammed had dictated that Dubai should stand for elite quality. Therefore it was incumbent upon us to be at the vanguard of the Dubai Quality Awards.

By the end of the year there was more, in the unlikely surroundings of Malacañang Palace, official residence of the President of the Philippines, located along the north bank of the Pasig River in Manila. Dubai Duty Free was to be honoured by the Philippine government, with a pair of top awards in recognition of its employment of Filipino workers in Dubai.

"It is another of those awards that can be traced back to our employees themselves, particularly in this case of those from the Philippines," says McLoughlin. "If they weren't brilliant we would not have gone back to Manila in order to secure more. If memory serves me correctly, around that time we had more than 1,000 employees and a shade less than half were from the Philippines."

McLoughlin received the Presidential Award of Distinction from Philippines President Gloria Macapagal-Arroyo, and in another ceremony later the International Employers Award of the Department of Labor and Employment, which was presented by Labor Secretary Patricia A. Santo Tomas.

Dubai Duty Free was one of 15 international companies to be honoured in this inaugural awards programme introduced by the government of the Philippines. In addition to formally recognising exemplary employers of Filipino workers, both awards acknowledged Dubai Duty Free's contribution to the financial wellbeing of its employees and also to the health, security, and social position of Filipino employees whilst employed by the company.

"As I have said, Dubai Duty Free's reputation was stellar. By 2002 there was a stampede every time we advertised jobs within the organsiation," says Angelito Hernandez, whose company handles recruitment in the Philippines. "At times, we were placing too many resources into the Dubai Duty Free account because the sheer numbers of applicants meant more man hours than normal were required to sift through the sheer volume."

*Dubai International Airport was in an almost constant state of change
as development work continued.*

Chapter Thirty

An Expanding Portfolio

The great thing in the world is not so much where we stand,
as in what direction we are moving.
– Oliver Wendell Holmes, American author

Sheikh Ahmed was overseeing the fruits of a $450 million expansion around the turn of the millennium. The Sheikh Rashid Terminal and Terminal Two were fundamentals of a $450 million expansion plan for Dubai International Airport. The airport now had capacity that stretched to 22 million passengers a year. In 2000, 10.7 million passengers passed through Dubai International Airport, which was serving 100 airlines, including new carriers that year such as Finnair, Angel Air, Ugandan Airlines, Condor, Mozambique Airlines, Tchad Airlines, Martinair, CSA Czech Airlines, and APA International Airlines, while scheduled arrivals rose by over eight per cent, to 57,632.

"It was apparent, even before the Rashid Terminal opened, that Dubai was shooting even higher," says Anita Mehra. "Sheikh Mohammed's vision was driving forward during this period with such an energy."

The Dubai government was rolling out projects and concepts that would transform the emirate over the next decade. In accordance with Dubai's wider master plan, the airport would need capacity to deal with a staggering 60 million visitors anticipated by the year 2010. Even before the Sheikh Rashid Terminal opened, the Dubai Department of Civil Aviation was continuing to plan for the future.

"The new shop floor was not completed when consultations began on further expansion," says McLoughlin. "The ambition shown by Sheikh Mohammed and the Dubai government was commendable."

As early as September 2000, airport development giants Aéroports de Paris were engaged to prepare plans for a Concourse 2 and Terminal 3 project. Terminal 3 was set to play a part in an aviation revolution that was being led by Emirates, but would also more than double Dubai Duty Free's floor space, including both the existing terminals.

"The chairman has approved a corporate plan to the year 2010, a dynamic period which will see us introduce the ultra-long-range [Airbus] A340-500 on non-stop services from Dubai to North America and Australia," said Maurice Flanagan. "Later, we will have non-stop services to South America and Japan penciled in."

Emirates was looking to Toulouse, where Airbus Industries was proposing the most dramatic civil aviation projects of the last few decades, the A3XX 'superjumbo', later called the A380, an engineering masterpiece that would transform the industry.

"The case of the A380 was compelling," says Maurice Flanagan.

The 'superjumbo' was to seat up to 555 passengers in a double-decker configuration, making it the world's largest passenger airliner, topping the Boeing 747.

In 2000, the average duty free spend for all passengers at Dubai International Airport was approximately $30, far above the world duty free average. With Aéroports de Paris behind the scenes working on Terminal 3, in October 2000, six months into the operational life of the Sheikh Rashid Terminal, Sheikh Ahmed unveiled these new ambitious plans for the emirate.

"Once again we had been involved in some serious discussions that would indelibly affect the future direction of Dubai Duty Free," says Horan. "There was no room for mistakes."

Aéroports de Paris had been charged with developing arguably the most

With a capacity of up to 555 passengers the A380 would bring more duty free customers into Dubai International Airport.

extraordinary airport terminal in the world, a vast edifice, an airport city, in which Dubai Duty Free would not just be a stakeholder, but an integral and unique part.

Given the importance of this phase of airport work on the long-term success of the company, Dubai Duty Free's consultations with Aéroports de Paris during the initial design phase were understandably comprehensive. It was more than a shop floor, Dubai Duty Free's vast needs including staffing facilities, on-site stock handling, logistics, and stock systems. An edifice such as was being planned would dramatically change the face of the company.

"Although Terminal 3 was years away from being completed at that stage, when you are planning something of this magnitude you have to start then, planning for how the company would grow to accommodate an expansion of this size," says Nic Bruwer.

In 1998, Dubai Duty Free employed under 700 staff. This would rise to over 900 by the time that the Sheikh Rashid Terminal opened, and was planned to cross 1,000 sometime in 2003 as the existing floor space grew busier. But encompassing the giant Terminal 3 project was estimated to require 3,000 employees.

This increase in staff levels would also require Dubai Duty Free to bring about what McLoughlin believes to be one of the most important developments of recent years.

"We should have built our own staff accommodation at the beginning, a top class complex," says McLoughlin. "But we rented, and as we grew it got messy, with our staff accommodation in several locations dotted around Dubai. This was not just difficult, if we had our own site, we could have made it a better class than was available."

T3 would also see a jump in terms of turnover, and therefore the stock required to fill Dubai Duty Free's shelves. Since its inception in 1983, the company had effectively been playing catch-up, its steeply rising turnover at odds with the process of running a smooth logistical operation.

Dubai Duty Free had gone through several warehouses. The time had come, along with T3, to invest in the most advanced warehousing operation in the industry.

"As much as C2 and T3, the new warehouse was to be vital to securing the future of Dubai Duty Free," says Ramesh Cidambi.

It was purpose-built, computerised, with state-of-the-art internal systems, constructed in a far more logical position near the airport and — most importantly of all — big enough to absorb T3 and other, almost inevitable, airport expansions.

Fly *Buy* Dubai

In 2002 work began on T3, a project that would cost $650 million. It was a year earlier than expected under the old master plan. Terminal 3 would have 36 to 37 gates and would be a replica, but bigger, of the Sheikh Rashid Terminal, handle 18 to 20 million passengers a year, and have 62 to 64 aircraft parking bays.

By 2007, on projections produced in the 1990s, the airport was expected to be handling 12 million passengers a year, making it one of the top 20 busiest airports in the world. In April 2001, it was announced that Dubai International Airport, with 12.3 million passengers, had jumped in global league tables from 83rd busiest in 1999 to 75th in 2000. The facility was rated by Airports Council International as one of the world's 10 fastest growing airports. By 2010 this would jump to 60 million.

This would only grow. The Dubai master plan projected that by 2018 the airport would have the capacity to handle 40 to 45 million passengers per year. Even as T3 was being unveiled, and in order to ensure capacity, word had begun to circulate that a plan was being drawn up to open an airport in the Jebel Ali area of Dubai.

While the Department of Civil Aviation and Aéroports de Paris were locked in discussions that would shape the future of the aviation industry in Dubai, and its burgeoning airside retail arm, Dubai Duty Free was tweaking its existing operation.

"I think of the duty free as a living thing, it is constantly changing and morphing," says Horan. "In order to remain relevant, we needed to be adept at changing ourselves in order to be at the vanguard of modern retail thinking."

In 2000, Dubai Duty Free had refurbished the Arrivals Duty Free, but it was on the main shop floor, following the opening of the Sheikh Rashid Terminal, that change was a constant factor.

"We had always known that when we became operational there would be plenty of tweaking to be done, and plans were ready when the Sheikh Rashid Terminal opened for a gradual roll-out of new spaces," says Sean Staunton.

Dubai Duty Free satisfied many of its premium brands, like Dunhill, Montblanc, and Cartier, by opening a Luxury Watch Shop.

"Colm and his team are, foremost, innovators," says Sany Nahhas, managing director of Visions, agents for both Dunhill and Montblanc. "

Dubai Duty Free was defined by its space. It was Dubai Duty Free. Standing policy was that outside branding should remain reasonably minimal, Dubai Duty free being the most important brand. The era of concessions ended in 1983.

An Expanding Portfolio

*Sean Staunton, Dubai Duty Free's Manager, Operations, was influential
in the expansion into the Sheikh Rashid Termial.*

"The advent of the Luxury Watch Shop emphasised our brands better,"
says Nahhas. "It had an immediate impact on sales."

"Some of the big luxury brands pressed a case for stand-alone boutiques.
That is not our policy. Dubai Duty Free is Dubai Duty Free," says
McLoughlin. "But as we bedded down and tweaked our own operations in
the Sheikh Rashid Terminal, there was a clear opportunity for some
complementary, luxury lifestyle brands to have cohesive spaces, if this
would benefit our operation overall."

Before this would happen, in the wake of the opening of a Luxury Watch
Shop, there was a great deal to the bedding down process. According to
Horan, two years were required to build the shop floor toward 100 per cent
maturity. This included a dedicated sunglasses outlet, opened in 2003, while
Swarovski opened an expansive counter the same year.

Swarovski is a Swiss luxury brand name, noted for its swan logo,
producing a range of precision-cut lead crystal glass and related products,
including crystal sculptures and miniatures, jewellery, couture, home décor,
and chandeliers.

Fly *Buy* Dubai

Dubai Duty Free had famously struggled with Irish Waterford Crystal during the mid-1980s, despite Waterford being perhaps the world's premium crystal glassware brand. Yet Swarovski was far more tailored to the average consumer and had superseded Waterford in terms of worldwide sales volume.

But undoubtedly the most important Dubai Duty Free development of 2003 was the company's continuing success story with the most malleable and ductile of the known metals. On the eve of the company's trading debut, December 20, 1983, Colm McLoughlin made his way to the Dubai gold *souq*. A few hours later he returned with a briefcase full of gold jewellery, relieved to hand over the burden.

"I was carrying so much gold that I was constantly looking over my shoulder with the fear of being mugged!" says McLoughlin.

The operation had got underway in 1983 with just a briefcase of gold on sale.

Gold has been highly valued since prehistoric times, possibly the first metal used by humans, and much sought-after for ornamentation and rituals. Egyptian hieroglyphs from as early as 2600 BC describe gold, which king Tushratta of Mitanni claimed was "more plentiful than dirt"!

But times changed, and Egypt had been supplanted as the capital of 'aurum' ('Au' is the chemical symbol for gold). Particularly in Asia, and especially India, there was a centuries-old tradition of buying gold as a store of value. By 1983, when one thought of gold, India was king.

"In those early days we quickly learned that gold would be a major component of our turnover," says Horan. "And we adapted to ensure that the Asian customers were well served. This meant subcontinent-leaning jewellery designs and the ubiquitous gold bars which are so beloved of small Indian investors."

Running a major gold operation was not without its risks for Dubai Duty Free, and a great deal of care was required to ensure the company was not hurt by fluctuations in the gold price.

"The reason we went off to buy our gold on the very eve of the opening of the shop floor in 1983, was that I did not want to risk losing money overnight," says McLoughlin. "Even a moderate dip in the price would have wiped out our profits. When dealing in gold, you need to be deft."

With this in mind, McLoughlin kept a close eye on the Dubai Duty Free gold counter more than any other during the early years, the potential for gold to 'hurt' the company's bottom line being apparent.

The high price of gold is due to its rare amount. Only three parts out of

An Expanding Portfolio

(top) Sheikh Ahmed, Colm McLoughlin, George Horan, Jamal Al Hai and Sany Nahhas at the opening of the Mont Blanc brand space.

(right) Chart topping songstress Fergie models a Swarovski dress. The well marketed Swarovski brand has become a big seller on Dubai Duty Free's shop floor.

*Gold would become one of the most important elements of
Dubai Duty Free's turnover.*

every billion in the Earth's crust are gold. When alloyed with other metals the term carat, or karat, is used to indicate the amount of gold present, with 24 carats being pure gold and lower ratings proportionally less.

The price of gold is determined on the open market, but a procedure known as Gold Fixing provides a daily benchmark figure to the industry.

With such a large Asian population in the UAE, and millions more transiting, gold quickly grew in importance for Dubai Duty Free.

India was the world's largest consumer of gold. Official gold imports into India were estimated at 700 tonnes in 1998, and this figure was conservative as it was based upon data collected from gold importing banks, official bodies, and declared imports by non-resident Indians. This figure did not include gold jewellery imported by Indians returning after foreign travel, and gold smuggled into India, of which there was a great deal.

One factor had conspired to help McLoughlin and his team. Prior to 1992, the official import of gold into India was banned except against value-added export of jewellery. At one point in time there was 97% income tax in India. This resulted in large-scale tax evasion.

Even Indians returning from foreign travel were not even allowed to bring in jewellery in very small quantities for personal use. In 1992, New Delhi liberalised its policy and permitted 'non-resident Indians' to bring in five kilograms of gold per person on payment of import duty in hard currency at a reasonable rate of about seven per cent of the gold price. Later there was further liberalisation.

"Liberalisation in India created a legitimate market and Dubai Duty Free was well positioned to cater for this," says Raju Maliekal, an Indian bullion investor. "The company seems to have worked its gold operation effectively. Indians talk, and reputations can be won and lost easily. Dubai is known for its competitive gold pricing, and the Duty Free is at the vanguard of that."

The predominant Hindu population finds mention of gold as a commodity of immense value in their religious books. Hindus believe that gold is a metal of demi-gods and monarchs. From ancient times gold enjoyed safe-haven status. Gold jewellery is worn by all women irrespective of their religious beliefs. A large number of Indian men also wear gold jewellery as neck chains, bracelets, and rings.

But there is also economic reasoning. Banks were either not trusted, or not present in many areas of India. There is also a widely held perception that gold is the only way to protect against depreciation of the Indian rupee against dollar. Although this is not always the case, inflation has continuously, year after year, eroded the value of currency.

Fly *Buy* Dubai

"Due to import duty and other limitation on imports, the price of gold in India is always higher than the international price," says Maliekal. "And when one is buying precious metals, tiny fractions in price are important. Dubai Duty Free is always among the best vendors in Dubai. Therefore, as India continues to import gold year after year, Dubai Duty Free will always be successful."

During its early years, despite the success of its gold operations, Dubai Duty Free had traded in a negative market. For example, the average price of an ounce of gold in 1980 (adjusted to the dollar in 2006) was $1,567.73. By 1990 this had dropped to $654.02, and by 2000 sat at a miserable $318.68. However, the bear market was showing signs of a return to a bullish environment.

According to the World Gold Council, during this period annual mine production of gold hovered around 2,500 tonnes, yet annually about 3,000 tonnes was going into jewellery or industrial/dental production, and around 500 tonnes was being utilised by retail investors and exchange-traded gold funds. This deficit was certainly going to have an effect on price.

Also 'freshened up' was Dubai Duty Free's Finest Surprise. Launched in 1989 to mark the company's first major expansion, the concept was perhaps expected to be a one-off. But it had lasted, and only served to strengthen. As watered-down versions of the competition swept the industry.

"Winning Finest Surprise was an incredible surprise, a great moment," says Satish Seemar. And Seemar, who trains thoroughbreds and Arabians for the Ruling Al Maktoum family of Dubai, and who has claimed the UAE Trainers Championship twice, knows great moments. He has saddled hundreds of winners, skillfully picking off some of the UAE's finest races. Indeed, it was he who was handed responsibility for handling a problem horse from Britain.

The two-year-old filly arrived in his care that winter, with bags of potential but also a reputation for having behavioural problems. The following spring she returned from Dubai, the first ever UAE-trained racehorse to compete in Europe, to finish fifth in the 1000 Guineas at Newmarket. Some months later she won a listed race at York, in doing so opening the door for the phenomenon that would be Godolphin.

"I bought tickets for a long time. Then, after not winning, I stopped for a few years," says Seemar. "When I won, it started with a joke. I was going to Argentina and asked my wife what she wanted me to bring her back. She said a Porsche, and as I passed through duty free I saw that they were offering a Porsche, so I thought why not.

(top) The gold shop would prove both a profitable and risky business.

(right) Several times UAE Champion racehorse trainer, Satish Seemar won a Finest Surprise car.

441

Fly *Buy* Dubai

"It was an extraordinary shock! And my wife got her Porsche."

The advent of Millennium Millionaire was, like its sister competition, originally planned as a one-off, this time to mark the opening of the Sheikh Rashid Terminal. But it too had set down roots. Instead of a single edition, before the first draw was made tickets were already on sale for a second cool $1,000,000.

As Millennium Millionaire began to pick up steam and hogged much of the publicity and kudos, the same naysayers outside of the company saw another opportunity to bleat. Both competitions could not survive together, they said.

"We never believed that," says Salah Tahlak. "The fact was, the advent of Millennium Millionaire hardly caused sales of entries in Finest Surprise to drop. Just as many people were now buying two tickets, one in each."

Indeed, Finest Surprise was still giving away as many cars each month after Millennium Millionaire came on the scene.

"There was a case that we could freshen up Finest Surprise. It was, after all, a competition that was well over a decade old," says Tahlak.

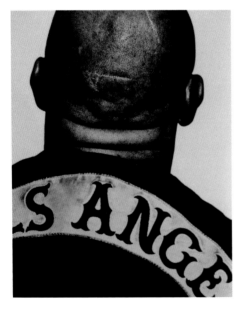

Hell's Angels are closely associated by the media with the iconic Harley-Davidson, but the truth was somewhat different.

An Expanding Portfolio

As McLoughlin and his marketing team considered the future direction of Finest Surprise, it was with the thought that having catered to discerning millionaire wannabes, and well served a crowd who could afford Dhs. 500, even as part of a consortium, perhaps a more fiscally accessible addition to Finest Surprise's array of prizes was a good idea.

Having given away an array of top-of-the-line Rolls-Royce, Ferrari, BMW and Mercedes-Benz cars, only a 'marquee' brand would do. One could not envisage these marques on the duty free shop floor next to a Smart car, for example.

"Then discussion turned to two wheels instead of four. And when you think of motorcycles there is only one real marquee brand that has crossed into the mainstream," says Tahlak.

In the 1920s, a group of enthusiastic American farm boys who liked racing their Harley-Davidson motorcycles were dubbed 'hog boys'. The group had a pig as their mascot. After each success, they made it a tradition to go on a lap of honour with the pig. Within a few years, 'Hog' became a generic name used for big motorcycles, especially the ubiquitous Harley.

Today, the Harley-Davidson Motor Company sells heavyweight motorcycles designed for cruising on the highway. Harleys have a distinctive design and exhaust note, and are noted for the tradition of heavy customisation.

The crossover into the mainstream began with Hollywood, which damaged Harley-Davidson's image with many outlaw biker gang films produced from the 1950s through the 1970s, and later when the Harley became synonymous with the Hell's Angels.

But the Harley-Davidson's enduring quality and iconic status endured these challenges. In the UAE there was a burgeoning Harley community, with some 500 bikes, several owners' clubs, and some 500 'Hogs' on the UAE's roads. Indeed, instead of the preserve of Hell's Angels and hoodlums, the UAE's owners' clubs were peopled by young executives, bank managers, policemen, and doctors.

"In 1987, the median household income of a Harley-Davidson rider was $38,000," says Kevin Morrissey, one of the UAE's best known Harley-Davidson enthusiasts. "By 1997, the median household income for those riders had more than doubled, to $83,000."

The glamour of the Harley-Davidson made it an ideal addition to Finest Surprise. What was more, on identical terms as the car draw, a total of 1,000 tickets was sold, the cost of a ticket for a Harley-Davidson was only Dhs. 100, or $27.

Colm McLoughlin presents a 'Hog' to a winner of the Dubai Duty Free
Finest Surprise Harley-Davidson.

An Expanding Portfolio

"The Harley-Davidson made enormous sense, and appealed to a different type of customer. Firstly, there are a surprisingly large number of people who are more keen on two wheels, for whom a Ferrari has less appeal," says El Sibai. "Secondly, a less expensive entry appealed to a great many people for whom a car ticket was just too much."

In 2002, Finest Surprise offered its first draw for a 'Hog'. Again, it was up to the travelling public to determine if this was a one-off, or the beginning of something more long-term. In the event, the general public snapped up tickets.

By the autumn of 2003, McLoughlin and his team had tweaked and developed the Sheikh Rashid Terminal operation for 18 months. Turnover was surging, the dark days of the various Gulf political problems were history, and the success of Dubai International Airport as a whole was sending ever more passengers on to the shop floor.

It was time for a party.

By 2004, the Dubai Duty Free Finest Surprise promotion had given away well over 1000 luxury cars.

Chapter Thirty One

$700 per minute

I am opposed to millionaires,
but it would be dangerous to offer me the position.
— *Mark Twain, American author*

The year 2004 started out well for four people in particular. On January 6, Lebanese businessman Becher Traboulsi won his second Finest Surprise car in three years, scooping the 1,102nd car given away in the long-running promotion. A Porsche 911 Carrera would soon arrive in his garage, alongside the Mercedes-Benz S500 he had scooped in April 2000. On the same day, another Lebanese, Annie Parseghian, found herself the owner of a red Jaguar XK8 convertible, ideal for ultra-trendy Beirut; while Bahrain-based Pakistani Rehan Ashraf would potentially find himself tearing up the streets of Manama aboard a Harley-Davidson.

Five weeks later, inside three days, there were two Millennium Millionaire draws. On February 14, Indian Mathath Beeran Kutty won a seven figure-fortune, rapidly followed by 41-year-old Lebanese Youssef Khoury on February 16.

Khoury was Dubai Duty Free's 36th millionaire.

It was a good few weeks for the Lebanese, for sure, but the company's overall success was impacting further afield. On December 20, 2003, Dubai Duty Free had celebrated 20 remarkable years in business.

"It was a big, big day for us," says McLoughlin. "We wanted to mark the occasion in some way, something to stamp it as 'our' day."

In addition to planning a series of events that would reward the company's staff, "our family" as McLoughlin puts it, it was decided to roll out a promotion that would go on to become an annual tradition.

For a period of 24 hours, customers could avail themselves of a 20 per cent discount across a wide range of merchandise. The offer began at midnight on December 19 and ended at midnight 24 hours later, a period in which there were 35,733 sales transactions, worth $1.9 million. This smashed a $1.6 million record set the previous day, December 19.

"Not imagining this would be just under $2 million, we had also pledged that all revenues on our anniversary day would go to charity," says Horan. "There were some very happy charities!"

These included the Sheikh Mohammed Foundation, Rashid Pediatric Centre, Dubai Centre for Special Needs, the Al Noor Centre, Dubai Autism

Fly *Buy* Dubai

Centre, the Emirates Diving Association, and what was to become the Dubai Duty Free Foundation.

"The ramifications of that $1.9 million, and the growth of the Dubai Duty Free Foundation, were profound," says McLoughlin.

In addition to donations and good works all over the world, 2004 would be the year of the Beslan school hostage crisis, when a group of armed rebels took more than 1,100 schoolchildren and adults hostage in the town of Beslan, North Ossetia. After a chaotic gun battle, at least 334 hostages were killed, including 186 children. Hundreds more were wounded. The Foundation made funds available to support local families in the aftermath of that atrocity.

In the wake of December 20, the year ended with Dubai Duty Free posting quite remarkable results. Turnover for the 12 months stood at $380 million, representing a 24 per cent increase over 2002.

Based upon CIA World Factbook estimates for the year of global, nominal GDP, this sent Dubai Duty Free from roughly matching the GDP of Guinea-Bissau to leapfrogging Samoa, The Gambia, and the Solomon

A Samoan Fireknife dance. Dubai Duty Free was now generating more revenue than Samoa's GDP.

$700 per minute

Islands. The latter, consisting of nearly 1,000 islands in Melanesia, east of Papua New Guinea, exports gold from a mine at Gold Ridge, on Guadalcanal, which finds its way onto the Dubai Duty Free shop floor.

"A rise in turnover of almost a quarter made Dubai Duty Free one of the most successful corporates in the world in growth terms," says Jersey-based financial analyst Malcolm Corrigan. "Duty free continued to be viewed as a fringe industry within retail, but what we were seeing during this period was volumes, and growth, that made the rest of the retail world sit up and take notice."

The year's turnover also equated to a further milestone, pushing the company across a daily average of over one million in sales per day, more accurately $1,013,699, equating to over $42,000 per hour.

"That is a shade over $700 per minute, every minute, 365 days a year," says Krishnamurthy Kumar, Finance Manager, Dubai Duty Free. "In December, turnover for the month had more than doubled that of Dubai Duty Free's turnover for the entire 1984, our first full year of operations."

Alcohol continued to be the largest area of revenue, followed by electronics and then perfumes. Revenues from the expanded, redesigned, and repositioned gold shop, although not operational for the full year, increased markedly. Indeed, in the first quarter of 2004 turnover from gold sales rose by 43 per cent over Q4.

During 2003, staffing levels had crossed 1,000 and several hundred new employees were due for recruitment in 2004. This was for good reason.

"It was just getting busier and busier at Dubai International Airport. This meant additional pressure on staff, and as we grew busier the whole operation built around the shop floor had to grow," says Nic Bruwer. "There was such growth within Dubai Duty Free that we needed capacity in order to meet the volumes that were being dealt with."

There had also been a discernible shift in passenger volumes. As well as greater numbers of passengers flowing through Dubai International Airport, the innovations of the previous two years had noticeably driven up spend per passenger. The new gold shop, luxury watch shop, and sunglasses shop, in addition to basic tweaking of all shop floor areas, had sparked a seismic shift in spending.

Across the duty free industry as a whole, only the most successful operations reach double figures in terms of dollars per passenger passing through the airport. The industry norm was said to be around $25. During the years when retail guru Tom Ellery had been associated with the company this had risen in Dubai, gradually, to reach $20 and over. By 2002, the first full trading year from the Sheikh Rashid Terminal, this was $32. In 2004 this spiked to $39, belived to be among the highest anywhere in the world.

"This is an industry-leading figure down to several factors, the most important of these being our staff. We look after them the best we can and have, over the years, evolved into as effective a corporate entity as there is...anywhere," says McLoughlin. "Our boys and girls have underpinned the Dubai Duty Free success story."

That success story continued in Q1 of 2004, with sales up 45 per cent up over the equivalent period of the previous year. The company was embarking upon a highly successful year, one which would see a slew of awards, including a Raven Fox award as Middle East Travel Retailer of the Year and, in October, a record fourth Airport Retailer of the Year, at the Tax Free World Association's Frontier Awards.

At a packed industry gathering at the Hotel Martinez, Cannes, the venue for the 20th Frontier Awards, Dubai Duty Free stole the show. Dubai Duty Free won the first 'Airport Retailer of the Year' award in 1985 — at the very first Frontier Awards ceremony — and again in 2000 and 2001.

"This award is well deserved and underlines the international status that the operation has achieved over the past two decades," Sheikh Ahmed told the media. In addition to winning the top award of the night, Dubai Duty Free was also 'Highly Commended' in 'Best Marketing Campaign by a Retailer' category. McLoughlin was himself honoured, with only the second 'Lifetime Achievement Award' ever presented.

This slew of awards established Dubai not only as an industry-leader but, in Frontier Awards terms, the most successful duty free operator in the world.

In Frontier Awards terms it was undeniable. And there was another surprise in store. In June, Dubai Duty Free's position as an industry-leader took another step forward with the release of new statistics from Sweden-based Generation Group, which ranked the company as the third-largest duty free operation in the world in terms of turnover. The new statistics, based on 2003 figures, showed a jump of two places for the operation, and places Dubai behind London-Heathrow and Seoul's Incheon International Airport. Heathrow boasted in excess of 60 million passengers a year, while Incheon International Airport was approaching 30 million.

"While in a way this was satisfying, to be ranked third, it would only spur us on," says Horan. "It's not a race, of course, but our status in the industry, in terms of the Frontier Awards and others, showed that we were arguably

(top) The Dubai Duty Free team in Cannes in 2004, celebrate another big awards night.

(right) Colm McLoughlin is presented with the 'Lifetime Achievement Award', only the second ever given.

the best in the world. We wanted to be the biggest, not just for the sake of beating Heathrow and Seoul, but in order to serve Dubai International Airport better."

While there was much international success this year, the year had a domestic tone of which McLoughlin is personally quite proud.

'Emiratisation' is a proactive policy by the governments of Dubai and the United Arab Emirates to employ nationals in the public and private sectors.

Since the early 1990s the UAE has adopted this strategy, aiming to use the country's human resources, and to transfer skills and knowledge from expatriates to UAE nationals.

Expatriates still make up the vast majority of the work force, while there was, in some areas, an employment crisis among young Emirati graduates.

This was a difficult task. Many countries had been caught out in an expatriate trap. Expatriate workers fuel the domestic economy, but can badly affect domestic culture — especially in the numbers that are seen in the UAE. It is a challenging balancing act for governments.

"We did not have quotas," says McLoughlin. "We had traditionally hired talent, that was our prerequisite, and within Dubai Duty Free there were plenty of Emiratis."

In the 1980s there had been little appetite among Emiratis for relatively low-paid jobs, and indeed few Emiratis joining the private sector job market. The UAE's education system only grew after the formation of the country in 1971, and only several decades later was a generation of well-educated school leaders leaving the country's universities and high schools.

"Because we did not have a policy that discriminated against Emiratis, it was not a challenge," says Nic Bruwer. "Emiratisation targets set by the government into overall human resources strategy was simply a matter of going into the market to see who wanted to be a part of Dubai Duty Free."

Conventional wisdom, or rather gossip, was that the relatively young and inexperienced UAE workforce lacked the work ethic of expatriates. Expatriates, it was said, were more willing to work long hours and at a substantially lower wage.

"The thing about a poor ethic was rubbish," says McLoughlin. "All around us are examples that show what nonsense that is."

He adds: "We have been lucky to have UAE talent with us. Look at Salah Tahlak, as hard-working and talented a young man as you could find, someone who joined us as lower management level and through sheer force of professionalism went on to be a director and ultimately run our tennis."

What was true was that a majority of UAE Nationals preferred to seek

$700 per minute

(top) Emiratisation was never forced on the company and has come naturally, particularly in recent years when UAE employee numbers have spiked.

(right) Salah Tahlak is the highest ranking Emirati in Dubai Duty Free.

employment in the public sector due to better conditions, namely more attractive compensation packages, job security, and often shorter working hours.

But that was changing. As more and more Emiratis joined the employment market, there was a perceivable growth in willingness to join the employment market at ground level, work hard, and climb up the ladder.

Some of the UAE's leading companies, like Emaar Properties, First Gulf Bank, or Etisalat, were aggressively pursuing such people — and reporting excellent results.

"Colm signaled that it was time to adapt our human resources strategy and aggressively look for young Emiratis looking for a career in retail," says Bruwer. In the early years of the millennium, while hundreds of job positions were created, the number of UAE nationals on the Dubai Duty Free payroll remained largely static.

Experience is something that Dubai Duty Free could not expect, recruiting in a nation that was formed some 30 years ago and whose population is extremely young. Nearly half of the Emirati population was under 15 years of age. But where experience was missing, they found enthusiasm and a willingness to work hard. Most positions being created in 2004 were shop floor. That, as the company found, did not preclude there being plenty of Emirati applicants.

In August that year, a first batch of nationals entered a three-week training programme, and by early September they took up their positions.

"It was a huge success," says Bruwer. "They were engaged, adaptable, and willing. It was a decision that we have not looked back upon with anything less than satisfaction."

Indeed, so successful was the programme that even before the first batch had completed their training, Dubai Duty Free was recruiting more Emiratis for ground level positions.

"With their knowledge of Arabic and local culture they are a great addition to our sales force," says McLoughlin. "From a small number of Emirati employees, today they represent the seventh largest block in Dubai Duty Free."

For a retail-based organisation, in a culture where there is no culture of working in retail, this is indeed a success story. In 2008, only Filipinos, Indians, Chinese, Moroccans, Uzbeks, and Pakistanis numbered more.

And there was another Emiratisation effort underway in Dubai Duty Free during the same period.

"When we opened in 1983, it was difficult even to get what you would

$700 per minute

The Gifts from Dubai section in Dubai Duty Free in the 1980s. In those days it was difficult to source a wide array of goods.

consider tourist goods, let alone any serious goods produced in the UAE," says Horan, who then served as shop floor manager.

For many years little changed — even on a national level.

Oil and natural gas exports have allowed the UAE to sustain a trade surplus for many years, but changes in oil prices cause the surplus to fluctuate widely from year to year. The government does not provide statistics for workers' remittances, but some estimates had this as high as $30 billion of capital flight each year. In 2000 the US Central Intelligence Agency (CIA) reported a UAE trade surplus of $19 billion, yet with so much import of goods, so little domestic manufacturing, and so much money flowing abroad, there was potential for an economic black hole.

"Aside from the economic ramifications, it was incumbent upon us to encourage the economy in this young nation," says Horan.

During the formative years of 1970s, the UAE market opened its doors to a massive flood of imported goods and commodities. It was difficult for local entrepreneurs to compete, especially in a market in the habit of preferring imported goods. So many did not bother, turning to import.

Fly *Buy* Dubai

The spectacular gold counter on Dubai Duty Free's shop floor includes a palm tree made of simulated gold bars.

$700 per minute

'Made in the UAE' was not something we had stamped on, or sewn into, many of our products in those early days," says Horan. "Even Dubai post cards were produced abroad. It was hopeless."

So called 'Heritage Products' were the first to emerge, as tourism became viable in the UAE. This meant trinkets and tourist-orientated items like T-shirts and mugs.

"Dates were, of course, something that the UAE was known for, so we encouraged date producers, both by stocking their existing products, which were in those times basic and too simple, and working with them to build better packaging and to add to their range of products," says Horan.

The annual date production in UAE jumped from less than 8,000 tonnes in 1971 to more than 240,000 in 1995, an increase of about 30-fold that made the UAE the seventh biggest producing country, with six per cent of world date production. Most exports remain in the region — such as Saudi Arabia, Iraq, Iran, and Oman — where they are viewed as a food. Yet thousands of tonnes now go abroad, not in bulk, but in professional, international-standard packaging, as gifts.

"Dubai Duty Free was one of the first to encourage Emirati companies to explore this segment of the market," says Horan. "Today, there is a thriving industry that we helped pioneer. Many small farmers sell into this segment."

There have been other successes. Tourist-oriented goods now have a stand-alone space in the centre of Dubai Duty Free, which generates millions of dollars in turnover.

"There is a demand now for indigenous products," says Horan, "in areas like perfumes, furniture, and food products. The quality of products manufactured in the UAE today are on par with those manufactured in any of the developed countries, and this is a fact that we need to be proud of. And within our remit, and what is possible, it is our policy to support this as far as possible.

"Brand UAE has truly arrived."

Salah Tahlak and Sinead El Sibai were delighted with the media exposure generated by the tennis match on the helipad of Burj Al Arab, which was 'seen by half the planet'.

Chapter Thirty-Two

The $500,000,000 tennis match

Never discuss love with a tennis player, it means nothing to them.
— Author Unknown

'Yes. How about these pictures coming up? Tennis stars Andre Agassi and Roger Federer could have used a bigger net. Look at where they're playing. This is Dubai. They were hitting groundstrokes 700 feet above ground level in Dubai. The helipad of the exclusive Burj Al Arab Hotel was turned into a tennis court for publicity. Agassi and Federer are competing in the Dubai Open. They said they loved playing tennis up there. And there wasn't much argument about when they hit one out. Yes, out is out.'

For 40 seconds, CNN co-host Daryn Kagan spoke over footage of the two tennis maestros going through their paces on the helipad at Burj Al Arab. The footage was repeated 23 times, mostly as a link, in CNN's regular programme. A segment of footage of the pair was also included in CNN's sports regular round-up. Within this particular news cycle, Dubai, Dubai Duty Free, Burj Al Arab, and tennis received some 28 minutes, almost half an hour, of airtime on CNN. Over the ensuing news cycle it was repeated several more times.

Britain's BBC went further. Dubbing it 'The Helipad Open', footage of the clash went onto every domestic news and sports bulletin over the next 24 hours, on all the Beeb's satellite channels and international feeds.

In the US, ABC quickly picked up coverage, both on its World News programmes, and with a quirky piece on 'Good Morning America', which used footage of Andre Agassi's post-match interview on the helipad, coupled with some interested chat from Diane Sawyer. Fox News, MSNBC, CBS, and NBC also showed the intriguing clash in various programming throughout the news cycle. Sky News Australia, Sky News New Zealand, and Sky News itself took up the story, the latter repeating a one-minute segment for virtually 24 hours.

According to Nielsen TV Ratings data, CNN is available in 93 million USA households and more than 890,000 American hotel rooms. CNN International has combined branded networks and services that are available to more than 1.5 billion people in over 212 countries and territories. Sawyer's 'Good Morning America' is seen by around five million Americans every day. As of January 2005, Fox News was available to 85 million households in

Fly *Buy* Dubai

Roger Federer and Andre Agassi play their famed game on the helipad at Burj Al Arab. (inset) Agassi launches a ball over the side.

The $500,000,000 tennis match

(top) Roger Federer and Andre Agassi in action.

(left) Colm McLoughlin and Sinead El Sibai with Venus Williams.

The $500,000,000 tennis match

the USA and, more internationally, the BBC's news coverage is estimated to be available to more than 274 million households worldwide.

Across Europe, North America, Asia, and the Middle East, particularly, television channels were fed with footage of 'The Helipad Open'. Dubai Duty Free, the ATP, and the world's biggest news agencies fed newspapers, magazines, and Internet news sites with photographs.

The project began when Sinead El Sibai and Salah Tahlak were working on a publicity angle for that year's Dubai Tennis Championships. When the Burj Al Arab concept was hit upon, and Dubai Duty Free and the Jumeirah Group had sorted out logistics, the ATP and the players were approached. All jumped at the chance.

"They could see that this was going to be big, right from the start," says El Sibai.

A few months later, the two biggest names in the sport at the time were filmed and photographed going through their paces in one of the most iconic places a tennis court has ever been situated.

"The interest was phenomenal," says El Sibai. "Agassi and Federer actually played for 15 minutes, but we were fielding calls from the media for weeks and photographs and press releases were going in publications for months. Even today, three years on, film footage of the match is all over the Internet and photographs appear in many books and magazines."

The world's highest tennis court and the unusual one-off match played there became an iconic tennis moment. While one would not dare to compare a PR stunt with some of the greatest matches in the history of the sport — such as Tracey Austin and Chris Evert in the 1979 US Open Final; John McEnroe and Jimmy Connors in the 1984 Wimbledon Final, Bjorn Borg and John McEnroe in the 1980 Wimbledon Final; and Roger Federer and Rafael Nadal in the 2008 Wimbledon final — this game in Dubai was huge not only for emirate, but for tennis itself.

"In terms of the publicity generated, I have been told that it ranks in the hundreds of millions of dollars," says El Sibai. "Certainly, as I said, until the present day it represents enormous value to Dubai in terms of exposure."

Unlucky for no-one, the men's version of the Dubai Tennis Championships were in their 13th year in 2005. It was also the third year under Tournament Director Salah Tahlak, a man who came through the ranks from within Dubai Duty Free and now commands a position as one of the highest-ranking Emiratis in the world of international sport.

"It was a great, great year, 2005. We were already regarded as one of the top spots on the calendar, but that made Dubai a tennis capital," says Tahlak.

Legendary Martina Navratilova appeared in Dubai several times. (inset) Bharat Godkhindi, an influential figure in the growth of the Dubai Tennis Championships, with Andre Agassi.

The $500,000,000 tennis match

Fly *Buy* Dubai

Justine Henin-Hardenne would come to dominate Dubai through her four tournament wins.

Tahlak joined Dubai Duty Free in 1992 — the company's first Emirati employee — the year of the Aviation Club Tennis Cup, the one-year forerunner of the tour. He was in customer services in 1992. A decade later he was a director in the company and made Tournament Director.

"I started in the tennis as a 'gofer'!" he says. "I helped the organising committee handle the Arabic media, arranging trophies, and arranging for police for security.

"I quickly learned that there is an enormous amount involved in a world class tennis tournament. Preparations for the following year's event began with a couple of days of the end of its predecessor.

"Being director of the tournament means that my life is saturated, it's all tennis. There's a lot of things to do, you have to deal with the WTA, deal with the ATP, with the agents, with the players, there are new things and new ideas to absorb and bring to Dubai, TV, new technology for the tennis and the courts."

"Dubai has emerged not only because of the prize money, but also because of the level of organisation and care," says Tahlak. "This is why the

The $500,000,000 tennis match

Rafael Nadal enjoyed a photoshoot at Wild Wadi water park. Media coverage was carried extensively in his native Spain and around the world.

best players in the world come here. We are better. They look forward to a week in the UAE. Players are provided with drivers and a hostess, they are cared for extremely well in excellent hotels, given access to excellent practice courts, and generally feted."

When Swiss star Martina Hingis won the inaugural Dubai Duty Free Women's Open in 2001, she told the post match press conference: "There are so many things going on around this tournament that it is hard to concentrate on the tennis."

Tahlak and El Sibai ensure that as much as possible is done to ensure that the stars of the sport – and the journeymen and women – get an opportunity to fulfill their dreams. French star Amelie Mauresmo, for example, loves horses, so a tour was arranged at Sheikh Mohammed's Zabeel Stables (coincidentally the base of Finest Surprise Porsche-winning trainer Satish Seemar). On the women's tour, Dubai Duty Free-arranged trips to Dubai's lavish and alluring shopping centres have become legendary. There is even a story that superstar Martina Navratilova delayed her departure flight by two days so she could take in as many malls as possible.

Fly *Buy* Dubai

On one memorable occasion, Venus Williams had programmed a two-hour visit to the Bur Juman Shopping Centre and stayed for six. At the annual tournament party, held at the beginning of both weeks, one of the famous stories told was of US star Jennifer Capriati who, although it was her first time, was a finer belly dancer than the belly dancer booked for the occasion.

Aside from the malls, the most requested destination by both men and women players is Dubai's famed gold *souk* (*souq*).

In 2004, Justine Henin-Hardenne, who would go on to claim the Dubai title four times, stated: "I think all the players are feeling great here. They take care of us extremely well. My husband had a great time this week. I did not see him because he was water skiing and in the desert. It's a great tournament..."

"It's much more than a tennis tournament. The reason we get involved is to promote Dubai as a destination," says McLoughlin, "and one of the reasons we are able to attract the best players year-after-year is because they have such a magnificent time when they are here."

Within days of the end of a Dubai Tennis Championships the organising committee meets to debrief. It's a process that should be completed within two weeks. In recent years mundane issues such as badges, ticketing, and car parking have featured heavily.

Having ATP and WTA events back-to-back, which is in itself a success, also throws up problems because in many cases one organisation accepts something the other does not. There are many subtle changes between Week One and Week Two of the Dubai Tennis Championships.

Tahlak admits that, as a tournament organiser, he finds the men's event easier: "Be it your mother, your sister, your wife, it is a woman's world out there, they have it *their* way," he sighs. "I find the top women players have a long to-do list. They are complicated and sophisticated...they demand extra..."

While too seasoned a professional to name names when it comes to the prima donnas of the sport, he points to Swiss legend Roger Federer as the consummate professional, ever accessible and willing to do things for the good of the tournament he is competing in and for the sport itself.

"His career took off around the time Dubai Duty Free came on the scene. We have grown up with him, and the first tournament he won was one in Milan, the one we own," says El Sibai. "We are very proud of him"

Tahlak adds; "I've enjoyed working with the Williams sisters, Ivan Lendl, Tim Henman and would make special mention of Andre Agassi, a super guy, very nice..."

The $500,000,000 tennis match

Maria Sharapova is considered an asset to tournaments for the media circus which follows her.

Fly *Buy* Dubai

*American star Venus Williams poses before the iconic
Dubai landmark Burj Al Arab.*

The $500,000,000 tennis match

At the end of the day the success of the tournament can be measured in several ways. One is the virtual sell-out of tickets for the fortnight in Dubai. A second is the positive media coverage. A third is the slew of ATP and WTA awards that Dubai has won.

For Tahlak, two things stand out. One is personal.

Sheikh Mohammed is himself known as being handy on the tennis court, and in 2005 Tahlak and El Sibai accompanied Agassi to the palace for an audience with the Dubai Ruler. At that meeting, Sheikh Mohammed told the American star that he was a fan, and stated that he always watched the tennis championships on television as his diary allowed.

The second was that afternoon on the helipad at Burj Al Arab.

"It was not easy. Sinead, in particular, worked for months to ensure that happened smoothly," he says. "For the rest of the year we were inundated by people commending us on the idea. I remember the head of ATP said, 'Salah, this thing that you did, it hit half of the planet.'"

And it did. PR gurus in Dubai talk of the stunt attracting anything up to $500 million in free television and print media coverage.

In its very early years Dubai attracted only a handful of Top Ten player from the men's rankings. In 2008, the Dubai Tennis Championships had nine out of ten women playing (the other was injured), and seven out of the top ten men. Allowing for injuries, this means that Dubai gets the very cream.

Says Tahlak, "I think honestly it is not fair to have Grand Slams just in North America, Europe, and Australia and not in Asia and the Middle East when this region is spending so much money on developing players and staging top class tennis tournaments.

"I will say this: one day, and it may be a way into the future, the sport is going to look at the Slams. Dubai will be one of the few tournaments with the quality and class to become a Grand Slam.

"I genuinely believe that it can happen."

*Former England Captain David Beckham transcended football and became a global icon —
even in the United States where 'soccer' is not among the biggest sports.*

Chapter Thirty-Three

David Beckham walks into a room...

I don't consider myself as the best player in the world.
I'm not obsessed with individual titles. I'm much more interested
in being part of a team which wins trophies.
– *Ronaldo Luis Nazário de Lima, Brazilian sportsman*

At the end of October 2004, McLoughlin and his management team had headed to Cannes for the annual Tax Free World Association exhibition. They were pretty buoyant. There was a certain optimism that Dubai Duty Free would claim its fourth duty free industry 'Oscar' confirming the company as the best duty free in the world.

"Airport Retailer of the Year is the equivalent of Best Picture at the Academy Awards," says George Horan. "It says that you are the best in the business."

Indeed, although the Academy of Motion Picture Arts and Sciences organised the first Academy Awards in 1929, some 66 years before the first Frontier Awards, only two people had ever collected four, legendary director John Ford (for *The Informer*, *The Grapes of Wrath*, *How Green Was My Valley*, and *The Quiet Man*) and Katharine Hepburn (*Morning Glory*, *Guess Who's Coming to Dinner*, *The Lion in Winter*, and *On Golden Pond*).

Jack Nicholson only ever won three! In 2004, McLoughlin took the short walk to the stage to collect a fourth statuette after Dubai Duty Free had been named Airport Duty Free Operator of the Year.

The 76th Academy Awards ceremony that year, when *The Lord of the Rings: The Return of the King* won best picture, drew 43.56 million television viewers in the USA and hundreds of millions more abroad. By contrast the Frontier Awards are not televised — but that does not make them any less important to those for whom the duty free industry is important.

"The Frontier Awards are the top accolade in our business and, without meaning to seem conceited, the fact of the matter is that no organisation had claimed four nods as Airport Duty Free Operator of the Year," says McLoughlin. "That is an enormous testimonial to our staff. I'm a team player, so is George, so is Salah, Ramesh, Nic, Sean, Anne, Kumar and Sinead, we all are part of a group.

"And, to be perfectly honest, that ethos has come down from Sheikh Ahmed. From Sheikh Ahmed to the boys and girls on the shop floor, we have succeeded thanks to a team spirit above anything I have encountered in any other organisation of comparable size."

But this particular night would end on a personal hue, even for someone who prides himself on ensuring the Dubai Duty Free "team" is the entity that gets recognition in time of success.

Dr Brendan O'Regan, the sagely father of the industry, stated: "If you're involved in developing an important idea, you have to let it possess you. If you keep knocking on the door, the door will open." It was an ethos he had lived by from being appointed as manager of St Stephen's Green Club in Dublin, to his time as Catering Controller at Foynes and on to the airbase at Rineanna — later to become Shannon Airport.

In 1997, in an emotional Cannes evening, and in a year that marked the 50th anniversary of Shannon Duty Free, O'Regan had been presented with the first, and only, Frontier Lifetime Achievement Award.

Seven years later it was the turn of the man who, in a manner of speaking, had picked up the duty free concept and built into a global industry, building on the legacy of the industry's founding father. For only a second time the Frontier Awards would see the presentation of a Lifetime Achievement Award.

"This award acknowledged an outstanding leader," says Sinead El Sibai. "Cannes is a gathering of the great and the good of the industry, so it was an ideal setting for this kind of recognition."

"If you have a room full of footballers and David Beckham walks in, there is deference that everyone understands," says Barbara Saunders, one of the UAE's leading public relations experts. "That is how it is with Colm."

The 'Lifetime Achievement' Award was an unexpected addition to the annual Frontier awards line-up, and a major surprise because McLoughlin was not informed in advance. Yet he regained his composure to state: "This is overwhelming, I am thankful to Frontier for this great honour. I would like to dedicate this award to HH Sheikh Ahmed bin Saeed Al Maktoum, who has always been a great support to the operation. This award is also dedicated to all of the duty free staff who do a great job and to my former colleagues at Shannon, where my career in the duty free industry began. Last, but by no means, least, I would like to thank my wife, Breeda."

Back at home there were more seismic events underway that would, perhaps, guarantee more award-strewn nights in Cannes.

In 2003 projections showed that 30 million passengers would be passing through Dubai International by 2010. It seemed an amazing number. But that figure turned out to be very conservative. By 2007, the airport was on the way to touching the 33 million passenger mark.

David Beckham walks into a room...

Colm McLoughlin makes an emotional address as recipient of only the second Lifetime Achievement Award presented at the Frontier Awards.

Fly *Buy* Dubai

(top) Concourse 2 at Dubai International Airport pictured weeks before its opening.

(left) Empty shelves waiting to be filled at Dubai Duty Free's Concourse 2 shop floor.

David Beckham walks into a room...

"Before the Sheikh Rashid terminal opened we had realised that every projection we had was wrong," says Sheikh Ahmed. "The experts were too conservative. I think they did not factor into their calculations the 'Dubai factor'. Sheikh Mohammed was driving the emirate into an unprecedented boom.

"We were living in extraordinary times."

Such a throughput — even based on early estimates — required some hard thinking by Dubai's government. Sheikh Mohammed worked quickly.

"It seemed we had only just finished working with project managers on the Sheikh Rashid Terminal when we began working with another set of designers on the next expansion for Dubai International Airport," says George Horan. "I don't think anyone was quite prepared for the scope of what was being planned."

Dubai International Airport was to be developed to create a Terminal 3 and Concourse 2 to be open late-2008. And for Dubai Duty Free, the new Terminal and Concourse 2 would equate to even more floor space. Some 10,000 square metres was allocated as retail space. While 117 airlines operated through Dubai in 2005, serving 194 destinations, this figure continued to rise. Such expansion has demanded that the airport stays ahead of the game in providing facilities for both airlines and their passengers and the non-stop development of recent years has enabled the airport to do so. Concourse 3 would later provide a further 7,000 square metres of floor space.

"This took care," says McLoughlin. "Almost as soon as discussions ended with designers on the Sheikh Rashid Terminal, meetings began on a new swathe of developments. Perhaps, in the history of Dubai Duty Free, there was no more an important period in its history away from the shop floor. The planning period they were about to embark upon would propel the company, or harm it, well into the next decade."

The impact of C2, C3, and T3 on Dubai International Airport would be profound.

What fuelled this surge in building work was a combination of factors. First was the dramatic development of Dubai itself, now firmly established as the region's leading business and leisure hub, which is continuing to grow at a pace never before witnessed anywhere in the world. Added to this is the ongoing expansion of Emirates, the airline, which continued to be the world's fastest-growing, and now a truly global operation with new routes being introduced on a regular basis.

The expansion involved the construction of Terminal 3 and Concourses 2 and 3 — all exclusively for Emirates. Concourse 2 quickly changed the shape

Fly *Buy* Dubai

David Beckham walks into a room...

Weeks before opening to the general public construction workers are the only ones walking the Concourse 2 shop floor and the shelves wait stock.

of the Airport skyline. It was to have a similar fuselage profile to the existing Sheikh Rashid Terminal, to which it is linked via a distinctive air traffic control tower. When the new development came on-stream, the airport would be able to handle up to 70 million passengers annually.

No sooner had Dubai Duty Free signed off on plans on the Sheikh Rashid Terminal than they had been asked to participate in the development process of C2, C3, and T3.

"This was, perhaps, the biggest undertaking in the history of Dubai Duty Free," says Nic Bruwer. "The ramifications of such huge expansion were like dropping a pebble in a pond. There are not just shop floor layouts and attendant facilities to consider. From my perspective, Human Resources, there is staffing to consider, numbers of staff, recruitment, training, payroll, transport, housing, etc. And it is the same for every department within the company.

"C2, C3, and T3 would see our staffing levels treble. Any company would require enormous forward planning in order to absorb an expansion of this size and scope."

Even while Dubai Duty Free was executing its first major expansion, into the Sheikh Rashid Terminal, meetings were going on that would set in motion the company's C2, C3, and T3 expansion.

"It was a big, big thing for us," says McLoughlin. "This took hundreds of man hours each week. Retail is such a rapidly growing and quickly evolving business, but we needed to articulate, in some parts of the development process, a vision as much as half a decade into the future. This required we anticipate the industry's movement and that we have an ability to look ahead."

Excavation work was completed by mid-2003, and by mid-2004 construction was well underway. Excavation and foundations for Terminal 3 and Concourses 2 involved the excavation of 5.6 million square metres of earth and 1,500 piles being drilled and poured, some to the depth of 50 metres. The work also included 450 anchors for diaphragm walls.

The spectacular view of Concourse 2 was to be achieved by building Terminal 3 underground, beneath the apron and taxiway area. On several levels, it would boast first class lounges and dedicated counters, restaurants, 180 check-in counters, and 2,600 underground parking spaces. The Departures and Arrivals halls within the terminal were planned to be located 10 metres below the apron and taxiways, and passenger orientation was to be heightened by maintaining visual contact with the landside through a fully-glazed façade at one end. Concourse 2 would feature a bright, naturally-lit atrium at the other end. Passengers would be able to access the terminal via 'travelators'. The two concourse buildings would be linked, enabling transiting passengers to move freely between the two buildings. Concourse 3 is a smaller version of Concourse 2, and this was expected to be operational after its sister building. Upon completion, it will be the world's first totally dedicated Airbus A380 facility and will have 20 contact gates, 18 of which will be reserved for the A380s. Electric buses will connect the two new concourses.

"It will be stunning. Breathtaking," says McLoughlin. "The enormity never ceases to amaze."

Taking the design process from concept to opening day required from Dubai Duty Free an exhaustive process, working with designers and architects.

"For four years there have been, somewhere in Dubai Duty Free, two or three internal planning meeeings a week," says McLoughlin. "Then there are half a dozen meetings with the designers each month. It is an enormous exercise."

Concourse 2 is directly connected to Terminal 3, meaning a minimum of walking for passengers. It has 27 contact gates and 59 passenger-loading bridges. The Concourse also includes a 235-room hotel and health club — and a further 10,000 square metres of commercial space allocated to Dubai Duty Free.

"The planning also included huge administrational shifts," says Ramesh Cidambi. "If we're pushing paper and have a bottleneck, that's a problem."

New software needed to be considered, through both external and in-house development. We began to experiment with home-grown software systems, but these needed to be flexible, able to provide a turnkey service for our shop floor operations.

If we were considering sales of one million pieces a week by 2007, then when C2, C3, and T3 were operational that could be four or five times that figure."

Another consideration was to ensure harmony between operations. With a vast majority of operations being directed to one main shop floor, in the Sheikh Rashid Terminal (Terminal 2 and Arrivals representing a far smaller percentage of business) there was a central focus. With the eventual creation of C2, C3, and T3, millions of transactions would be made in each. Creating separate platforms would create confusion.

"If we were looking at many platforms, and getting bogged down over how one part of the business speaks to the other, the complexity was going to kill us," says Cidambi. "There aren't a lot of great off-the-shelf products. We would eventually go with an off-the-shelf solution and our IT department spent a great deal of time fine-tuning a detailed, comprehensive, and ultimately successful system that is unique to us."

Perhaps the biggest challenge for Dubai Duty Free was bridging the gap between the planning stage and the years that the project would take to roll out — even allowing for the speedy nature of construction in the emirate.

In the mid- and late-1990s there was a catch phrase, 'retailing for the next millennium'. It was a slogan. "But it was a reality for us," says Horan.

Retailing had come a long way since the days of Shannon's kiosk and had morphed into a radically different business since Dubai Duty Free had opened for business in a former kitchen in the airport. In the period between planning and opening of C2, C3, and T3, retail would change, as it always had. Changing demographics had altered everything, despite the fact, as Cidambi observes: "Human nature doesn't change, never has, and never will. We thought the Internet would be a big challenge to retail, but it falls short because it cannot replace the human touch."

The Internet would have far lesser impact upon retail than the soothsayers originally claimed, but retail was an evolving beast, requiring retailers to morph themselves within an ever-changing environment. The number one enemy is stagnation. Planning for buildings that would be completed in 2008 presented grave risks.

While Dubai Duty Free's corporate image was strong worldwide, it remained an industry given that the least expensive form of advertising was an exciting, and dramatic shop floor, a visual display that pulls the eye. Staggered merchandising, uneven shelving, vignettes, flexible wall and floor fixturing, and gondolas would all play a role, but also the flexibility to absorb new concepts, many of which would only emerge after building work had started.

Another consideration was logistics. A cluster of shop floors around the airport would require an enormous logistical operation. For example, by 2008 it was projected that the Sheikh Rashid Terminal would see over one million pieces a week sold. If this was only partly replicated on C2, C3, and T3, Dubai Duty Free's supply chain would be charged with bringing to the site, one with tight controls, millions of items. Getting this right would be even more important than ensuring flexibility on the shop floor.

Building from the winning design formula of the Sheikh Rashid Terminal, the new area would have similar designation of sections and departments.

"It will not be as much one unit but spread a little more than the present

David Beckham walks into a room...

Dubai International Airport was now home to one of the biggest civil construction projects ever seen in the Gulf.

one," said McLoughlin. "There will be several different zones separated in-between by lounges and other airport facilities as needed." The new area will host sections of many of the brand names popular in the existing duty free — and some additional names are promised. Getting the logistics together for an operation of this scale has ensured that the management and their teams have been working flat-out during 2007.

"Apart from increasing staff levels and the inherent training this brings about, we have to introduce new stock controls, stock systems, pilferage controls, and proper security. We need to have a logistical system set up whereby we can manage a lot of deliveries."

The ambitious programme has required a serious re-configuration of existing information and management technology systems to cope with the increased volume of business generated by the expansion.

"We do over 60,000 transactions every day," said McLoughlin. "One of our difficulties is that when we have customers, we very often have them for only 20-30 minutes and we have to make the most of them while they are here."

Fly *Buy* Dubai

With the higher volume of orders expected across a larger and more dispersed retail area, warehousing will also play an important role. To this end, IT and business services company Enabler has been called in to design and implement a warehouse management system for a new Distribution Centre facility and Head Office which has been built on a designated 50,000 square meter site in Umm Ramool, near the airport. This became partly operational midway during 2008 and was completely up and running by the end of the year.

The Distribution Centre's system is based on an Oracle retail Warehouse Management System. The new facility has been designed to handle 10,000 pallets in the first phase. The warehouse is semi-automated with storage and retrieval for palletised merchandise. There are plastic totes for perfumes and other non-palletised goods, and a special handling area for delicate items such as fashions, accessories, and cigars.

The new facility will allow a quicker turnaround of goods for the shelves of Dubai Duty Free; currently it takes up to two days from receiving and picking the goods to having them on sale. To ensure this faster turnaround and yet not compromise on security, it has been proposed that trucks arriving at the airport from the new warehouse be scanned for security, thus preventing the time-consuming business of loading and unloading merchandise.

"So much is measured against turnover," says Horan. "But look at the warehousing. We have rolled out a 27,000 square metre warehouse, with 28,000 square metres of trucking bay, along with a large Head Office. When we opened in 1983 we had a tiny shed-type structure, and had trouble stocking chocolate and perishables as there was a single small refrigerated room."

David Beckham walks into a room...

Opened in mid-2008, Dubai Duty Free's new Headquarters and Distribution Centre building would represent a huge step forward for the company.

485

Hawaii, famous for its grass skirts and hula dancing, was also one of the world's early leaders in the duty free industry.

Chapter Thirty-Four

Grass Skirts and Hollywood

> While the miser is merely a capitalist gone mad,
> the capitalist is a rational miser.
> — *Karl Marx, German philosopher*

For many, Hawaii sums up hula-skirts and cocktails with mini umbrellas. For others it's the birthplace of the father of surfing, Duke Kahanamoku, Barack Obama, and entertainment stars Nicole Kidman and Bette Midler. Then there is the Island of Hawaii, 'the Big Island', well developed Oahu, mountainous Maui and the garden isle of Kauai.

But one of Hawaii's lesser known features was its duty free.

Located on an archipelago in the central Pacific Ocean southwest of the continental America, the 50th state of the United States is well located southeast of Japan, and northeast of Australia. In 1959, Qantas began the first jet service to Honolulu as a stop on its flights between Australia and California. Because of its strategic location, Honolulu International Airport became the principal aviation gateway for the United States to the Far East and Asia and one of the busiest airports in North America.

Yet with the advent of ultra-long range aircraft, most trans-pacific flights were now able to over fly Honolulu and there was notable decrease in international passenger traffic over the years, particularly to Australia, the South Pacific and southeast Asia. Although Honolulu International Airport fought back and helped foster a growth in its domestic market as a tourist destination in its own right, the ultra-long range aircraft that so decimated passenger numbers for a time did have a long-term effect — Honolulu's record breaking duty free would never recover.

In the 1970s and 1980s Honolulu Duty Free was a record breaker, helped by the Japanese. Japanese travelers were, during this period, the Holy Grail of the industry. With liberal import allowances they copiously purchased products not available in Japan, were attracted to nation speciality products like watches made in Switzerland and French perfumes, and were very 'brand-oriented', hunting brands with the image of high price and known for their ostentatiousness and social status.

At their height, in the 1980s, Japan's penny-pinching savers and earnest salarymen loosened their purse strings when they traveled. America was an important destination for those holidaying or with family ties. For a great many a visit to Honolulu Duty Free was a high point of their trips.

During this era Honolulu Duty Free was easily the world's highest earning duty free in terms of spend per passenger and passenger penetration — in no short measure due to the Japanese connection.

The ultra-long range aircraft of Boeing and Airbus would sound a death knell, however, to the golden days of the free spending Japanese tourist in Honolulu, with time to kill in Transit and a penchant for luxury goods.

If this era was over in Honolulu, however, there was soon to be a new kid in town. In 1984 Dubai Duty Free earned revenues of around $20 million, to record a spend per passenger of around $5.5. This was really quite reasonable.

"The industry norm around that time was around $5, but I felt that this was in no way indicative of what could be achieved," says McLoughlin.

Within three years of opening, during the 1987 financial year, Dubai Duty Free had reached double figures, $12 per passenger. In 1990 the figure reached $20 that year. In 1999 it was something of a milestone to record $30 per passenger.

This figure was way in excess of the industry standard, at the time believed to hover around $20 worldwide. But the Sheikh Rashid Terminal, opened in 2000, represented something new for Dubai Duty Free, another opportunity. From its inception, the shop floor had been housed in a former kitchen, essentially a basement. While passengers were directed there by prominent signage, it was hardly centre stage. In the Sheikh Rashid Terminal, the duty free floor was visibly at the centre of life.

"Placing the duty free where it is accentuated our already established positives. Like our very high level of staff, the excellent value, the world class service…" says McLoughlin.

The Dubai Duty Free boss adds that, even today, he cannot understand why airports are built and duty free shops are planned as an afterthought.

"Unused spaces are co-opted at a late stage for retail. Retail is given what's left. It does not make sense to me as there is ample evidence, not least in Dubai, showing that duty free can be a major contributing factor to airport profitability," says McLoughlin.

Honolulu's success was not particularly based upon its management's attention to a duty free operation, rather a liking to the concept displayed by the travel retail-orientated Japanese. But a generation on, a successor to Barack Obama's birthplace was on the horizon.

"In 2004 we reached $39 per passenger, which was a huge figure, as good as, if not better than, any other airport duty free operator in the world," says McLoughlin. "The Sheikh Rashid Terminal placed its duty free front and centre, at the heartbeat of Dubai International Airport. It worked so well."

Grass Skirts and Hollywood

(top) Barack Obama's homeland Honolulu set a duty free industry standard in the 1970s and 1980s.

(right) By 2004 Dubai Duty Free was generating one of the highest spend figures, per passenger, of any duty free in the world.

Fly *Buy* Dubai

So well, in fact, that with a little tweaking, in 2005 Dubai Duty Free crossed a remarkable threshold. That year, for every single departing passenger who passed through Dubai International Airport there was an average of $40 per passenger spent in the duty free.

In reaching this milestone, the company was undoubtedly helped by demographics. The term 'capitalism' was coined in the mid-19th century by Karl Marx, the brilliant German philosopher, economist, sociologist, political theorist and revolutionary.

The father of Communism argued for socio-economic change and claimed that the structural contradictions of capitalism would cause capitalism to collapse, which would then see society embrace Communism. In the Communist Manifesto he wrote: 'The development of Modern Industry, therefore, cuts from under its feet the very foundation on which the bourgeoisie produces and appropriates products. What the bourgeoisie therefore produces, above all, are its own grave-diggers. Its fall and the victory of the proletariat are equally inevitable.'

'Bourgeoisie' is a term used describe members of the upper or merchant

Karl Marx believed Capitalism would collapse.

490

class, whose status comes from employment, education, and wealth as opposed to aristocratic origin. 'Proletariat' is a term used to identify a lower social class.

There is near-universal agreement that the gap in wealth between the richest and the poorest is widening, but it is also true that less and less people view themselves as working class, or, to borrow Marx's definition, part of the proletariat. Middle class used to be defined as white-collar workers, while blue-collar workers were working class, but there is a blurring line and a far wider portion of the population rank themselves as Middle Class than do statisticians. This blurring is also enhanced by the definition of Middle Class in different world economies. What a Westerner may consider a proletariat salary can be viewed as being bourgeoisie in some parts of the subcontinent, for example. And the recipient of a subcontinent bourgeoisie salary will aspire to show himself as such to family members, neighbours and friends when he returns home.

This also helps the duty free industry, particularly in Dubai, where millions of passengers use the airport as a hub. Those considering themselves Middle Class buy more, and shop for higher quality and look for brands. Perhaps it can be argued that this is the age of the international salaryman, once a cultural phenomenon of Japan.

The success of Dubai Duty Free's shop floor: its merchandising, shelving, vignettes, attractive wall and floor fixturings and gondolas, had succeeded in driving up spend per passenger. But the other secret, according to McLoughlin, is penetration.

If the Honolulu Duty Free era of the 1980s were the years of the 'Reagan revolution', Tiananmen Square, the Rubik's Cube, Raybans and MTV, then the early years of the Millennium belonged to Dubai. Not only had Dubai International Airport seen an industry revolution as its duty free crossed the $40 barrier, it probably also reached more passengers than any airport in the world in terms of penetration – bar none.

Customer penetration which makes arguably the biggest difference.

"Around the world perhaps 20 to 22 per cent of travelers through any given airport shop in the duty free," says McLoughlin.

Penetration rocketed with the advent of the Sheikh Rashid Terminal.

"The placing of the duty free floor in the crux of the Sheikh Rashid Terminal is indicative of the attitude and style of Sheikh Mohammed and Sheikh Ahmed, and indeed the entire history of Dubai," says George Chapman, a six-decade veteran of living in the emirate. "Clever, targeted commercialism has been behind the success of the emirate since the days of

Fly *Buy* Dubai

Dubai Duty Free also boasts the highest passenger penetration in the world. (inset) Sean Staunton presides over one of the company's innovative promotions — which further drive up revenue.

Fly *Buy* Dubai

*The revamped Dubai Duty Free shop floor in the arrivals hall at
Dubai International Airport.*

Sheikh Mohammed's great- great-grandfather, who set up what was perhaps the world's first free trade zone in the late 1800s in order to capitalise upon the demise of the port of Lingah."

Whereas McLoughlin observes, around the world duty free is often the last item considered when airports are being designed, by placing Dubai's shop floor in the very heart of the new terminal it became the focal point.

In 2008 Dubai Duty Free would record a 42 or 43 per cent penetration, almost double what is generally considered to be the global norm.

It's not just the positioning, although that is admittedly the major factor," he says. "Its about our brilliant staff and their excellent training, our IT, our prices, so many factors."

The search for turnover and serving customer needs also led to work on a revamped arrivals shop. Worldwide, historical perception was that land-side shopping, which came after passport control and security, comprised of smaller shops, offering less choice. Dubai had been one of the first airports in the region to boast a duty free for arriving passengers, and indeed the store was considerably smaller than in departures. The array of stock was smaller

and based around the fundamentals — mainly alcohol, cigarettes, children's gifts, a few small electricals and mobile telephones. "We saw a fundamental shift, and were of the belief that this was becoming a more important retail area," says McLoughlin. "By 2005, when our main shop floor was seeing $40 per passenger, arrivals was still hovering at around $6.

"We will drive this figure up."

Departures would always be the most important aspect of the business, in 2005 accounting for a vast majority of Dubai Duty Free's total revenue. Departures' importance is expected in the Middle East and Europe. Yet in other markets the reverse is true. In the USA, for example, Departures could account for as little as ten per cent of turnover. But arrivals and other revenue points, such as Landside, needed exploration. Indeed, the business plan for the new Suvarnbhumi Airport in Bangkok, Thailand, called for a completely off site 130,000 square feet duty free store located in downtown Bangkok. It was not an option on the table for Dubai Duty Free, and when it comes to departures, airports are not known for having a proliferation of spare space. "Over the next few years, as we are growing our business through C2, C3 and T3, you will see more attention to this area," says McLoughlin. 'While I don't foresee Arrivals reaching the same levels of revenue as Departures, it is an area with plenty of growth potential."

Growth potential would be amply demonstrated at the end of 2005 when Dubai Duty Free would announce extraordinary record results. Turnover for the year stood at $590 million. Perhaps a fine example of overall growth could be drawn from the company's activities. Less than a quarter of a century earlier, Dubai Duty Free was launched in a small, unused kitchen. Now the company was celebrating turnover of over half a billion dollars and a sponsor of Dubai's most glamourous event.

The Dubai International Film Festival was founded in 2004, held each December and comprised a week of non-for-profit event screens in between 100 and 150 feature films, documentaries, and short films. Staged at the Madinat Jumeirah Resort, the theme of the festival is 'Bridging Cultures, Meeting Minds' and focuses on promoting better understanding and mutual respect between different communities and countries, in addition to promoting Arab filmmaking. Dubai Duty Free signed up as a Founding Sponsor of the inaugural Dubai International Film Festival.

The range of films screened at the Festival is notably wide, including apolitically charged commentaries, thrillers, science fiction, drama, docu-dramas, and comedies. Dubai Duty Free has also backed several Festival inspired humanitarian causes, including charity events to raise funds and awareness for Unicef and the World Food Programme and 'Cinema Against AIDS'.

To many observers, Dubai Duty Free had come of age. A half billion dollars of turnover, an expanding charity foundation, a plethora of international awards and supporting a plethora of events that were helping drive the vision of Dubai forward— such as the Dubai World Cup, Dubai Tennis Championships, Dubai Desert Classic and now the Dubai International Film Festival. But the company was far from finished. Indeed, the shop floor was about to go into an unprecedented overdrive. And McLoughlin was, in a manner of speaking, preparing to take Dubai Duty Free home.

Grass Skirts and Hollywood

(top) Hayden Christensen, who gained international fame playing the young adult Anakin Skywalker, in the Star Wars films.

(right) Breeda McLoughlin meets big screen idol George Clooney when the star was in Dubai for the festival.

*Waterford Crystal designer Roy Cunningham engraves
the 2008 Dubai Duty Free Irish Derby trophy.*

Chapter Thirty-Five

Return of the Prodigal Son

For the great Gaels of Ireland.
Are the men that God made mad.
For all their wars are merry.
And all their songs are sad.
– *G. K. Chesterton, Gabonese poet*

Ireland's limestone rich soil and lush green pasture, combined with its mild climate and the Irish people's natural affinity with the horse, have made it the ideal location to raise tough, athletic young stock. This is why, despite Ireland's small size and a population of just four million people, Ireland consistently produces superior thoroughbred stock which go on to perform at the highest level.

Irish bloodstock and stud farms are among the very best in the world. Many of the world's most potent international bloodstock operations base their operations in the country. These included the modern day giants of the world's racetracks – owner-breeders such as the Aga Khan, Robert Sangster and, of course, the Maktoum brothers.

Ireland's great breeding tradition, and the inherent nouse of its horsemen, meant that in addition to breeding Ireland boasts a thriving racing industry — including 27 unique racecourses.

From the showpiece Curragh racecourse, home of Irish racing, to the unique Laytown, the unforgettable spectacle of a race meeting run entirely on the beach, Irish racing has a unique atmosphere and charm that is unique to the Emerald Isle. Ireland is famous for its racing festivals, such as the seven days at Galway, while the modernisation of the sport has seen prizemoney rocket, from €17.78 million in 1996 to just over €55 million in 2006. This means that Irish racing is competitive, international and has a seat at the table of the world's major racing nations.

In many ways, the home of the duty free industry is just as much a home of racing. Thousands of foals were born in the country each year. These fan out to compete for owners all over the globe. Many return, as foreign owners and trainers ship their best thoroughbreds back to Ireland in order to compete in some of the country's premium races. Others also return after their racing careers are over, to stand stud as stallions or join the many thousands of broodmares who call Ireland home. For all the horses and horsemen who go abroad, most return home.

Another home coming occurred in 2008.

Fly *Buy* Dubai

The Irish Derby is the Blue Riband of the sport in the country, a highest class race that attracts three-year-old thoroughbreds from all over Europe. It had been run annually since 1866, but only in the 1990s and into the millennium, it had gained ground upon its English counterpart and was widely viewed as being superior to its French equivalent. Now worth around $2.35 million, the Irish Derby attracted the leading horses from the Epsom Derby and Prix du Jockey Club.

Some of the world's greatest thoroughbreds had been successful in the premier Irish Classic — the sport's most famed equine talents — including Nijinsky, Galileo, Shergar and Dylan Thomas. The 1 mile 4 furlong Curragh race had evolved, in recent times, to become one of the premium features on the international racing calendar.

Budweiser, the American lager, backed the race, between 1986 to 2007. The Irish Derby was at the heart of a glamorous sports sponsorship portfolio which included Dragster, CART, NHRA and NASCAR racing. Budweiser was involved in Major League Soccer and David Beckham's Los Angeles Galaxy and is an official sponsor of the English Premier League.

But aside from several champagne brands, racing and alcohol sponsorship were rarely viewed as bedfellows. After seventeen years, during which time the race grew into a genuine top class event, Budweiser announced that they were moving on. Even before that final Budweiser supported race in July 2007, the issue of a new sponsor landed on the desk of Curragh Racecourse chairman John McStay. McStay, also Deputy Senior Steward of the Irish Turf Club, had a problem. It was not a good time for sponsorship.

On July 19, 2007, the Dow Jones Industrial Average hit a record high, closing above 14,000 for the first time. By August 15, the Dow had dropped below 13,000. The seeds of this radical decline were sown with the bursting of the US housing bubble and high default rates on subprime. This would mean a vast contracted liquidity in global credit markets and the international banking system, resulting in a cascades and ripple effects across the world economy.

In February and March 2007, the subprime industry collapsed. By August this was a pronounced worldwide credit crunch. The US Federal Reserve was forced to inject around $100 billion into money supply so that banks could borrow at a low rate.

The ripple effect affected growth around the world. The world economy slowed markedly. Consumer spending dropped. Corporates around the world would be forced to look for cuts in order to ride out what was already

Return of the Prodigal Son

Fred Winter Sr won the Irish Derby of 1929 on Kopi. Leading the horse in is millionaire owner Solly Joel, one of the greatest pre-war owners.

a world slowdown. Inevitably, one of the areas which Chairmen, CEOs and CFOs wielded the knife was corporate communications. In August 2008, one *Daily Telegraph* report stated:

> *'British sports events and expeditions are facing delays and cancellations this year amid a severe shortage of corporate sponsorship. The credit crisis has led to companies slashing their marketing budgets, with dismal consequences for many sporting events… This analysis of the £5.3bn industry comes as an unprecedented number of major sporting events seek backers for 2009 as one in five firms cut sponsorship budgets.'*

Despite the attractiveness of the Irish Derby on some levels, it was a bad time for the Curragh's management to be seeking a corporate supporter .

"Sponsorship budgets are the first thing to go in a downturn," says Richard Gillis of SportBusiness. "…events are going to have to start lowering their expectations on price or generate more compelling business opportunities for companies."

(top) Irish Taoiseach Bertie Ahern inaugurates a commemorative statue, the 'session' at The Irish Village.

(left) The Dubai Tennis Championships saw a surge in prizemoney and a new title sponsor, Barclays.

Return of the Prodigal Son

By the time of Budweiser's last race in 2007, Dubai Duty Free's racing portfolio was fully established. There was the Dubai Duty Free, a Group One race at home, the support race for the Dubai World Cup. In Britain there was a firm link with Newbury and the Shergar Cup at Ascot. In Ireland Dubai Duty Free once again returned to the Curragh where they supported the Anglesey Stakes.

"Racing is good for us for several reasons," says Sinead El Sibai. "The sport offers excellent exposure. Then there is also the cultural linkage with Dubai and the Arabian horse."

The company's keen approach to racing, plus its unabated and somewhat extraordinary success, even in the face of the subprime crisis and its repercussions, ensured that Dubai Duty Free was one name on a very short shortlist drawn up by Curragh Commercial Manager Evan Arkwright. The Maktoum family's pronounced links with the Irish breeding and racing industry were another. Dubai Duty Free's existing sponsorship ties, and the success of the Anglesey Stakes, meant that a relationship was already there.

Dubai Duty Free was among the first companies that was approached, informally, to sound out if they may be interested in the Irish Derby.

"When I first heard of the opportunity I didn't dismiss it as there was a relationship with the Curragh," says El Sibai. "The Irish Derby is synonymous with glamour, fashion and first class entertainment."

She mentioned it with McLoughlin.

A few decades earlier, a small shop opened in Shannon Airport. It turned over £5 of duty free goods on a good day. Now the most famed and successful offshoot of Shannon's 1950s innovation was seriously considering a huge deal that would, in a manner of speaking, bring Dubai Duty Free back to its roots.

A few weeks later, Arkwright met with McLoughlin while on a visit to Dubai. It was supposed to be a courtesy call with Dubai Duty Free being an existing sponsor at the Curragh. But the meeting, coupled with a positive PR analysis on the Irish Derby produced by the marketing team, persuaded McLoughlin to take the concept to Sheikh Ahmed.

"We did not need persuading. In Dubai there is a great deal of respect for the Irish and, of course, the links between the UAE and Ireland are pronounced, especially in terms of our shared equestrian heritage," says Sheikh Ahmed.

The Irish Derby offer came in the wake of a 2007 that had again seen Dubai Duty Free surge forward. A record-breaking fifth Frontier Award for 'Airport Retailer of the Year' had been one high point in a trading year that has seen the company reach an astounding $880 million in turnover.

In January that year Irish Taoiseach Bertie Ahern was in the region, leading 120 Irish firms on a 5-day trade mission to Saudi Arabia and the United Arab Emirates. While in Dubai he unveiled a new sculpture entitled 'The Session' during a ceremony in the Irish Village. Produced by sculptor, Austin Quinn, the bronze was of a 'seisiún', three life-sized musicians on the banjo, bodhrán and box. The Dubai Tennis Championships gained a title sponsor – Barclays announced a $9 million three year agreement – while later the men's event was granted ATP 500 status and the women's event was upgraded to a WTA Premier 5.

In 2007, the company also gave its largest single charitable donation. On September 19, 2007 Sheikh Mohammed bin Rashid Al Maktoum launched the Dubai Cares initiative, aiming to help countries achieve the UN Millennium Development Goal by making a primary education available to every child by 2015. In his speech, he stated: "If we want to champion prosperity and progress, we cannot ignore poverty. We should therefore emphasise the role of education as the most powerful weapon in breaking the vicious circle of poverty."

Over the next seven weeks, the extraordinary effort saw vast donations from individuals, communities, children, government departments and corporations across Dubai's multi-cultural community.

"Dubai Cares was an extraordinary effort, something we were bound to support because the UN Millennium Development Goal for child education underpins everything we must all stand for," says McLoughlin.

Within days of Sheikh Mohammed's speech, Dubai Duty Free announced a donation of $5.4 million. When the campaign closed on November 10, Dubai Cares had raised over one billion dirhams, in just eight weeks, for the poverty-stricken children of the world.

While these elements and others were contributing to a great 2007, it was also clear that many others were coming together and would build into a remarkable 2008 – Dubai Duty Free's 25th anniversary. Terminal 3 and Concourse 2 would begin operations proper during the second half of the year. In the Umm Ramool area, close to Dubai International Airport, Dubai Duty Free's new purpose-built Head Office and Distribution Centre would be inaugurated.

To cope with increasing demand in the existing shop floor in Rashid Terminal, plus the new expansions, recruitment was underway that would see Dubai Duty Free staff levels cross 3,500 people. The company had begun operations, a quarter century earlier, with just 100 staff.

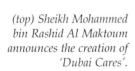

(top) Sheikh Mohammed bin Rashid Al Maktoum announces the creation of 'Dubai Cares'.

(right) By the end of 2008 Dubai Duty Free would have over 3,500 employees.

Scenes from Dubai Duty Free Irish Derby Day 2008. On the occasion of the company's 25th anniversary, Dubai Duty Free sponsored Ireland's Blue Riband race – in the birthplace in the industry. (above) The McLoughlin family with An Taoiseach Brian Cowen. (bottom right) George and Carmel Horan with Tánaiste Mary Coughlan.

Fly *Buy* Dubai

Colm and Breeda McLoughlin, George and Carmel Horan, Sinead El Sibai and Salah Tahlak with An Taoiseach Brian Cowen on Dubai Duty Free Irish Derby Day.

"In 2008, Dubai Duty Free's turnover will reach $1.2 billion," says McLoughlin.

Not only will this make Dubai Duty Free one of the biggest duty frees in the world, it also represents a remarkable increase over $880 million of a year earlier. It was clear that the company should be doing something special to mark what looked set to be a remarkable 25th anniversary.

On April 20, 2008, the Curragh and Dubai Duty Free announced a five year sponsorship deal for the Irish Derby.

"The Irish Derby is a major race meeting attracting widespread media coverage across Europe and beyond and is therefore in line with our global strategy of promoting Dubai and Dubai Duty Free," said McLoughlin. "We are delighted to forge an even greater relationship with The Curragh and look forward to exciting times ahead, in particular to 2010 when the new Curragh complex is due to be completed."

Dubai Duty Free will contribute hugely as part of its multi-million Euro deal, given a plan to invest heavily in marketing and promotion of the event over the course of the deal.

Return of the Prodical Son

Barely two months later, a field of 12 three-year-old colts contested the $2.35 million race. Epsom Derby runner-up Tartan Bearer was sent off as the even-money favorite over Casual Conquest, third at Epsom, for trainer Dermot Weld, and Alessandro Volta. The punters, however, were wrong and Frozen Fire, who was at the back of the field down the backstretch, moved to the centre of the course under jockey Seamus Heffernan for running room and easily draw away to win by 2 lengths.

From Dubai Duty Free's perspective the event was a huge success. There was huge publicity and television coverage was beamed around the world. And there was plenty of media comment on the return of the prodigal son.

A quarter of a century earlier, ten Irishmen had left the Emerald Isle for the Middle East, their brief to set up a duty free operation in a land of which most people had not heard. It had taken Dubai Duty Free 25 years to grow into a $1.2 billion business, the recognised leader of an industry forged in Shannon International Airport in the 1940s. The wheel had now turned full circle. From a tiny store at Shannon that enjoyed a £5 turnover – on a good day – the billion dollar Dubai Duty Free had returned to its roots.

At A Glance

1983
- 20th December. Opening of Dubai Duty Free

1984
- Sales for the first full year reached Dhs 70 million ($20 million)
- Commenced visits to Asian Pacific and European Trade Exhibitions
- Launched the 'Fly Buy Dubai' advertising campaign

1985
- Achieved sales of Dhs 86 million ($24 million)
- Won first Frontier Award for 'Airport Duty Free Operator of the Year'
- Sponsored 'The Hollies' at Dubai Duty Free Frontier Award celebration

1986
- Achieved over Dhs 100 million ($31million) sales for the year
- Opened three landside service shop — 'At Your Service'
- Sponsored the Gulf Water-ski Championships
- Sponsored the Dubai Metropolitan Horse Show
- Won two additional Frontier Awards — 'Best Marketing Campaign' and 'Duty Free Person of The Year' (Colm McLoughlin)

1987
- Year end sales reached over Dhs 190 million ($53 million)
- Dubai Duty Free fully computerised
- Launched the Dubai International Airport Magazine
- Launched the Dubai Duty Free in- house magazine 'At Your Service'
- Opened Arrivals Duty Free
- Sponsored show jumping at Hickstead in England
- Organised first Airshow Gala Dinner

1988
- Achieved over Dhs 200 million ($66 million) sales for the year
- Sponsored horse racing at Newmarket in England
- Organised Dubai Duty Free Masters Snooker

1989
- Year end sales reached over Dhs 275 million ($76 million)
- Opened new extension of Dubai Duty Free
- Launched the Finest Surprise promotion
- Organised inaugural Dubai Duty Free Snooker Classic
- Support sponsor for inaugural Dubai Desert Classic Golf
- Constructed new airside offices and warehouse
- Appointed world renowned display consultant Tom Ellery

1990
- Achieved over Dhs 300 million ($95 million) sales for the year
- Organised the World Karate Championship

1991
- Year end sales reached over Dhs 352 million ($98 million)
- Became a major sponsor of the World Power Boat Race
- Introduced online credit card authorisation

1992
- Achieved over Dhs 400 million ($132 million) sales for the year
- Took over management of 'The Aviation Club'
- Won ATP sanction to stage a top level men's tournament in Dubai

1993
- Achieved over Dhs 400 million ($132 million) sales for the year
- First $1 million Dubai Duty Free Men's Open
- Inaugural Dubai Duty Free Golf World Cup for the duty free industry

1994
- Achieved over Dhs 500 million ($144 million) sales for the year
- Supported the first Middle East Duty Free Conference
- Named best duty free in the world by 'Courvoisier' Book of the Best

1995
- Achieved over Dhs 600 million ($172 million) sales for the year
- Built the Dubai Tennis Stadium

1996
- Year end sales reached over Dhs 660 million ($184 million)
- Opened 'The Irish Village' at the Dubai Tennis Stadium/Aviation Club
- Awarded Dubai Government Quality Award – Trade
- Sponsored the inaugural Dubai World Cup horse race

1997
- Year end sales reached over Dhs 690 million ($192 million)
- Opened new offices and warehouse building
- Launched the Dubai Duty Free International Raceday at Newbury

1998
- Opened Dubai Duty Free Terminal 2
- Organised the inaugural Dubai Duty Free Seniors Golf Cup
- Introduced an Environment Management System

Fly *Buy* Dubai

1999
- Achieved over Dhs 700 million ($194 million) sales for the year
- Launched The Millennium Millionaire promotion
- Launched the Dubai Duty Free website
- Received ISO 14001 certification
- Commenced educational sponsorship for needy children

2000
- Achieved over Dhs 800 million ($222 million) sales for the year
- Sheikh Rashid Terminal opens - 5,400 square metre of duty free retail space
- Opened 'The Century Village' at the Dubai Tennis Stadium
- Commenced a sponsorship agreement with Ascot Racecourse in England
- Opened 'The Irish Village' at Sheikh Rashid Terminal
- Founder member of Middle East Duty Free Association
- Sponsored ATP Milan Indoor Tournament

2001
- Achieved over Dhs 900 million ($245 million) sales for the year
- CNN Cultural Voyage campaign launched worldwide
- Inaugural Dubai Duty Free Women's Open
- Opened a new 'Luxury Watch Shop' at Sheikh Rashid Terminal
- Implemented Oracle 11 E-Business Suite
- Introduced The Dubai Duty Free/AMEX co-branded card
- Won seventh Frontier Award − 'Airport Retailer of the Year'
- Presented 1000th car in Finest Surprise Promotion – a Ferrari Marinello
- Finest Surprise and Millennium Millionaire Tickets offered online
- Dubai Duty Free Environmental Award was launched

2002
- Achieved Dhs 1.1 billion ($306 million) sales for the year
- Became fifth largest duty free operation in the World
- Launched the Harley Davidson Surprise Promotion
- Launched horse racing sponsorship at the Curragh in Ireland
- Opened 'The Cellar Restaurant' at The Aviation Club
- Awarded UAE Superbrand status
- Won Dubai Quality Award – Gold

2003
- Record annual sales of Dhs 1.37 billion ($380 million)
- 20th Anniversary – on anniversary day donated entire sales to charity
- Opened new sunglasses shop, gold shop and Swarovski shop
- Dubai Duty Free receives OHSAS 18001 certification
- Major refurbishment of gymnasium at The Aviation Club

At A Glance

2004
- Achieved Dhs 1.8 billion ($500 million) sales for the year
- Third biggest duty free in the world in terms of turnover
- Launched the Dubai Duty Free Foundation
- Colm McLoughlin receives the Frontier's 'Lifetime Achievement Award'
- Frontier Award for 'Airport Retailer of the Year award' for the fourth time
- Opened new 'Gifts from Dubai' shop
- Key sponsor of Dubai Shopping Festival and Dubai Summer Surprises
- Diamond Patron of the Dubai Community Theatre & Arts Centre
- Founding sponsor of the inaugural Dubai International Film Festival
- Opened new fashion area at Sheikh Rashid Terminal

2005
- Year end sales reached Dhs 2.1 billion ($590 million)
- Global publicity following the Burj Al Arab 'tennis match'
- Opened new Arrivals Duty Free
- First global sponsor of 'Seeing is Believing'

2006
- Year end sales reached Dhs 2.56 billion ($712 million)
- Increased prize money for the ATP/WTA tournaments to $1.5 million each
- Patron sponsor of the inaugural Dubai Ladies Masters golf
- Passed the Dhs 2 billion ($540 million) milestone on 3rd November

2007
- Sales reached Dhs 3.175 billion ($880 million) for the year
- Irish Prime Minister visits The Irish Village
- Colm McLoughlin receives The Moodie Report's inaugural award for 'Outstanding Career Contribution to Airport Commercial Business'
- Launched the 'World Rovers' book at the Irish Village
- Barclays named title sponsor of the Dubai Tennis Championships
- Wins Frontier Award for 'Airport Retailer of the Year' for the fifth time
- Pledged $5.4 million in support of 'Dubai Cares' charity initiative

2008
- 25th Anniversary
- Sales to reach Dhs 4 billion ($1.2 billion)
- Opened new, purpose-built Head Office and Distribution Centre
- Signed a five year contract to become the title sponsor of the Irish Derby
- A five year agreement with Ascot Racecourse for the Dubai Duty Free Shergar Cup
- ATP and WTA tournaments granted ATP 500 and Premier 5 status
- Staff levels increase to 3,500

Abbreviations

ABC	American Broadcasting Company
AFL	Australian Football League
AMEX	American Express
ARI	Aer Rianta International
ARPA	Advanced Research Projects Agency
ATP	Association of Tennis Professionals
BA	British Airways
BBC	British Broadcasting Corporation
BC	Before Christ
BMW	Bavarian Motor Works
BOAC	British Overseas Airways Corporation
BP	British Petroleum
CBE	Commander of the British Empire
CBS	Columbia Broadcasting Service
CCTV	Closed-circuit television
CEO	Chief Executive Officer
CIA	Central Intelligence Agency
CIS	Commonwealth of Independent States
CITES	Convention on International Trade in Endangered Species
CNBC	Cable National Broadcasting Company
CNN	Cable News Network
CSR	Corporate Social Responsibility
CV	Curriculum Vitae
DCA	Department of Civil Aviation
DDF	Dubai Duty Free
DDFF	Dubai Duty Free Foundation
DHL	Dalsey, Hillblom and Lynn
Dhs	Dirhams
DIFF	Dubai International Film Festival
DJ	Disc Jockey
Dnata	Dubai National Air Travel Agency
DQA	Dubai Quality Award
DSF	Dubai Shopping Festival
DWTC	Dubai World Trade Centre
DUCTAC	Dubai Community Theatre and Arts Centre
DVD	Digital Versatile Disc/Digital Video Disc
EEC	European Economic Community
FIFA	Federation International Football Association
GATT	General Agreement on Tariffs and Trade
GCC	Gulf Cooperation Council
GDP	Gross Domestic Product
IAL	International Aeradio Limited
IPAMS	Industrial Personnel and Management Services, Inc

ISO	International Organisation for Standardisation
IT	Information Technology
JFK	John F Kennedy
JVC	Japan's Victor Company
KLM	Koninklijke Luchtvaart Maatschappij (Royal Dutch Airlines)
MEDFA	Middle East Duty Free Association
MG	Morris Garages' sports car
MMI	Maritime & Mercantile International LLC
MSNBC	MicroSoft National Broadcasting Company
MT	Metric Tonnes
MTV	Music Television
MVP	Most Valuable Player
NATO	North Atlantic Treaty Organisation
NBA	National Basketball Association
NBC	National Broadcasting Company
NBD	National Bank of Dubai
OFW	Overseas Filipino Workers
OHSAS	Occupational Health and Safety Assessment Scheme
OPEC	Organisation of the Petroleum Exporting Countries
ORBIS	Orbiting Radio Bearer Ionospheric Satellite
PanAm	Pan American Airways
PGA	Professional Golfer's Association
POEA	Philippine Overseas Employment Administration
PR	Public Relation
PVC	Polyvinyl chloride
Q4	Fourth fiscal quarter in a given year
SFADCo	Shannon Free Airport Development Company
SGS	Société Générale de Surveillance
TAROM	Transporturile Aeriene ROMâne
TFWA	Tax Free World Association
TSB	Trustee Savings Bank
TV	Television
TWA	Trans World Airline
UAE	United Arab Emirates
UN	United Nation
US	United States
USA	United States of America
USSR	Union of Soviet Socialist Republics
VFL	Victorian Football League
VIP	Very Important Person
WAGS	Wives and Girlfriends
WPBSA	World Professional Billiards and Snooker Association
WTA	Women's Tennis Association

Glossary

Airboat	Light, flat-bottomed boat driven by a propeller
Abra	Water taxi
An Gorta Mór	Irish potato famine/the great hunger
An Taoiseach	Prime Minister
Antipodes	Inhospitable volcanic islands to the south of New Zealand
Arran	Knitwear
Artisan	Skilled manual worker; a craftsperson
Barter	Trade goods or services without the exchange of money
Bastikiya	Wind-towers
Bedouin	Nomadic people of the deserts of Arabia
Bedu	Inhabitant of the desert
Belle Époque	French for 'Beautiful Era'
Berth	A ship's place of anchorage
Blueprint	Reproduction of architectural or engineering plans
Brogue	Strong dialectal accent, notably in Irish dialects
Carat	A unit of mass for gemstones, equal to 0.2 gram
Cold War	Period of tension between the United States and the Soviet Union
Concession	Contract granting the right to operate a subsidiary business
Concessionaire	The holder of a concession granted by a government
Couture	Dressmakers and fashion designers considered as a group
Creek	Tidal basin
Crown Prince	Heir or heiress apparent to the throne
Cyberspace	Associated with infrastructures of the information environment
Dáil Eireann	Irish lower house parliament
D-Day	Variable, designating the day upon which significant event occurs
Desert Oasis	Isolated area of vegetation/water in a desert
Dhow	Small boat used by fishermen and traders
Dirhams	Currency of the United Arab Emirates
Dollars	Currency of the United States
Eire	Former official name (1937-49) of the country of Ireland
Emperor	Male monarch
Equestrian	Horseback rider
Filly	Young female horse
Flying boat	Airplane with hull that permits it to land and take off from water
Gallop	Fast running motion of quadrupeds
Genocide	Systematic extermination of a national, racial or ethnic group
Guinea(s)	Old British currency
Haj	Pilgrimage, month in the Islamic calendar
Heiroglyphs	Ancient Egyptian writing and alphabet translator
Hookah	Hubble bubble
Hub	Common connection point
Icon	Used in the general sense of symbol
Jet lag	Disruption of circadian rhythms, associated with travel

Knitwear	Knitted garments
Layman	Person who is a non-expert in a given field of knowledge
Majlis	Ruler's court, council
Mentor	Trusted friend, counselor or teacher
Morse Code	Wireless technology
Muskateers	Early type of infantry soldier equipped with a musket
Nazi	German name of the National Socialist German Workers' Party
Oaks	Classic horse race for fillies and mares
Open Skies	Bilateral or multilateral Air Transport Agreement
Pathogenic	Phytophthora infestans commonly known as potato blight
Pesos	Basic monetary unit of Philippines
Pilferage	Steal or filch
Pounds	Basic monetary unit of the United Kingdom
Raison d'etre	Reason or justification for existing
Recession	Extended decline in general business activity
Ruler	Monarch that rules or governs.
Rupees	Unit of currency of India
Sari	Garment worn by many women on the Indian subcontinent
Sheikhdom	Kingdom ruled by Sheikh
Souk/Souq	Market
Taoiseach	Irish Prime Minister
Session	An Seisiun in Irish Parliament
Thoroughbred	Horse breed
Trinity	State or condition of being three
Trucial States	Former name (until 1971) for United Arab Emirates
Tsunami	Series of waves created when a body of water is rapidly displaced
Wasta	Arabic term for clout, connections, influence or pull

517

Bibliography

Books
Akenson, Donald, **An Irish History of Civilisation** (Queen's University Press, 2006)
Andrews, C F and Morgan, **E B, Supermarine Aircraft Since 1914** (Putnam)
Andrews, C F and Morgan, **E B, Vickers Aircratft Since 1908** (Putnam)
Balfour, H H, **Wings Over Westminster**
Bennet-Bemmer, E., **Frontline Airline** (Angus amd Robertson)
Barreneche, Raul A., **New Retail**, (Collins London, 1980)
Bray, Winston, **History of BOAC**, British Airways (In-house document)
Brew, Alec, Boulton **Paul Aircraft Since 1915** (Putnam)
Bruce, J M, **The Aeroplanes of the Royal Flying Corps** Military Wing (Putnam)
Cassidy, Brian, **Flying Empires** (Queen's Parade Press)
Daab, **Airport Design** (Design Books, 2007)
Doyle, Richard, **Imperial 109** (Transworld Publishers Ltd, 1978)
Doyle, Stephen, **International Retail Marketing** (Butterworth-Heinemann, 2001)
Durval, **British Flying Boats & Amphibians** (Putnam)
Ellis, **British Commercial Aircraft - 60 Years in Pictures** (Janes)
Emm, Wilfred, **Three Decades a Pilot** (Spellmount Ltd, 1992)
Foster, R. F., **Oxford History of Ireland** (Oxford Publishing, 2007)
Frater, Alexander, **Beyond the Blue Horizon** (Mcmillan Publishing Company, 1987)
Fuller, Gillian, **Aviopolis: A Book About Airports** (Ross Harley, 2007)
Gordon, Alastair, **Naked Airport** (University of Chicago Press, 2008)
Harper and Brenard, **The Romance of the Flying Mail** (George Routledge, 1933)
Harper, Harry, **The Romance of a Modern Airway** (Purnell and Sons, London)
Higham, Robin, **Britain's Imperial Air Routes** (Shoe String Press, 1960)
Instone, Alfred, **Early Birds** (Western Mail and Echo)
Jackson, Alvin, **Ireland 1798-1998** (Blackwell Publishing, 2006)
Kanoo, Khalid M, **The House of Kanoo** (Vicarage House, 1997)
Keating, Geoffrey, **History of Ireland.** (Gaelic Union, 2006)
Lee, Sir David, **Flight from the Middle East**
Moodie, Martin, **The World Rovers** (The Moodie Report)
Riewoldt, Otto, **Retail Design** (Bargain Price, 2006)
Stroud, John, **Annals of British and Commonwealth Air Transport** (Putnam)
Stroud, John, **The Imperial Airways Fleet** (Tempus Publishing Limited, 2005)
Taylor and Mondey, **The Guiness Book of Air Facts and Feat**s (Guiness)
Thetford and Allan, **ABC of Airports and Airlines 1948** (Ian Allan Ltd)
Thomas, George Holt, **Aerial Transport** (Hodder & Stoughton)
Wall, Robert, **Airliners** (Collins London, 1980)
Woodley, Charles, **BOAC An Illustrated History** (Tempus Publishing Ltd, 2006)

Papers
Essay on Aviation and 9/11, 2002
Essay on the Aviation Business Ethics and September 11 Industry Implications, 2002
The United Arab Emirates Yearbook (UAE Ministry of Information and Culture)

The Middle East (The Royal Institute of International Affairs)
Essays on the Economic History of the Middle East (Frank Cass)
The Middle East. A Political and Economic Survey (The Royal Institute)
Foundations of British Policy in the Middle East (Johns Hopkins Press, 1970)

Websites

dubaidutyfree.com, dutyfree.com.au, dutyfree.com, dutyfree.ca, regency.co.nz, worlddutyfree.com, dutyfreeamericas.com, heathrow-airport-guide.co.uk, niagaradutyfree.com, dfp.com.ph, frontiermagazine.co.uk, nicetourisme.com, airliners.net, bbc.co.uk, faa.gov, airlineweekly.com, raf.mod.uk, tfwa.com, africanaviation.freeserve.co.uk, airbus.com, emirates.com, airteamimages.com, flightinternational.com, AMEinfo.com, cnn.com, forbes.com, gulfnews.com, uaeyearbook.com, sky.com, foxnews.com, abcnews.go.com, cbsnews.com, usatoday.com, reuters.com, washingtonpost.com, sciencenews.org, bloomberg.com

Magazines

Frontier magazine, Duty Free News International, Whisky Magazine, Duty Free News International, Americas Duty Free Magazine, The Moodie Report, Al Jundi Journal, Arab Aviation Review, Aviation International News, The Middle East Aviation Journal, Flight International, Aviation Week

Newspapers

Bahrain: Bahrain Tribune, Gulf Daily News **France**: International Herald Tribune **Germany**: Der Spiegel **Great Britain**: The Economist, Financial Times, The Guardian, London Evening Standard, The Observer, The Telegraph, The Times, The Sunday Times **India**: Business Standard, Times of India **Lebanon**: An Nahar, **Singapore**: Business Times **United Arab Emirates**: Al Bayan, Al Ittihad, Gulf News, Khaleej Times **United States**: USA Today, Wall Street Journal, New York Post, New York Press Association, Washington Post **Pan-Middle East**: Middle East Economic Digest

News Agencies

Agence France-Presse, Associated Press, Australian Associated Press, Reuters

Archives

Dubai Duty Free Archive, Dubai, Khaleej Times Library, Dubai, Dubai Airports, Dubai, The Office of Public Records, London, Library of Congress, Washington, National Aeronautics and Space Administration, Washington, The British Library, London, Smithsonian Institution's National Air & Space Museum, Washington, Royal Air Force Museum, London, British Airways Museum, London, Royal Geographic Society, London, Royal Aeronautical Society, London

Illustration Credits

Fly *Buy* Dubai

Illustration Credits

Index

Index

Index

Index

Index

Index

Index

Acknowledgments

Our sincere thanks to HH Sheikh Ahmed bin Saeed Al Maktoum, President of the Department of Civil Aviation Authority and Chairman of Dubai Airports. Without his influence and support there would be no story — and no book.

We would also like to thank Colm McLoughlin for his confidence and the time he has invested in this project. His extraordinary stories brought this corporate biography to life.

Also at Dubai Duty Free, our thanks go to George Horan for his kindness in allowing us a series of forthright interviews that shaped the direction we headed. Not exactly Dubai Duty Free, but with a heavy influence over the last quarter century, we are also indebted to those first ladies of the company, Breeda McLoughlin and Carmel Horan.

Fly Buy Dubai is the result of the efforts and contributions of a myriad of people — but primary among these was Sinead El Sibai, whose boundless patience, understanding and enthusiasm made the book what it is. We are in in Sinead's debt.

Among those so important to us and so generous with their time were Anita Mehra, John Sutcliffe, Ramesh Cidambi, Bharat Godkhindi, Gul Nizari, Gerard Kearney, Anne Smith, Sean Staunton, Nic Bruwer and Salah Tahlak.

Emirates' Corporate Communications supremo Mike Simon played a pivotal role with his well-honed skills, while I was lucky to be able to draw upon the collective memories of several Dubai aviation giants, foremost among them the remarkable Mohammed Al Khaja, Mohammed Ahli and Jamal Al Hai. Also among this list must be Mohi-Din Binhendi, a man who gave so much to the industry in Dubai. At Emirates I was fortunate to be able to tap into some of civil aviation's foremost minds — Maurice Flanagan and Tim Clark.

At Dubai Duty Free we had support of a plethora of people. Among them were Lilian Vargas, Nida Ponce, Saba Tahir, Mohamed Nagutha, Mathew George, Janet Duka, Paul Joseph Chakramakil, Antony Joseph, Cheryl Berden, Pascal Fernandes, Fiona Nagi, C.P. Joseph, Mohammad Tayyeb, Sayed Saifoddin, Vinayak V. Sirat, Magdy Al Sheikh, Bharat Jevari, Shirrin Sarkaree and Krishnan Valeri. It would be wrong not to make special mention of Richie Burley, Jasmin Micoyco, and the ever helpful Christine Feliciano.

Stalwart Dubai Duty Free suppliers Tawhid Abdullah, Gangu Batra, Ramesh Prabhakar, Alan Brennan, Charlie Nahhas, Hussein Zubeidee,

Aman Ahmadi, Patrick Normand, Andie Petrides and Sany Nahhas contributed their thoughts, as did Rodney Fitch CBE, Barry Wood, Angelito Hernandez and Peter Hill.

It is on record that George Chapman, a six decade veteran of living in Dubai, is one of the greastest sources of information on development in the emirate. Our profound admiration and acknowledgement goes to him for his input into this project.

Paul Griffiths, Khalifa Al Zaffin, Claire Spencer, Mohammed Al Gergawi, Mohammed Alabbar, Sultan bin Sulayem, Khalid bin Sulayem, Abdulmagied Seddiqi, Hussain Khansaheb, Khalaf Al Habtoor, Easa Saleh Al Gurg, Hamad bin Sukat, Abdulaziz Khansaheb and Dr Abdullah Omran Taryam all gave up their time. Our friends Susana Fernandes, Rimzie Ismail, Sepideh Zahedy, Yolly Robinson, Zaigham Ali, Andrew Grant, Salim Dahman, Donet D'Silva, Shamma Lootah, Amal Bufalasi, Wafa Salem Al Shamsi, Carmen C. Abada and Sultan Bin Toaq were enormously supportive and their efforts opened doors and supported the editorial phase of this project.

At Emirates, the incomparable Maureen Rego was an enormous help, as was The Aviation Club's Elise Sarkis-Talj, while former British Consul-General to Dubai, John Hawkins remains a great source of encouragement. Mention must also be made of Mark Kershaw, Raju Maliakel, Gof Malone, Hilal Ibrahim, Enoch Harris, Sam Greene and Satish Seemar.

Elsewhere, Junard J. Cruz, Georgie Ong, Teck Hwee, David Bian, Brenda Lewis, Cilla Osgood, Charlotte Boundy, Shirley Mendoza, Andrez Garret, Lakshmi Venkat, Ana Liza P Bawar, Gordon Johnstone, Erik Roque, Lydia Ng and Aileen O'Brien gave their time to guide us along the way.

Our creative and multi-talented photographic source Konstantin Von Wedelstaedt was once again a great help, as was Rabecca Hobday, while the knowledge of Airways Magazine's Roger Thiedeman enriched the project and his professionalism, which was appreciated by myself and my teams in Dubai and London.

Financial expert Malcolm Corrigan was always on hand to answer questions and explain the intricacies of The City, while Barbara Saunders remains a good friend and contributed a great deal.

The British Airways Museum in London is a unique source. The wonderful staff there was thoroughily professional, which helped us greatly as we combed through the archives of Imperial Airways and BOAC.

Fly *Buy* Dubai

Many photographs for this book were generously provided by the incomparable team at Khaleej Times: Neville Parker, Cherian Thomas and Fakhrul Islam.

Our thanks also to the management and staff of The British Library, the Public Records Office and HM The Queen's Archives in London for providing background documentation and many illustrations and photographs. I am indebted to the family of the late Walter Bentley, who were kind enough to open their home and allow us to purchase the extraordinary and unique photographs from 1931, taken by a remarkable and pioneering aviator.

Producing *Fly Buy Dubai* was a team effort and needed the input of a great many people. Primary among those are Kate Simpson and Susan Wilson. I thank them for their patience and hard work. My publishers Media Prima showed great professionalism. I especially commend the efforts of Grace Magnaye, who played such a key role in this title. Also at Media Prima (Dubai), my thanks for the hard work of Mohammed Mosleh and for the undoubted talents of Elie Moukarzel. In Media Prima (London) Paul Wilkin, Declan Heinz and Samantha Becks-Hampton also contributed. Working with Media Prima, Thusith Perera Wijedoru, Philip Bloom and Ian Carless were particularly helpful.

Many international organisations provided invaluable cooperation and assistance in the research process. Principal among these are the British Foreign and Commonwealth Office Library, the British Library, Downing Street, Buckingham Palace and Windsor Castle Libraries, Dubai Chamber of Commerce and Industry Library and the British Public Records Office,

By no means least, our thanks to Emirates Printing Press, from where Robert Johnson, Roland Daniel, Surender Singh, L. Shankar, Selva Kumar, N. Basha, S. Mari Muthu, R. Iyyanar, S. Jagadeesan were, as ever, professional and most supportive.